Managing in Complexity: How Our Fears of Uncertainty Can Hurt Us and What To Do About It

Challenging traditional ways of thinking, leading, and managing based on cutting-edge research and real-world examples, this book provides an insightful and accessible perspective for leaders and managers in the 21st century who seek to become more effective in an increasingly uncertain and complex world which limits their ability to get results.

Just how significant this is has become all too evident in the Covid-19 pandemic. Many books have been written to address these leadership and management challenges, but they are based on the premise that there are ways to simplify, organise, and control what is going on in the workplace. In our complex world this is not possible, and there are no magic tools and techniques that will ensure success. This book explains why and offers an alternative approach, incorporating social theory and the sciences of uncertainty, written in plain English by a leader with over 40 years of experience in the private, not-for-profit, and federal government sectors. Each chapter focuses on a single key concept and is introduced by a story illustrating how these key ideas can be applied in the workplace and includes practical suggestions for leaders and managers at all levels and across sectors to incorporate these perspectives into their day-to-day work practice, making it easy for readers to use the book as a reference guide.

All who manage in complex times and uncertain environments will appreciate this accessible and actionable book that will inspire a radical rethink of current management orthodoxy and help them to become more effective.

Sara Filbee's (B.Sc., MBA/LLB, D Man) career has included being a corporate commercial law partner, President of Atlantic Provinces Economic Council, Director Corporate Banking, and Assistant Deputy Minister with the Canadian federal government. Sara is active in the voluntary sector and is currently adjunct at Dalhousie University. She lives in Chester, Nova Scotia.

Managing in Complexity

How Our Fears of Uncertainty Can
Hurt Us and What To Do About It

Sara Filbee

Routledge
Taylor & Francis Group

NEW YORK AND LONDON

Designed cover image: Cover design by Mary Filbee.
Photographs courtesy of Mary Filbee and Karen Filbee Dexter.

First published 2024
by Routledge
605 Third Avenue, New York, NY 10158

and by Routledge
4 Park Square, Milton Park, Abingdon, Oxon, OX14 4RN

Routledge is an imprint of the Taylor & Francis Group, an informa business

Library of Congress Cataloging-in-Publication Data
Names: Filbee, Sara, author.
Title: Managing in complexity : how our fears of uncertainty can
    hurt us and what to do about it / Sara Filbee.
Identifiers: LCCN 2023038463 (print) | LCCN 2023038464 (ebook) |
    ISBN 9781032334059 (hardback) | ISBN 9781032334011
    (paperback) | ISBN 9781003319528 (ebook)
Subjects: LCSH: Management. | Organizational change. |
    Uncertainty.
Classification: LCC HD31.2 .F54 2024 (print) | LCC HD31.2
    (ebook) | DDC 658—dc23/eng/20230817
LC record available at https://lccn.loc.gov/2023038463
LC ebook record available at https://lccn.loc.gov/2023038464

ISBN: 978-1-032-33405-9 (hbk)
ISBN: 978-1-032-33401-1 (pbk)
ISBN: 978-1-003-31952-8 (ebk)

DOI: 10.4324/9781003319528

Typeset in Optima
by Apex CoVantage, LLC

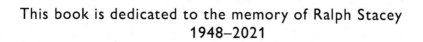

This book is dedicated to the memory of Ralph Stacey
1948–2021

Contents

Preface

The sciences of complexity are a substantial but minority tradition within the natural sciences. What distinguishes them from more orthodox scientific disciplines is that they rely on nonlinear computer-based models, which are probabilistic rather than predictive. Because the relationship between variables in the model is nonlinear, they demonstrate qualitative changes over time rather than having predictive value. As an everyday example, the complexity models with which we are all most familiar, and which most obviously demonstrate this distinction between probability and certainty are weather forecasts, which Sara Filbee mentions in this book. In more temperate, changeable climates, the weather can change frequently. But forecasts are framed in terms of likelihood of weather events, which tend to be very accurate over the shorter term of three to four days. The longer the forecast is projected into the future, the less confident and accurate the prediction. In nonlinear relationships, a small change in activity can bring about a complete transformation of conditions over time. Meanwhile a large disruption might bring about very little effect over the longer term. This nonlinear relationship is referred to in everyday parlance as the butterfly effect, where something as minor as a butterfly fluttering its wings over Sao Paolo may lead to a storm over Florida if one could measure nonlinear patterning to an infinite degree of accuracy. With the weather, it is not possible for just anything to happen (although we have had snow in Texas and heat waves in the Northern hemisphere in spring because global heating has changed the parameters of activity), but the amount of variability produced by nonlinear relationships creates a great deal of change. Modelling is undertaken on the basis of constant adjustment and revision to reflect small changes in the data which can make a big difference to population-wide patterns.

Similar models are used in zoology to simulate ant nests or termite mounds, in biology to simulate the human brain, or in urban planning to simulate traffic flows and population changes across neighbourhoods. The models are very helpful in deepening our understanding about relationships between actors and variables, and offer insight into complex patterns, which would be inexplicable using simple cause and effect. Complexity models are not useful for predicting end states.

About thirty years ago, a handful of organisational scholars became interested in what these models might tell us about organisational life, and social life more generally. You don't need to be a complexity scientist to recognise that organisational life has exactly the predictable unpredictability and nonlinearity that complexity models demonstrate. Despite our elaborate plans and strategies and the time and care we put into managing people, it is hard to predict with certainty over the longer term what will happen and how people will behave, what the organisation will become. Small changes in an organisation can escalate into completely different ways of doing things, meanwhile organisation-wide culture change programmes can result in very little change at all as weary employees dig in and resist the latest fad. The early complexity scholars noticed that the majority of organisational scholarship still assumed that with enough application managers could predict, plan, and organise organisational ends that they wanted despite evidence on a daily basis that they might be in charge, but they were not necessarily in control. Complexity models offered a different explanation of stability and change, the precariousness of prediction and the inadequacy of linear logic. It isn't necessarily the case that managers aren't trying hard enough or are using the wrong tools and techniques.

One of the original pioneers of the movement to take up insights from the complexity sciences in organisational scholarship was Ralph Stacey, who latterly with Doug Griffin and Patricia Shaw, developed a body of work which they termed complex responsive processes of relating. They named their perspective in recognition that the most relevant complexity models for them were complex adaptive systems (CAS), but they also wanted to spell out the differences. Computer models only take you so far, and they wanted to combine insights from natural and social sciences in an interdisciplinary way. So taking the formulation of complex adaptive systems, Stacey, Griffin, and Shaw thought that human beings are not just adaptive, they are also responsive; we do not form systems when we interact but are instead already and always involved in social processes; and we are always in relation with one another. While the term complex responsive processes of relating is rather a mouthful, it sets out the interdisciplinary, human-centred perspective which puts experience and our relationships with one another, front and centre.

Stacey, Griffin, and Shaw were alive to the dangers of taking up insights from the complexity sciences in an instrumental discipline such as management, which many of the early scholars did. Even Stacey was guilty of this kind of assumption in his early writings until joined by Griffin and Shaw, who helped him hammer out some of the inconsistencies in his position.

And it is still a tendency today to assume that managers can mobilise complexity for the good, or that complexity only applies in certain conditions of the manager's choosing, or that the manager is somehow outside the complex conditions that everyone else is experiencing and can direct complexity this way or that. Instead, Stacey, Griffin, and Shaw tried to cleave to what they understand to be the radical implications of the complexity sciences, which are that if social life is complex, it is always so, even if it appears ordered and regular, and that there is no standing outside looking in, no God's eye view of directing complexity for predetermined ends. This does not imply that there is nothing we can do, that we shouldn't try to improve and become more effective, merely that we give up on our certainties and hold our tools and techniques lightly because they will only take us so far.

Stacey, Griffin, and Shaw founded a doctoral programme, the Doctor of Management at the University of Hertfordshire. This is a practice-based programme, which is run experientially and both Sara Filbee and I are graduates. Students are invited to take their everyday experience seriously and to theorise from it drawing on the four pillars of thought underpinning complex responsive processes of relating. These are the complexity sciences understood by analogy; pragmatic philosophy, which also focuses on human experience; process sociology, which is concerned with patterns of human relating in flux and change; and group analytic theory and practice, which, again, is interested in the patterns that humans produce, conscious and unconscious when they are engaged in joint activity. Relationships are never at rest, always in flux, so students are asked what sense they can make of them. Sara explores the ideas which underpin complex responsive processes more fully in the book. Over more than 20 years the programme has produced 75 graduates and continues to this day. It is Stacey, Griffin, and Shaw's lasting legacy to have produced publications, an annual conference, and a thriving doctoral programme, which adheres to the radical implications of the complexity sciences without collapsing into stepwise prescriptions for managers. The programme, and the insights it offers, can be very unsettling viewed in the light of the dominant orthodoxy of management. As an explanation of the relationship between the individual and the group and stability and change, it only offers managers good enough ground for now, and provocations to think, rather than certainty.

In this book Sara Filbee develops and extends the research that she undertook for her doctorate to address a wide range of organisational themes and to make what are a complex set of ideas accessible for the curious reader. She grounds the book in the key ideas of complex responsive processes of relating, adds in in her own reading and research, and illuminates recognisable examples from everyday organisational life to bring the complexity perspective alive. Dealing with important and contemporary themes, such as the fluctuating bonds of trust, the ubiquity of metrics and targets, and the complex dynamics of groups, Sara adds an important new volume to the growing literature from a perspective which takes the radical implications of complexity seriously.

Chris Mowles
Professor of Complexity and Management
Oxford, March 2023

Acknowledgements

It is rather daunting to write an acknowledgements section for a book project such as this. It reminds me of the song "You'll Never Walk Alone," from the 1945 musical, *Carousel*, because I owe a huge debt of gratitude to so many people that to thank them all here would read like an interminable Academy Awards acceptance speech. I know that I will likely miss thanking some of those who helped me to get to this point, so my apologies in advance—and please attribute it to my forgetfulness rather than to any sense that I do not appreciate all you have done.

It is impossible to say definitively where the journey that led to this book began. In the book I talk about the two strategic planning initiatives in the not-for-profit sector with the United Way and how the differing results prompted my inquiry into why we have difficulty in dealing with change. During my time with the United Way, both at the national and local level, I worked with many tireless and dedicated volunteers and staff who cared deeply about the health of the communities in which we live. My experience working with them was highly formative in terms of who I am today and my interest in managing in complexity.

If I am going in order, I would then want to thank Dr. Robin Armstrong, former president of University of New Brunswick, Fredericton, who introduced me to Mitchell Wardrup's book on complexity, thus inspiring this journey.

Thanks to my close friends (and roommates when I am in Ottawa), Professors Emeritus Barb Orser and Allan Riding of the University of Ottawa, for pushing me to do a doctorate sooner rather than later, which ultimately led to this book. Their friendship and our many debates and discussions have been a tremendous support during what was (for me) a rather daunting challenge.

Thanks also go to my dear friend and colleague Professor James Barker at Dalhousie University who I reached out to on the advice of a friend to discuss my plans for doing a PhD in the field of complexity. Without his help, I might never have heard about the work being done on complexity in management at the University of Hertfordshire or found the professional doctorate programme that introduced me to the perspective developed by Ralph Stacey and his colleagues. Later, when I was working as Public Servant in Residence with the School of Public Administration at Dalhousie University, Halifax, Nova Scotia, Canada, he was the one who inspired me to write a book for managers and leaders in the field.

Many thanks also to my colleagues and friends from the public service of Canada, where I worked for many years. I learned so much from you and saw firsthand how dedicated you were—at all levels—to the health and welfare of this country I am honoured to call my home, Canada. While we often have different perspectives, we are all doing the best we can in our complex world, and I am so glad that you have been a part of the research project that I call my life! I would be remiss if I didn't single out John Banigan who took a chance on a young woman who wandered into his office looking for a chance to serve in the federal government and jousted valiantly with the human resources processes needed to make it happen. Or Deputy Minister (and later Clerk) Michael Wernick with whom I worked for five years and from whom I learned so much. My appreciation goes to him for taking the time to read my book and to write a very kind endorsement of it. Or my boss, Louise Levonian, who believed in me and supported me to study in this field, without whom this book would never have been written. Or Graham Flack and Lori MacDonald, deputy ministers in the Department of Employment and Social Development Canada who supported me in becoming Public Servant in Residence at Dalhousie, which gave me the time and space to write this book. Or my friend and colleague, Darlène de Gravina, who has encouraged me throughout the process.

Dalhousie University has likewise been very supportive of this work. Thanks to Kim Brooks, Lori Turnbull, and Krista Cullymore, as well as my many colleagues in the Faculty of Management who despite their being in the middle of dealing with Covid's disruption of their work, graciously welcomed me into their midst.

And of course, my thanks and appreciation to the entire faculty of the University of Hertfordshire Professional Doctor of Management programme in the UK: Chris Mowles, Emma Crewe, Karina Solsø, Nicholas Sarra, Karen Norman, Kiran Chauhan, and Ralph Stacey—for inspiring and guiding me, and for their advice, support and friendship. Thanks also to all those who were students and colleagues during my time in the programme. I couldn't have asked for better colleagues during what can be a challenging exploration of productive doubt. Of note, my friend Majken Askeland was the first fellow student that I met when I arrived at Roffey Park (site of the programme residentials) and has become a close friend since then. Our many walks and discussions have also informed this work.

Of particular note, I would like to recognise Ralph Stacey in whose memory this book is dedicated. I count myself lucky to have worked with him. He, with his colleagues Doug Griffin and Patricia Shaw, developed the perspective on managing in complexity that is the subject of this book. While I understand Ralph's early frustrations with being unable to predict effectively, we have all reaped the rewards of the insights and thinking that it engendered. Chris Mowles has continued to steward this important field of research and the programme together with the support of the faculty, students, and the many alumnae of the Doctor of Management programme. He was my thesis supervisor and has continued to support me through the process of writing this book. Thanks to him for everything and for agreeing to write the preface despite all he has on his plate.

Thanks to Routledge, Taylor & Francis Group, for taking a chance on a first-time book writer. In particular, I want to acknowledge the support of Meredith Norwich, Bethany Nelson, and Sathyasri Kalyanasundaram during the publication process.

One of the challenges of writing (at least for me), is that it can be all too easy to get completely enamoured with one's own perspective. My dear friend, Liz Crocker, supported me with advice and counsel from the very inception of the concept of this book and then provided editorial and conceptual feedback on the first draft of the manuscript. Her insights and generous commentary led to many a revision and rethink and for that I will always be grateful.

Many others have either encouraged me or provided me with comments and critiques of the work. In addition to Michael Wernick, Annette Verschuren O.C., Dr. Kim Brooks and the Hon. Scott Brison took time out of their busy schedules to read an early version of the manuscript and to provide me with their support. Thanks go to them and to Donna McCready, Susan Crocker, Sherry Porter, Steve Mabey, Rod McCulloch, Clair Duff, and Gerry Griffin, whose support and input have been invaluable.

It is very common in acknowledgements to give credit to all those that gave advice on the writing and to assume full responsibility for all errors and misconstructions of that advice. I now fully understand why that is such an important inclusion. I have tried to do justice to all the wonderful input that I have received, but where I have failed to do so, I alone bear that responsibility!

Writing can be a lonely business. Thanks to my many friends and colleagues for their interest in my work, encouragement, and support—especially those who, with a straight face, insisted that they would want to read the result. I love them for their gift of friendship.

A special thanks to two dear friends of the family, Sir Iain Anderson and Professor Jaye Mehrishi, with whom I have had many interesting conversations, including about complexity. Their comments and input have enriched this project.

Thanks to my wonderful family. My sisters Mary (who worked on the cover for the book and is the source of some of the photographs) and Jane, two of my closest friends and supporters and without whom this book would not have happened. My brother-in-law, David Archibald, is likewise a wise and caring source of advice. My niece Karen Filbee Dexter and my two nephews, Paul Filbee Dexter and Dave Filbee Dexter, are a never-ending source of inspiration, joy, and love in my life. Ditto for Dave's wife, Kate (Katie) Stockdale and their son and my great nephew Henry Dexter. I consider myself so blessed to have all of them in my life.

The photographs on the book cover include ones of kelp courtesy of my niece Karen. She and her partner, Thomas Wernberg, are two of my scientist heroes for their dedication to the study of kelp, a fundamental part of marine ecosystems worldwide. Their work to preserve, and in some cases to restore, these ocean forests has opened my eyes to their importance as powerful carbon sinks—greater in area than the Amazon and in some areas just as much at risk. As one of the existential challenges that I write about in my book is climate change, I felt it appropriate to feature important natural ecosystems, both land and aquatic, of this planet we call home on the cover. We may be a very talented species, but as we are an inextricable part of the natural world, we are nothing without it.

Recognition of my family would be incomplete if I didn't mention my much loved and dearly missed parents, John and Shirley Filbee, who always believed in and supported me. They are now gone but are never the less still always present in my life. I truly hit the birth lottery with them!

Lastly, thanks to you the reader. My best wishes to you as you explore the concepts in these pages and for your own journey in this giant research project we call life.

Sara Filbee
Chester, Nova Scotia
May 2023

Cover Description

The photo design on the book cover shows a composite of photos from nature that exhibit what is called fractal patterning. Fractals are common in complexity and describe a pattern in which the laws of nature repeat at different scales in a way which is both predictable and unpredictable. They can be thought of as never-ending patterns; however, they never repeat in exactly the same way, and there is no way of knowing what future patterns will look like. They are regularly irregular and predictably unpredictable. Rivers, trees, flowers, snowflakes, sunflowers, seashells, ferns, broccoli, and humans are all fractal.

The arrangement of the individual photos is based on the *sectio aurea* or "golden section proportion," which also is found in nature. Artists often use what they call "the Golden Rule" to guide their composition. This **Golden Ratio** describes a sense of perfect balance or **proportion**.

Mary Filbee, Creative Designer, Chester, NS

Glossary

Acronyms. (abbreviations formed by using the first letters of other words, such as NASA or UN or YMCA)

ADMs. Assistant Deputy Ministers

Attachment. The bond that forms with the caretaker present at a crucial stage of development of the infant, usually in the second half of their first year of life.

Boids. An early and well-known example of complex adaptive systems. A computer program created to reproduce the patterns known as murmurations seen in certain flocks of birds or shoals of fish.

COO. Chief Operating Officer

Complex adaptive systems. Abbreviated CAS, they are computer programs which model the behaviour and interactions of many individual agents, each of which follow certain rules as to how they will relate to each other as determined by the computer programmer. No leader or single agent coordinates the actions of the others but through their interactions, patterns emerge.

DCMT. Departmental Crisis Management Team

DGs. Director Generals

Emergence. A universal process of becoming or creation in which the resulting outcomes cannot be predicted by understanding the behaviour (or composition) of the interacting parts or actors that are involved in creating the resulting phenomena.

Episteme. One of the three types of knowledge identified by the Greek philosopher Aristotle. *Episteme* is abstract or universal knowledge.

Figurations. Figurations are used to describe the web of interdependencies formed among human beings which connects them, a particular patterning of power relations and how we relate to one another.

Fractal. Fractal patterning describes a pattern that the laws of nature repeat at different scales. They are formed from nonlinear equations that contain self-similar complex patterns which increase with increase in scale or magnification. When a fractal pattern is divided into parts, you get a nearly identical copy of the whole in a reduced size.

Groupmindedness. The process of keeping both the group *and* the individual in mind at the same time.

Groupthink. Groupthink is a phenomenon that occurs when a group of individuals reaches a consensus without critical reasoning or evaluation of the consequences or alternatives. Groupthink is based on a common desire not to upset the balance of a group of people.

Habitus. The environment that has developed over time based on our individual and shared histories and the resulting patterns and themes of how we relate to one another, which determines the way we do things around here.

Nonlinearity. A relationship in which there are very complex connections between cause and effect which means that the effect is not necessarily proportionate to the cause and thus, a small change can lead to large differences in outcomes. This is sometimes described as the *butterfly effect* in complexity theory or sensitivity to initial conditions.

Paradox. A paradox represents what would appear to be two self-contradictory statements which are both true at the same time. It is the coexistence of one thing and, at the same time, its opposite.

Path dependence. A concept in economics and the social sciences found in complexity sciences in which past events or decisions can constrain future events or decisions.

Performative. With respect to words and/or actions, performative means that their very use or presence effects a transaction or constitutes the performance of an act. A common example would be the words "I do" in a marriage ceremony which changes the legal status of the relationship between two persons or the ritual expressions that are used in a court that confirm the authority of the speaker and their entitlement to speak.

Phronesis. One of the three types of knowledge identified by the Greek philosopher Aristotle, it is practical wisdom and good judgement associated with *praxis* or what we would call practice or experience.

Pragmatism. A philosophical movement or system having various forms, but generally stressing practical consequences as constituting the essential criterion in determining meaning, truth, achievement, or value.

Praxis. The practice or experience of an individual.

Reductionism. An analysis which reduces what is being studied to its component parts, on the assumption that doing so will allow us to do a proper scientific analysis of the subject.

Reflexivity. The ability to examine one's own feelings, reactions, motives, and intentions and how they influence what we do. Being aware of the impact upon how we think of both our own personal history and experiences as well as the traditions of thought and history of colleagues and our communities.

Self-organising. A property of complex adaptive systems found in complexity in which what is going on is because of what all the individuals are doing together, each according to their own programme or principles, as they relate to their neighbours. Out of the multitudes of these interactions, patterns of relating between individuals emerge which continue to affect their local interactions, creating never-ending cycles of acting and reacting, forming and being formed. There is no one individual in charge, and the resulting patterns are unknowable and unpredictable.

Symbol. The word symbol is generally employed to refer to something that is taken to represent something other than itself. Symbols are the medium through which we interact and communicate with one another thus making possible a shared understanding of our social world.

Techne. One of the three types of knowledge identified by the Greek philosopher Aristotle. *Techne is* technology associated with production, e.g., applied knowledge.

Trust. Trust is a "felt confidence" that an individual and/or group will meet our expectations about a particular outcome.

Value slogans. These are values that are adopted by organisations as branding statements or motivational slogans. In other words, they are values which are expressly adopted and made public.

Introduction

The journey that led to this book started early in my legal career. I was actively involved with the United Way as a volunteer, both in my hometown and nationally, and ended up leading two separate strategic planning type initiatives. The one at the local level was considered highly successful while nationally, we were unable to even raise what many of us considered important questions about issues facing the organisation. I had followed many of the same principles, and in fact, some of the same people had been involved and yet the results of our efforts were as different as night and day.

I could never understand why this was the case. In the local United Way work, we had to deal with some very difficult issues, and yet by the conclusion of the process, there was a broad and strong consensus that we were on a good path. And our ability to work together collaboratively had significantly improved. In contrast, at United Way of Canada, when we handed down our report for discussion, we were told that it was wrong, unhelpful, and highly risky, and both the discussion and the process were rejected outright. Our work was shelved with no follow-up consultation or report.[1] All of us who had been involved in the work were frustrated. It just didn't make sense.

This led to an ongoing fascination on my part with how one brings about change. At that time, I did not use the term complexity, but grabbed on to the language used in organisations, that of managing change. I became convinced that this was the issue and that it was just a question of learning how to do it properly.

I ultimately left law because I did not enjoy the practice, and perhaps more importantly, I did not feel I was making a difference. At the time I considered starting a PhD in change management, but my desire to not be a poor student got the better of my good intentions. Instead, I took on a job leading a career counselling and downsizing practice for a consulting company. That was followed by gigs as president of an economic think tank, a corporate banker, and a VP of operations for a start-up application service

DOI: 10.4324/9781003319528-1

provider in the human resources space. I used to joke that I couldn't keep a job, but the basic problem was that I never did find a job that fed my soul.

It was during my time as president of the economic think tank that I first stumbled onto the concept of complexity. The president of a regional university introduced me to Mitchell Wardrup's *Complexity: The Emerging Science at the Edge of Order and Chaos*. This book told the story of the founding of the Santa Fe Institute for the Study of Complexity and some of the initial scholars in the field who became its faculty. For the first time, this book helped me to understand just why management and change making are so difficult, and I decided that one day I would study in this area.

I joined the public service halfway through my career and spent the next twenty years as an executive in the Canadian federal government in three different departments, ultimately at the level of assistant deputy minister. Despite the aspersions often directed towards bureaucrats, I found myself finally in a place where I felt I could make a difference (albeit a small one) and was working with colleagues who felt the same way.

But I never let go of my interest in complexity. In fact, working in the government I became seized with just how complex the work was. There were so many interests and stakeholders that needed to be considered as well as the significant interconnections and interdependencies between them. I used to joke that anyone anywhere could wake up with a cold and it could change dramatically what was going on for the community and thus for us as public servants. When I got the chance to study in the field, I leapt at it and started the doctoral programme at the Complexity and Management Centre at the University of Hertfordshire in the UK.

In the Doctor of Management programme (we referred to it in shorthand as the DMan), I found myself studying and writing about a theory called *complex responsive processes of relating*. My thesis was on trust and its role in how we work together. I found that the insights from this way of considering the challenges of complexity helped me to make better sense of the world and the times in which we live. In fact, the more that I study in this area, the more I see how what on the surface seem to be very simple insights (albeit ones that resonate significantly for me given my career experience), can have quite major, or even radical, implications for one's management practice.

What made this theory so different was the integration of social theory into the science of complexity. The original scholars in this area, Ralph Stacey, and his colleagues, Patricia Shaw and Doug Griffin, were pioneers in using these social concepts to help understand the challenge of managing in uncertainty. As managing necessarily involves people working together, it is in retrospect quite astounding that it took so long for the substantial body of research, which seeks to understand our social condition to be consulted to inform management practice.

While this book is written for a general and not an academic audience, I have included references to relevant literature and some commentary in the end notes for those who wish to explore the issues further. You will also find a glossary of some of the key terms that you will encounter in these pages and a bibliography of resources.

As you will discover, in a complex environment it is rarely, if at all, possible to rely upon evidence such as used in the natural sciences that will allow you to know with confidence what *will* happen. Instead, our experiences are our data, and we need to rely upon reasoning (often by analogy) to help us determine what is going on. In this book, I draw heavily upon my experience throughout my career and have included several stories as illustrative anecdotes. Some of these experiences feature differences in perspectives between me and others. This is not necessarily to suggest that colleagues were wrong, or I was right, but to show how well meaning, talented, and caring people can differ and how our challenge is to try and respectfully understand the nature of the patterning of our relationships so that we can figure out how to go on together.

This ability to inquire into what is going on and why that may be the case is referred to later in the book as reflexivity. It turns out that this capacity is key for managers seeking to understand what may be happening. Drawing upon the social sciences such as sociology, philosophy, anthropology, and history can also help us to learn from our experiences. As I say in the final chapter of the book, living is effectively a giant research project as we seek to make our way in this complex world.

The book is in four parts. The first two chapters discuss the challenges of complexity and provide a high-level view of the work from the University of Hertfordshire to set the stage for what is to follow. The second part, Chapters 3 through 6, covers some of the key implications and concepts of this way of looking at management practice. Part 3, Chapters 7 and 8, examines in more detail, two aspects of management from a complexity perspective, the use of metrics and meetings. The chapters in both Parts 2 and 3 all conclude with a section titled "Implications for Your Practice" which aims to provide you, the reader, with practical suggestions for how to incorporate the concepts in the book into your practice. Chapter 9 summarises the book and leaves the reader with parting thoughts on leadership and the challenges ahead of us.

Traditional management theories, at least since the 1990s, have tended to make a distinction between leaders and managers. However, one of the consequences of taking complexity seriously is the realisation that what is going on in our workplace is the consequence of what everyone is doing. While leaders may have more influence than others, no one is an authority on their own. It is always a question of the interplay between individuals and groups.

For that reason, you will find that I use the terms managers and management for the most part, although I do refer to leaders and leadership when it involves considering aspects of positional authority and/or some way in which an individual leads others.

I am writing this at a time when we are (I hope) starting to emerge from the worst days of the Covid-19 pandemic. We see the horrendous brutality and destruction of the Russian invasion of Ukraine, which has put a spotlight on the worldwide conflict between authoritarianism and democracy. International reports on the climate change emergency increasingly warn us that we may have run out of time to mitigate the worst of outcomes. At the same time, we face high and increasing levels of income inequality; the legacy of colonialism; questions of social justice and racism; and the impacts of social media and big data upon our lives. At the risk of making my reader want to run home and pull the blankets over their head (which I must admit sometimes appears to be the wisest course) the complexities and challenges we currently face are likely to pale before what is ahead.

And so how we cope—let alone thrive—is a very real question for all of us. We have seen during the pandemic how many of the traditional theories about management were not suited to dealing with the radical uncertainty that we encountered. Most of the time, all we knew was that we had to do something, to decide, while everything we knew was likely to change—literally overnight. Assumptions that we would have evidence and data for our decisions were shattered. Modelling tools, while helpful, were shown to be flawed and incomplete. Any pretence that we could predict and determine our future was out the window. Half the time we didn't even know what questions we should be asking, and as the scientists worked hard to understand the science behind this virus, what did and did not matter. And yet we pressed on and did the best we could.

Maybe now is the time we acknowledge the lessons of the pandemic and re-examine how we think about managing and leading in this uncertain and complex world. This book is my contribution to that effort. This is not to say that everything you have been taught or have learned through your experience is to be tossed out. You will recognise many of the concepts discussed in these pages, such as trust, power, culture, values, and metrics. However, this new perspective, and the implications of taking complexity seriously may cause you to look at them differently.

This is not a recipe book. There are no answers in these pages, but I hope that you will find some of the alternative ways of understanding your work as a manager to be helpful. You may find that this book contradicts or questions what you may previously have taken for granted about your work. This type of reflection is not everyone's cup of tea. Instead, we are used to the legions of consultants who, granted often with the best of intentions, are happy to relieve us of our uncertainties and our cash in return for their prescriptions, assurances, and advice. However, what if you are not and cannot be in control? What if uncertainty is an inevitable part of our complex existence?

Any change in understanding requires you to let go of control in some way. That can feel like a high stakes manoeuvre. The reality is, however, that some of our ways of trying to impose certainty because of our fears of uncertainty are counterproductive. Depending upon your position in the hierarchy, you may have more, or less, leeway to change the way things are done around here (although all levels are constrained to a greater or lesser extent). Regardless, I hope that this book will provoke you to question some of the orthodoxy of your organisation, profession, or sector (even if only quietly) and to use that exploration and this perspective on managing in complexity to adjust your practice. If this book can do that in even a small way, then I shall consider this work to have been worthwhile.

Note

1 Ironically, the next time this strategic thought piece came to my attention was a decade later, when someone pointed to the document as being particularly prescient in its identification of the issues then facing the organisation.

Part 1

Managing in a Complex World

Chapter 1

Why Is Our World
So f&*$#@%! Difficult?

The Challenge of Living in Interesting Times

We live in interesting times. And in early 2020, just how interesting they can get became clear as the Covid-19 pandemic swept the world and gave all of us a crash course on the perils, pitfalls, and challenges of complexity. Covid brought home to many of us just how uncertain and unpredictable—how f&*$#@%! difficult and complex—the world around us is.

I was working in senior management in a large federal department of the Government of Canada during the early days of this crisis, and overnight we found ourselves struggling to maintain our essential services to Canadians at the same time as we were balancing and prioritising the health and safety of our employees. Most of us left our offices and headed home to work virtually in a department in which, prior to the epidemic, telework had been a definite no-no. At the same time, brand-new questions kept surfacing. How were we going to maintain our in-person services to Canadians? Was that even possible? We dealt with confidential documents and the private information of Canadians. How could we keep those secure once individuals were working from their homes?

Our policy and programme development folks worked day and night to re-invent our systems, policies, and procedures to get essential benefits—including some wholly new programmes—developed and delivered to Canadians, in many cases online. Those of us in the benefits and service delivery side of the department had to figure out how to implement and deliver these new or reconfigured programmes now that employees were not necessarily in their regular offices or able to meet with Canadians in person. Where and what type of masks did we need? Where could we find hand sanitiser as it quickly became a precious and scarce commodity? Some of our early supply arrived in wine bottles as distilleries and wineries repurposed their processes to manufacture this now essential elixir. One of my colleagues joked that she had become way more of an expert on plexiglass partitions to ensure distancing than she had ever expected or wanted to be!

DOI: 10.4324/9781003319528-3

Going online was not easy. Our technology was dated, and we had been actively engaged in traditional planning to move to an updated digital platform knowing that we had some time to do so. But then, we had to be online in a week. Procurement worked overtime to secure the necessary equipment for a virtual way of working. Staff drove to employees' homes delivering computers while others came into the office in a socially distanced way to pick up their belongings. Seemingly overnight, our IT department had to upgrade our bandwidth so that we could work online.

At the same time, we were all, to a greater or lesser extent, dealing with personal issues, hopes and fears that the pandemic had brought to life. Working relationships with our colleagues, unions, managers, and political bosses were intense. And throughout, along with the rest of the world, we were operating in a time of radical uncertainty as scientists raced to understand the nature and dynamics of the brand-new virus we now know as Covid. Key questions that were unanswered were how it spread, how (and if) one could protect oneself from it plus many other details such as what social distancing was and just how much distance was necessary. Often, it was hard to even know what questions we should be asking. Many a time we found ourselves trying to make a key decision with data and information that was unclear or incomplete all the while knowing that what we thought we knew was likely to change the next day. And in such extreme uncertainty, what was a right or wrong decision also seemed to change from day to day. Truly any manager's worst nightmare! Data or no data, however, all we could do was our best and then adjust as more information became available.

While I highlight the Covid pandemic as a time of radical uncertainty, complexity is not new, and it is not going away. For those of you who yearn for the simpler times, they never really were. As you will see when we examine complexity a little closer, the human existence is necessarily complex and has always been so. Even now as we are repeatedly promised that the pandemic is over and that it will become endemic and manageable, its knock-on effects in terms of labour shortages, supply chain disruptions, sustained damage to our health care infrastructure, and continuing health challenges from infectious diseases make it clear that our lives will continue to be more complex and uncertain.

If anything, the roller coaster ride that we have been on is likely to become even more challenging. As a society and species, we currently face several seemingly intractable issues that challenge the way we live and, in some cases, potentially our very existence. The climate change emergency poses just such an existential threat to humankind and the planet as we know it. We already experience unstable and severe weather patterns, wildfires, warming oceans, and sea levels rising around the world. As well, the staggering and increasing level of income inequality has had a damaging impact upon societal health and outcomes, further adding complexity and risk. We continue to struggle with the impacts of colonialism and questions of social justice and racism. And as if these weren't enough, the global tussle between autocracy and democracy as guiding principles for how we are governed is more evident than ever before.

You might have noticed that I omitted social media, big data, and the rapid exchange of information from the list of the pressures which have unalterably changed how we live and work, what we believe in, and what we care about. That is not because these factors are unimportant. To the contrary, the extent to which we are all connected and the speed and spread of issues and ideas is mind boggling, compared to the world before the world wide web came on the scene in the 1990s. This is particularly significant to understanding the levels of complexity that we currently face. Dr. Stuart Kauffman, an American medical doctor, theoretical biologist, and complex systems researcher who studies the origin of life on earth has shown that the extent to which what scientists call self-organising systems (for our purposes, a way of thinking about our world and also referred to as complex adaptive systems described later in this chapter) exhibit stability or, on the other end of the continuum, chaos or complete randomness is determined by the number and strength of the connections between the entities that comprise a system or network.[1]

Our global online interconnectedness now means that our connections and their potential impact have mushroomed to the point that a schoolgirl in Sweden protesting climate change inaction can become a global environmental icon. An incendiary tweet, and even lies, can move around the world in a flash. The concepts of fake news, echo chambers, and filter bubbles have unalterably changed global media and its societal impact. The number and strength of our connections with each other have exploded, and with it the uncertainty and complexity of our world.

Any one of these existential challenges would be daunting; the sheer number of them is terrifying. While the future is, by definition, uncertain and unpredictable, the risks and opportunities managers are having to manage and the extent of uncertainty they face is, to use what in these times has become a very tired word, unprecedented. We can no longer pretend that we have got everything under control as it is obvious that we have not. Clearly, learning how to function better in our unpredictable world is something we all need to do, both individually and collectively, in both our personal and work lives. And this means facing up to our collective fear of uncertainty, as the behaviours it inspires often cause us to make our circumstances worse and often more complex. That is what this book seeks to address.

A Quick Primer on Complexity

As a foundation for the concepts that we will explore in these pages, we need first to spend some time exploring the concept of complexity and its implications. My favourite way of doing so is to compare the process of bringing up a baby to completing a very difficult sudoku. A sudoku might only have a few numbers and be extremely difficult and complicated, but once you have done it, you can do it again. There will be a recipe, if you will, and you can solve it the same way you solved it the first time. Complexity, however, is more like bringing up a baby. You can bring up children (for arguments sake let's say four of them) in the same house, with the same parents, going to the same place of worship, schools, sports activities, community, and so on, and yet—inevitably—they will develop into four completely different individuals. And if you were to go back and do it all over again with the intent of replicating the experience, you would get different results. There is no recipe, and experiments or experiences, while they may be helpful, are not replicable. In other words, just because it happened this way once, doesn't mean that it will happen the same way the next time.

The difference between the complicated sudoku and the complexity of bringing up a baby is because human interaction is always complex, the future is unpredictable, and causation often nonlinear. We are always missing necessary information, our problems are never solved, and we find ourselves repeatedly confronted by the same issues and dilemmas. It's never just one thing that we must worry about. And often, in the words of Nassim Nicholas Taleb, the Lebanese American writer on randomness, uncertainty, and probability, we need to guess at problems more than we do at the solutions.[2] It is often challenging to figure out what is going on as it is not obvious. Could the observed issue be just a symptom of something else that is not working well? Is it perhaps opening the doors to an opportunity or new direction for the organisation? Or is it the crux of the problem facing us?

Complex issues, sometimes referred to as wicked, are inescapably dynamic. As we react to what we identify as a problem, we take actions that, in turn, have outcomes that change what we are dealing with, sometimes in highly consequential ways. As we make predictions about the future, we then react to what we think is going to happen and may change our behaviour, once again, affecting the patterning of events we are concerned about.

A good example is the stock markets. An event happens and traders react to it by making predictions about what will happen to the price of shares in the affected industry. They take actions based on those predictions which cause an increase or decrease in the price of the shares, while others, in turn, respond to these predictions and actions, further affecting the market.[3] In the workplace, we see the same patterning of action and reaction. We identify an issue that needs resolution and adjust our processes and procedures. In doing so we make changes that in turn prompt further actions and reactions which affect what is going on and potentially the issue that we were trying to solve to the point that we may be looking at a different problem.

What Do Boids Have to Do With This?

While the sudoku and baby comparison is helpful, we need to delve a little deeper into complexity science to fully understood why human interaction and our work together is inherently complex and what the implications are of taking this view. A useful place to start is with what are known as complex adaptive systems (CAS). This concept was developed by researchers at the Santa Fe Institute, an independent, not-for-profit theoretical research institute in Santa Fe, New Mexico, US, dedicated to the multidisciplinary study of complexity.

CAS are computer programs which model the behaviour and interactions of many individual agents, each of which follow certain rules as to how they will relate to each other as determined by the computer programmer. No leader or single agent coordinates the actions of the others but through their interactions, patterns emerge. With the advent of increased computational power, they have been able to model the weather, complex chemical reactions, traffic flows within cities, brain neural patterns, and so on.

An early, and well-known, example is called Boids.[4] This is a computer program created to reproduce the patterns known as murmurations seen in certain flocks of birds or shoals of fish. It is made up of several strings of code called agents, or in this case, Boids. Each is programmed to follow the same three simple rules: keep a minimum distance from other Boids and objects in the environment, match the speed of the others, and head for the centre of the cluster of neighbouring boids. With these three instructions, the complex patterns of flocking that we are all familiar with are generated.

Researchers didn't stop with Boids, however. As the capacity of computers has increased, so too have they been able to develop increasingly intricate models. For example, later models were created in which there were differences between the agents. These programmes led to the emergence of new patterns. In Boids, all we get are flocking patterns while heterogenous (e.g., not all the same) agents allow for the emergence of innovation and novelty of patterning, as well as changes to the agents themselves.

While these models can help us to understand the nature of complexity, they too are limited. In the real world, we deal with complex social phenomena, which are too multifaceted to be reduced to simplistic modelling.

First, in Boids all the agents are identical and operate based upon three specific instructions. Even in the programmes with heterogenous agents, they still have limited differences between them, not at all the almost infinite diversity of attributes and characteristics that distinguish individuals, one from the other.

Second, in these models, a limited number of agents interact with each other. Instead, we as employees, managers, and leaders interact not only with our organisational colleagues, but with friends, families, and neighbours. Further, we interact with and are affected by various aspects of the natural world as well as ideas and concepts from books, television, and other media.

Third, all the Boids do is flock, and the rules never change. There is no learning behaviour that shapes future patterning in any way, and there is no history in the sense that future murmurations will be different because of past flocking behaviour. When diversity of attributes is added to the programming of the agents, the patterning can change and some learning can occur, but again, the resulting patterns will be constrained by the instructions of the programmer.

Lessons From Boids

While Boids and other complex adaptive system models are significantly different from the human world, despite these differences, these computer programs can help us to understand the basics of complexity. This section discusses five of these basics under the following headings:

1. Just One Flocking Pattern After Another
2. Predictable and Unpredictable
3. No One Is in Charge
4. The Whole Is Not the Sum of Its Parts
5. Seagulls, Butterflies, and Nonlinearity

Just One Flocking Pattern After Another

The Boids computer model generates patterns of flocking, a flocking that is never at rest. The equations that generate this behaviour are never solved and continue to iterate and reiterate for as long as the programme is run. There is no equilibrium or steady state, challenging the traditional ways that we are taught to think about stability and change, order and disorder. While we talk in terms of beginnings and endings of projects, the reality is that there is always something going on. No sooner do we feel we have one problem under control, then something else happens that we need to attend to. Just when we figure we can draw a breath, that life is getting sorted out and we are on top of things, something else happens. As a friend of mine once said to me in a pitying tone when I complained that I had just cleared my desk and was once again snowed under, "Don't you know God hates an empty inbox"?

Our patterns of behaviour and relationships continue to evolve and change. Our interactions and reactions to and with each other lead to further interactions and reactions and in the words of the song first made popular by Sonny and Cher, *The Beat Goes On*. The action and activity never stop. To put it rather morbidly, equilibrium and steady state are only possible in the case of death.

Predictable and Unpredictable

While the general nature of the pattern may be predictable, e.g., in Boids we know that they are flocking; what the pattern will look like at any point in time is unpredictable. The patterns never repeat in exactly the same way, and there is no way of knowing what future patterns will look like. Still, we recognise them as flocking. They are both predictable and unpredictable. This type of patterning is evident in nature because the non-human world is also complex. Look around at nature and you will see very few straight lines and often what looks straight is revealed to be irregular when examined closely. This is known as fractal patterning, which describes a pattern that the laws of nature repeat at different scales. They are formed from nonlinear equations that contain self-similar complex patterns which increase as the scale or magnification becomes greater. Interestingly, if you divide a fractal pattern into parts, you get a nearly identical copy of the whole in a reduced size. Trees are natural fractals. While the branches and leaves all follow the same general pattern, they are regularly irregular and predictably unpredictable. As are their root systems. Snowflakes are also fractal as are humans. We are all different but similar. We all follow the same human pattern, but each of us is different, unique. And those differences are unpredictable. We are thus both predictable and unpredictable and regularly irregular.

The patterning of how we relate to each other is likewise fractal. Going into a meeting, we may have expectations about what will happen and how others will behave and what they will do based upon past experiences and the patterning of our relationships with each other. However, one cannot necessarily predict with accuracy what will actually happen. It is likely to be predictable but at the same time, unpredictable. As a result, our plans and strategies, no matter how wise and experienced we may be, rarely survive first encounter with the future, to paraphrase an oft used phrase.

No One Is in Charge

What goes on and the flocking patterns that develop, happen as each agent places constraints upon its neighbours and at the same time has its own actions constrained by others. Each of the three rules involve other agents: match their speed, keep a minimum distance from them, and head for the centre of the flock. At the same time, all other agents are also participating in the same dance and so as one Boid obeys the instruction to head to the centre of the flock, others must adjust their positioning to maintain the minimum distance. This leads to an ongoing negotiation of conflicting constraints and adaptations by the agents as they respond to each other.

This process is what is referred to as *self-organising*. What is going on is because of what all the agents are doing together, each according to their own programme or principles, as they relate to their neighbours. Out of the multitudes of these interactions, patterns of how these agents *will* relate to one another emerge. In turn, these themes of how the agents relate to each other continue to affect their local interactions, creating never-ending cycles of acting and reacting, forming and being formed. There is no boss, no one agent that provides instructions to the others and no one is in charge! Even the programmer, who is the closest thing to a boss in this situation, has only defined the principles guiding the actions of each agent. The resulting patterns are unknowable and unpredictable to them, despite their having created the program.

Notice that I am not saying it is an anything goes environment. Indeed, throughout this book we will be discussing the factors that do, in fact, both influence and/or affect how we interact with each other. However, these constraints and enablers predominantly occur as the result of our collective interactions and how we affect each other, rather than necessarily being due to the actions and reactions of any one individual. Thus, as a manager, while you may have influence over what is going on, you are still not able to control or determine what will happen.

The Whole Is Not Necessarily the Sum of Its Parts

These models and the state of complexity demonstrate what scientists call *emergence*. This is not necessarily in the sense that one action emerges because of another or that something becomes visible. Rather, in complexity science, the term *emergence* is used to describe a universal process of becoming or creation in which the resulting outcomes cannot be predicted by understanding the behaviour (or composition) of the interacting parts or actors that are involved in creating the resulting phenomena. What happens as the result of the interactions demonstrates properties and complexities that were not observed in its constituent parts; the behaviours and patterns that arise are not foreseeable. In other words, the whole is not necessarily the sum of its parts.

Seagulls, Butterflies, and Nonlinearity

In the 1998 romantic comedy/drama, *Sliding Doors*, Helen Quilley, played by Gwyneth Paltrow, gets fired from her public relations job and rushes to catch her train home on the London Underground. Just as she gets there, the doors close and the train leaves without her. This scene is then replayed, and she makes the train, slipping in just as the sliding doors shut. The film continues with the story alternating between these two separate timelines, only minutes apart, showing two paths Helen could have taken in life, love, and career, all depending on whether she caught the train or not. Spoiler alert, in the future version in which she catches the train, she meets someone on her journey who later becomes important to her. When she arrives home, she finds her boyfriend in bed with his ex-girlfriend . . . with foreseeable results. In the version of her future in which she misses the train, she is further delayed by an attempted mugging, resulting in a hospital visit. When she finally returns home, the ex-girlfriend is gone.

Sliding Doors was written and directed by Peter Howitt based on his novel by the same name. He was inspired to write the book by an experience in which he had deliberated crossing the road to make a phone call from a nearby phone booth. As he said in an interview with Haley Milotek in 2018,

> I had to phone a friend of mine about some play we were doing, and I saw this phone box on the other side of the road and for whatever reason, what I call the cerebral flipping of the coin—we make a thousand of these decisions a day—I came down on *phone him now*. I obeyed that instruction and just walked straight into the road without looking where I was going. And I nearly got hit square-on by a car, which screeched to a halt within an inch of me.[5]

He started to wonder what his life would have been like if he had been hit, and the thought experiment that turned into *Sliding Doors* was born. This book and film gave rise to the term "Sliding door moments"—the seemingly inconsequential everyday moments that can change the path and outcome of your life.

If we stop to think of all the little choices and decisions we make every day, let alone at work, we would be staggered by the number. Crossing the street or not. Catching the train or not. Phoning a friend or not. Turning left or turning right. Every day, individually and in our groups, we make millions of different decisions about what to do, where to go, who to speak to, whether to speak up or not, and so on. Some of these choices in themselves might seem inconsequential but might turn out to be life-changing for us and others. Small things can have a major impact, and all too often, we only recognise how important they were in retrospect.

Simply put, there's always a lot going on, a lot at play, and it's not necessarily linear in the sense that if X happens, then Y will be the result. This is what is called *nonlinearity*. A relationship that is typified by nonlinearity is one in which there are very complex connections between cause and effect, which means that the effect is not necessarily proportional to the cause. Thus, a small change can lead to large differences in what happens. This makes it impossible to assert with any certainty that X causes Y or that if X happens, then Y will result. Nonlinear relationships make the world around us intrinsically uncertain and unpredictable and are an important aspect of complexity.

This is sometimes described as the *butterfly effect* in complexity theory or sensitivity to initial conditions and is one reason why it is impossible to predict the future. This concept came from an American mathematician and meteorology professor Edward Lorenz in the early 1960s, who was conducting weather simulations on his computer. He had previously run the one in question and for some reason was re-running it. This time he reduced the number of decimal places of one of the variables from 6 to 3. Same number but to a different precision. In the time that it took to go and fill up his coffee, he returned to find that this tiny change had drastically altered the projected weather patterns over two months of simulated weather.

In his original paper, he suggested that the flap of a seagull's wings could lead to a tornado. His colleagues later proposed the use of the perhaps more poetic term, "butterfly effect,"[6] possibly inspired by the sci-fi novel, *A Sound of Thunder*, by Ray Bradbury (1953) in which a time traveller who goes back in time disrupts the future by stepping on a butterfly and discovers a completely different world upon his return to the present.

What this means is that the smallest of occurrences can lead to significant alterations in the resulting patterning of our experience, and thus, there is a high degree of sensitivity to initial conditions. This concept is also referred to as path dependence in the sense that past events or decisions can constrain future events or decisions. Such complex nonlinear patterning of the many, many interactions, choices, and events means the future cannot be predicted nor can it be controlled or determined.

Going back to *Sliding Doors*, we see a demonstration of nonlinear relationships. Helen who missed her train was clearly inconvenienced, but in the scheme of things, it could easily be regarded as a minor event. The thought experiment of following her two lives based on the differentiator of whether she caught the train or not, however, shows how this small event led to major changes in her life and in the lives of those around her.

This very brief look into complexity science gives some insight into the nature of complexity and the resulting uncertainty and unpredictability of the world around us. In turn, we start to see how this affects us in our lives and workplaces. As unsatisfying as it may be, we cannot predict what is going to happen and neither can we control or determine what is going on. This won't come as a surprise to the reader given that you have likely already experienced the challenges of getting ordinary tasks done or changes implemented in your organisation. All of us know the frustration of—and often anxiety—that comes about as the result of our expectations being unrealised and being surprised by what happens because of our (and others') actions. We all struggle to understand how we can do a better job of managing in such a crazy and complex world.

What Do the Experts Say?

Given the rather daunting task of leading in a world in which we can neither control nor determine what will happen, what do we do? Clearly, when things don't turn out well or as we intended, we can't turn to our bosses, shareholders, employees, citizens, customers, and other stakeholders and blame it on this darned complexity problem. Instead, we can only do the best we can. Luckily, or in some cases unluckily, one thing we don't lack for is management advice. There are legions of consultants, leaders, and academics researching, writing, and speaking on the subject and no end of theories and prescriptions for managers to follow.

This is not an inconsequential matter. Our theories about the world and reality are a part of what we know about the world and how we know it. There is much research that demonstrates that the perspective from which we view the world influences what we perceive.[7] Thus, we don't necessarily see things as they are, we see them as *we* expect to see them. And this, in turn, affects our actions and decisions.

This makes a lot of sense when you think about it this way. If you accept a particular theory about how something happens, then you are accepting the foundational assumptions upon which that theory relies. What is possible and what is not. What is important and what is not. What is relevant or irrelevant. What is noticed and is not. Thus, the theory itself may influence how you understand what is going on, what is in the realm of the possible— and thus what you can or should do about it. What we perceive is shaped by our theories of the world, which makes it important to understand what theories we are relying upon.

When we pay attention to one thing, we fail to notice others—no matter how obvious. One rather famous example of this is the experiment known as the "invisible gorilla" test. In this, a video of six individuals playing basketball is shown. The watcher is asked to count the number of passes made by those wearing white shirts. In the middle of this game a person dressed as a gorilla walks through the middle of the video, stands in the middle, thumps his chest, and moves on. In scientific experiments, about one half of those participating were so busy counting the basketball passes that they failed to even see the gorilla.

For simplicity, this book divides the theories about management into three categories: *Magico-mythical Thinking*, *Scientific Management*, and *Complexity Sciences Theory of Management*.[8]

Broadly speaking, the first two are based upon an individualistic approach to the world and to thinking about how change happens in organisations. In this individualistic view, we see ourselves as individuals, closed off, and separate from each other. In the past 30 years, this perspective has become much more pervasive and has informed our identities and theories about the world as well as generally accepted political, economic, and management policies and approaches. The approach named *Complexity Sciences Theory of Management* is based upon the sciences of uncertainty and, in particular, the research at the University of Hertfordshire. Rather than an individualistic approach, it emphasises the impossibility of separating the individual from the group.[9]

Magico-Mythical Thinking

Magico-mythical thinking, an expression adopted by Chris Mowles in his review of the dominant ways of understanding how change comes about in organisations,[10] focuses upon the special attributes and capabilities of individuals as being fundamental in unlocking or activating performance, innovation, and results in organisations. It represents a form of fantasy thinking, often related to the newest fads or fashions in management thinking. The American pragmatist John Dewey described magical thinking as hoping "to get results without intelligent control of means. . . . We think that by feeling strongly enough about something, by wishing hard enough, we can get a desirable result."[11]

A myriad of literature focuses on heroic and charismatic leaders, ascribing to them special abilities to engender the sought-after success in their organisations. Aspiring leaders are enjoined to follow their lead, to unleash their potential, and to be positive. If only you are positive or charismatic or have the right vision or possess the right leadership competencies, then all will work out well.

This is not to say that leaders or talents or skills are not important. While having a clear vision of what you want to see happen and the determination to pursue it may in some situations be assets, in a complex, predictable and unpredictable, nonlinear, and emergent world in which no one is in control, they can only get us so far.

Scientific Management

Management as a science is often traced back to the work of Frederick Taylor. In the early part of the 20th century, he proposed that management was an objective science with the goal of improving industrial efficiency through observation and study of the work. In fact, what Taylor called *scientific management* has since been referred to as *Taylorism* in tribute to his role in its development. In many ways, this type of approach relied upon a concept of science in which knowledge was obtained by means of the evidence of the senses and reason which emerged from the Scientific Revolution and Age of Enlightenment and the works of scholars such as Rene Descartes and Sir Isaac Newton.

Frederick Taylor was born into a wealthy Quaker family in Philadelphia in 1856. Despite initial dreams of studying at Harvard and then becoming a lawyer like his father, a Princeton man, his rapidly deteriorating eyesight led to him becoming an apprentice patternmaker and machinist and ultimately a machine shop labourer in 1878 at a company called Midvale Steel Works. There, several promotions followed in quick succession, driven partly by talent and partly by his fortunate status of being brother-in-law to Clarence Clark, son of one of the owners of the company, and he quickly became chief engineer of the works and machine shop foreman. At Midvale, he became interested in the productivity of both men and machines. His focus was on the human side of the production process which he originally called shop management but ultimately labelled *scientific management*. His 1911 seminal work, *The Principles of Scientific Management*, was voted the most influential management book of the 20th century by the Fellows of the Academy of Management.

Taylor's central concern was the efficient performance of a worker's tasks through the application of measurement, and it is this for which he is probably the most remembered. He analysed and synthesised workflows through the application of laws, rules, and principles. Processes and tasks were observed and split into the smallest possible parts. In what was to become known as time and motion studies, the required skills were identified and the time taken to complete each task measured, thus forecasting, or determining the quantity of the resulting production. Individual performance is governed by defined standards and rewarded by financial incentives to ensure a motivated workforce.

He enunciated four principles which he identified as fundamental to what he called *scientific management*. He used the term "scientific" because, in his view, if his methodology was followed, the best way of performing a task would be scientifically proven.

1. Rule-of-thumb work methods were to be replaced by a scientific study of the task.
2. Each employee was to be scientifically selected, trained, and developed rather than leaving them to train themselves.
3. Each worker was to receive detailed instruction and supervision in the performance of their tasks.
4. Work was divided between managers and workers; managers did the mental work of planning the work, and workers were responsible only for the manual labour.

One of the criticisms of Taylor's work is the overly mechanised way in which workers were treated. In fact, he specified directly that for some of the occupations that he was studying, e.g., the loading and unloading of pig iron, it was preferable that the workers not be intelligent. He noted that "The man who is mentally alert and intelligent is for this very reason entirely unsuited to what would, for him, be the grinding monotony of work of this character."[12] While Taylorism did lead to productivity increases, this was often accompanied by disruption and labour relations issues as owners sought to appropriate the economic benefits from these increases by hiring lower skilled and waged workers with less job security.

Competing management theories and methods continued to emerge rendering scientific management largely obsolete by the 1930s in the opinion of many. Newer theories included systems thinking, strategic choice theories, and approaches based upon organisational learning and knowledge creation or upon organisational psychodynamics. For purposes of simplicity, all these ways of thinking about organisations are included in the category of *scientific management*. Common to these theories is a view of the manager or leader as scientist and objective observer and in control of what is going on. The theories and prescriptions pay little attention to individual freedoms, politics, and the unknowable nature of the future. Proponents talk about management of systems or individual or organisational behaviours, disregarding our interconnections and interdependencies which extend way beyond the walls of the organisation.

While the original Taylorism may have been somewhat discounted, many of the professional and work practices that persist in the workplace today are a legacy of Frederick Taylor's work in scientific management. Many traditional views on organisational management and decision-making are founded on the primacy of the individual and based on the same often quite explicit assumption that management is a science, that there is a right or correct result, and that there is an evidence base (proof) justifying the approach. Management is often seen as the work of forecasting, planning, organising, coordinating, and controlling through setting rules for others to follow. Managers are supposed to be in control and to determine what will happen and what is to be done about it. It is assumed that they can control and change the organisational culture or create change by changing the rules. Some of the common tools that will be familiar to the reader include performance reviews in which individuals are measured against set standards and rewarded according to financial incentive systems, organisation charts, quality measurement and metrics, and production and sales targets. Time and motion studies are still used in organisations despite the increase in knowledge content of most occupations, which makes it even more challenging to apply such a reductionist approach to the measurement and optimisation of the work.

These classical approaches to uncertainty are typified by a reliance on quantification in which everything is reduced to numbers and metrics. There is a focus on deriving tools and techniques that will ensure a successful result if followed correctly. Also common is the reductionist simplification of issues by breaking them down into their constituent parts and ignoring their complexity and the nonlinearity of relationships. A common assumption continues to exist that the whole is the sum of its parts, and that causation is linear in the sense that if we do X, then we will get Y.

Another challenge with traditional management approaches is that they feature several taken for granted dualisms about organisations. For example, it is assumed that we can split things into objective or subjective, leader and follower, mind and body, and theory and action. Each of the two is separate from the other. In complexity, however, we encounter *paradoxes*. A paradox represents what would appear to be two self-contradictory statements which are both true at the same time. It is the coexistence of one thing and, at the same time, its opposite. A traditional paradox is the statement: "I always lie." Clearly if that is true, then the person saying it is claiming to always tell the truth. If, however, they always tell the truth, then they aren't doing so when they say that they always lie. In our discussion of complexity, an example of a paradox is when we say that something is predictable and unpredictable at the same time.

A quick reread of the description of our complex world will quickly dispel any illusion that these theories based on scientific management will suffice to meet the challenges facing managers. This is not to say that all such management practices are useless and should be thrown out. A more helpful perspective might be to say that they are necessary but not sufficient as they do not consider the complexity of human interactions, and, in some cases, may be dysfunctional or just not useful in the face of uncertainty where no metrics, models, tools, or best practices can ensure success.

Complexity theorists, Ralph Stacey and Chris Mowles, in their excellent survey of the research on the various traditions of thought related to organisational management, concluded that traditional management advice

> is a powerful way of thinking and managing when the goals and the tasks are clear, there is not much uncertainty and people are reasonably docile, but inadequate in other conditions. Truly novel change and coping with conditions of great uncertainty were simply not part of what scientific management and human relations theories set out to explain or accomplish.[13]

The challenge today is how to manage in an uncertain working environment while knowing that our work together is inevitably complex, never in equilibrium, and always evolving. Neither work nor life are predictable, nor can they be controlled. Important information is often lacking and sometimes it is even challenging to find the right question to ask. And if we ever think we have something all figured out, the dynamics change again!

We need a radical rethink of how we understand our work together. We need to incorporate lessons from the complexity sciences as well as the true sciences of uncertainty—the social sciences. This is what we will look at in Chapter 2.

Notes

1 Jeffrey Stamps and Jessica Lipnack, *A Measure of Complexity: Organizations as Complex Adaptive Networks*.
2 Nassim Nicholas Taleb, *Fooled by Randomness: The Hidden Role of Chance in Life and in the Markets*, p. x.
3 This is a type of complexity that goes beyond what we see in the natural sciences such as weather patterns. In history, politics, and the actions of humans, we react to the predictions about what we think will happen, thus increasing the level of complexity. See Yuval Noah Harari, *Sapiens: A Brief History of Humankind*, p. 267.
4 Chris Mowles, *Complexity: A Key Idea for Business and Society*, p. 19.
5 Haley Milotek, *The Almosts and What-Ifs of 'Sliding Doors'*, April 24, 2018, p. 2.
6 *When Lorenz Discovered the Butterfly Effect*, www.bbvaopenmind.com/en/science/leading-figures/when-lorenz-discovered-the-butterfly-effect/.
7 Ted Cadsby, *Closing the Mind Gap: Making Smarter Decisions in a Hypercomplex World*.
8 For those who are interested in exploring this in more detail, a much more extensive review of historical and current management theories is contained in the introduction and Part I of complexity theorists Ralph Stacey and Chris Mowles' book, *Strategic Management and Organizational Dynamics* as well as Chris Mowles' most recent book *Complexity: A Key Idea for Business and Society*, pp. 40–42.
9 This perspective on society and the individual is examined further in Chapters 2 and 4.
10 Chris Mowles, *Complexity: A Key Idea for Business and Society*, pp. 40–42 and 55–57.
11 John Dewey, *Human Nature and Conduct: An Introduction to Social Psychology*, p. 18.
12 Frederick Taylor, *The Principles of Scientific Management*, p. 59.
13 See Ralph Stacey and Chris Mowles' book, *Strategic Management and Organizational Dynamics*, p. 61.

Bibliography

BBVA. (May 22, 2015). *When Lorenz Discovered the Butterfly Effect*. www.bbvaopenmind.com/en/science/leading-figures/when-lorenz-discovered-the-butterfly-effect/, accessed February 5, 2022.
Cadsby, T. (2014). *Closing the Mind Gap: Making Smarter Decisions in a Hypercomplex World*. Toronto: BPS Books.

Dewey, J. (1922/2017). *Human Nature and Conduct: An Introduction to Social Psychology*. Globalgreyebooks.com.

Harari, Y.N. (2014/2016). *Sapiens: A Brief History of Humankind*. Toronto: McClelland & Stewart.

Milotek, H. (April 24, 2018). The Almosts and What-Ifs of 'Sliding Doors'. *Haley Milotek*. www.theringer.com/movies/2018/4/24/17261506/sliding-doors-20th-anniversary, accessed February 5, 2022.

Mowles, C. (2022). *Complexity: A Key Idea for Business and Society*. London, UK: Routledge.

Stacey, R.D., & Mowles, C. (2016). *Strategic Management and Organisational Dynamics: The Challenge of Complexity to Ways of Thinking about Organisations* (7th ed.). London, UK: Pearson Education.

Stamps, J., & Lipnack, J. (February 2009). A Measure of Complexity: Organizations as Complex Adaptive Networks. *NetAge Working Papers*. www.netage.com/pub/whpapers/whpapers/WP_Complexity.pdf, accessed January 6, 2023.

Taleb, N.N. (2004). *Fooled by Randomness: The Hidden Role of Chance in Life and in the Markets*. New York: Random House Trade Paperbacks.

Taylor, F. (1911). *The Principles of Scientific Management*. New York, NY: Harper & Brothers.

Chapter 2

Taking a Social Perspective on Management

Introduction

The young Ralph Stacey was first and foremost an econometrician. Early exposure to macroeconomics and Keynesian models had him so fascinated that he studied all he could find on the subject. Stacey was particularly interested in theories of economic cycles and the models used to explain them. He and his colleagues were convinced that with the right model, it would be possible to calculate the amount of investment that would be required to produce desired levels of outputs and jobs. In other words, to predict what would happen.

His PhD thesis at the London School of Economics was on assessing the predictive effectiveness of certain economic models which attempted to forecast patterns of industrial development. While his research persuaded him that significantly more research was required to find a better model, again, he never doubted that that was possible. The journey that led to his disillusionment with the predictive capabilities of economic modelling and eventually to his work in the field of complexity and management started after obtaining his PhD. He had returned home to South Africa to lecture on applied economics and was frequently asked by his undergraduate students whether anyone actually used the complicated models he was teaching. One of Stacey's strengths was that no matter how convinced he was of something, when confronted with an opposing view, he would often take it away and mull it over. In this case, he realised that as an academic he had no idea of what went on in the real world of industry, and ultimately, decided he needed to take a job in industry to find out.

His first posts at British Steel predicting steel demand and with the planning department of a construction company, involved forecasting and planning and started to sow the seeds of doubt that economic models were useful, at least at the national level. He still, however, held on to the hope that models would be helpful for companies. His third job was as an investment strategist for a stockbroker and fund manager firm, which was interested

DOI: 10.4324/9781003319528-4

in using his expertise to get a jump on understanding what was going to happen in the financial markets so that brokers and fund managers could be better prepared for their day. This proved to be the beginning of the end of any remaining convictions that it was possible to create models that could predict the future. In fact, Ralph found this part of his career to be incredibly stressful. He felt like an imposter as he had no clue what was going to happen on any particular day. Instead, he would find himself reading the financial papers on the train on his way in to work and summarising what he found there for the edification of the brokers and managers and feeling like a fraud.

To his great relief Stacey was made redundant and in September 1985, joined the Business School of the Hatfield Polytechnic, (now the University of Hertfordshire). There he continued to explore his increasing doubts about the ability to plan and forecast as none of the models or theories he had seen were able to do so successfully. Stacey began to inquire into social theory and the dynamics of groups and power relationships in the workplace. Bit by bit through studies of chaos theory and group dynamics (he qualified as a group psychotherapist at the Institute of Group Analysis), he started to realise that the reason for the inability to forecast accurately was because it was just not possible. In 1995 he met Patricia Shaw and Doug Griffin, and together they developed the theory of *complex responsive processes of relating* as a way of understanding the job of management in a complex environment.

The Perils of Complexity and Uncertainty

What Ralph Stacey was grappling with—and what most of us also struggle with in our workplaces—is the difficulty of managing in complexity. In Chapter 1, we explored the nature of this challenge: predictable and unpredictable, dynamic, and ever-changing, nonlinear and highly sensitive to initial conditions, self-organising and emergent. We don't know what is going to happen. The smallest of occurrences can prove to be pivotal for our future success. Problems are never solved. It is sometimes even difficult to know what we need to focus on as the nonlinearity of our world means that what we have taken for granted can change overnight. And what we think is the right thing to do at any point in time, may in fact turn out to be a huge mistake.

While clearly daunting, this is not a new problem, and over the ages, scholars and practitioners have worked to find ways to do a better job of leading in our topsy-turvy environment. Chapter 1, in a quick survey of three of the key streams of thought in management, referred to the magical-mystical and traditional science of management based on lessons from the natural sciences. Neither of these theories are up to the task.

The first is clearly not based on science. We need a reality-based approach and not one predicated upon magical or hopeful thinking. Hope is not a strategy. Neither is magic.

The second, scientific management, draws upon the sciences of certainty and suggests that managers can determine or control, can change the culture and ensure success. Again, in an uncertain world, we know that predicting the future or controlling and determining what will happen is impossible. While books are sold and consultants hired on the implied premise that the traditional approaches to management can provide the answer, sadly, there are no guarantees or sure-fire recipes for success in our complex world. Once one accepts that we are managing in complexity and cannot therefore predict or control what is going to happen, these prognostications are no longer as helpful to us. Notice I say not as helpful. One can never rule out the possibility of finding inspiration or useful considerations amongst the many tools and techniques that are out there. It is just that there is not an answer in a reductionist or deterministic way.

What is missing from both perspectives is a consideration of the sciences of uncertainty, the social sciences. This is an important omission given that the role of a manager involves, by definition, work with and through others. What was needed was to bring the perspective of the social sciences to the study of this issue. Ralph Stacey and colleagues were pioneers in doing just that.

The Power of Iterative Interactions—Predictable and Unpredictable

To understand the *Complexity Sciences Theory of Management*, we first need to revisit the theory of *complex adaptive systems* discussed in the last chapter and the computer programs which model the behaviour and interactions of a large number of individual agents. Each of these agents, heterogenous in the case of some of the more sophisticated programmes, follow certain rules as to how they will relate to each other which are determined by the programmer. In Boids, one of the simplest of the complex adaptive systems, the interactions that are enabled and constrained by three simple rules lead to the generation of dynamic and ever-changing patterns of flocking: Keep the same distance from others. Maintain the same speed. Head towards the centre of the flock. These three rules govern how the agents interact and mean that each Boid's action places constraints on the others as they are in turn constrained in terms of what they can do. The ongoing, nonlinear, and iterative interplay and interweaving of the actions and reactions of the Boids, or agents, leads to patterns of flocking that cannot be foretold based upon the individual actions of any one Boid.

If we argue by analogy, these computer programs are helpful in allowing us to have a better understanding of what is happening in complexity, and as discussed in Chapter 1, a different understanding of stability and change. Just as in the Boids programme, the uncountable interactions in our workplaces lead to the emergence of population-wide patterns of how we understand and relate to each other. There is no equilibrium. In complex adaptive systems, just as in our workplaces, what is going on is constantly evolving and dynamic.

In complexity speak, this is known as self-organising. This does not mean that each of us is empowered or in charge of determining what we will or will not do, but that what goes on happens because of what everyone is doing. The entirety is self-organising and not determined by any one agent or individual. Even the programmer in Boids does not know exactly what is going to result from the three simple rules. They know it will be flocking, but they don't know the exact patterning that will result. Similarly, in human existence, putting theological considerations to the side for now, there is no one in charge. No one determining what will happen.

Likewise, the perspective of *complex responsive processes of relating* proposes that what is going on—what is happening—is due to the interweaving and interplay of the actions, inactions, and intentions of the many interdependent individuals interacting with each other. Meaning emerges from our interactions, both direct and indirect, whether or not we agree or even share the same understanding or awareness of the outcome(s). For example, you are reading this book and the ideas and arguments will affect you in some way. You may agree or disagree. You may be prompted to think of something else or be reminded of an event in the past. You may take a different perspective on an issue or have your previous convictions confirmed as the result of what you read in its pages. You may be inspired to do something totally unrelated to the subject matter. You may experience emotions that affect how you feel about what is going on (It's really not that kind of book; however, it is still possible!). How you understand what went on in the past, your history, may be seen in a different light. What you expect in the future may alter. Direct or indirect, big or small, reading the book will alter your life in one way or another.

There is thus no master plan, strategy, or political decision that determines the future development of a group, organisation, or country. Instead, it is the multitude of interactions of interdependent individuals and groups that determines what happens. The resulting interplay and interweaving of the many intentions, choices, and actions of all involved leads to the development of population-wide patterns of how we relate to each other that organise and affect our experience of being together. As we work together and interact with each other, we both enable and constrain others in our gestures and responses.

For example, let's think about a meeting to discuss a workplace issue. You introduce a different perspective. You support what someone else says. You disagree but remain silent. You vociferously object to a statement. You compete and/or collaborate. All of these will influence the conversation, and how both you and other(s) are perceived and feel about themselves. In the process, we may confirm by our participation that we really know our stuff or perhaps that we haven't a clue about what is going on. We may create or destroy alliances and relationships with colleagues. In the process, through what we are all doing or not doing, the way that we relate to each other and how we think of ourselves is affirmed and strengthened or perhaps weakened or negated. The sociologist Norbert Elias would say that we are forming others, and at the same time we are being formed by the others.

A few words on these interactions. What comes to mind first, of course, are the direct interactions such as in a conversation or a meeting. Nowadays, courtesy of Covid-19, we have learned that these can be in person or through the means of any number of technological programmes (such as Zoom, Google Meet, Teams, etc.) that have become all too familiar to us. Interactions can also, however, be more indirect. The American pragmatist, sociologist, and psychologist G.H. Mead is known for his work on what he called "gesture" and "response." The gesture is an action or movement that enables others to become aware of the intentions of an individual and which in turn calls out a response in them. This is not as simple as it sounds. The meaning that emerges lies in the gesture and response *taken together*. I may have certain intentions as to what I am trying to convey in my gesture, but how you interpret my gesture and intentions is dependent upon your history and perspectives. If someone reminds you too much of a child that bullied you all through school, then that is likely to affect the meaning that you make from his or her gesture.

To elaborate, I make a comment, in Mead's terms, a gesture, and others respond to me by agreeing, disagreeing, or even (sadly enough!) pointedly ignoring me. Gestures can be written, enacted, or filmed. A book is a gesture. A movie or play is a gesture. It is an offering of a communication of some form of meaning. The response may or may not come back to the author, actor, or producer, but there is a response or a reaction as it were from the reader or viewer. Thus, when I use the words, "many, many" as I did earlier, I am indeed dealing in the universe of so many as to be uncountable in terms of numbers of interactions in our collective daily existence.

Our identities are created, strengthened, and/or weakened by these patterns of relating. While Boids has three simple rules, we have significantly more influences and constraints upon us as we work together. Our power relationships and who needs whom the most affects how we present and interact with colleagues. Our emotions can determine how we react, what we become aware of, and what is important or unimportant to us. Our individual and collective norms and values influence what we consider to be a wise or rash, proper or improper decision. Thus, we are in a constant state of flux, evolution, and emergence which leads to a dynamic and ever-changing patterning of how we relate to each other. No one is indeed an island.

The patterning that emerges is nonlinear in the sense that one thing in a process or series of events does not clearly or directly follow from another. We cannot necessarily say that if X happens, Y will result. We cannot know for sure what has caused what, as in complexity, what is going on is as a result of this nonlinear patterning of interactions. Thus, it is not just any one thing. And yet it is also not the case that anything goes. We are all enabled and constrained in different and similar ways as we form and are formed. While what is going to happen cannot be predicted and the whole is not necessarily the sum of its parts, nevertheless in the unpredictable patterning of our relationships, there is also some predictability in terms of the repetition of patterns. And while we cannot know for sure, we can hope to develop a better understanding of the themes and dynamics of what is going on.

If we take this way of thinking about interactions and patterns further, taking complexity seriously also has implications for how we understand our organisations and groups, which is the subject of the next section of this chapter.

We Interact Our Organisations Into Being

We often talk about organisations as if they are tangible beings, and legally, they are deemed to be a person, provided they have certain governance structures and follow the requirements in the applicable legislation. In fact, they are social objects which we have agreed as a society to treat as a being (in the same way as we have agreed to treat certain pieces of paper or metal as legal currency). They can also be thought of as social processes of communication and joint action.[1] Scholar Deirdre Boden, a film maker turned qualitative researcher, proposed that it is the activity of talk that structures our organisations: "When people talk they are simultaneously and reflexively talking their relationships, organizations, and whole institutions into action, or into 'being.'"[2] Of course, using the language of complex responsive processes of relating, you would say that they interact the organisation into being. This is so much more than verbal communication. It is written. It is body language and gestures. It includes what is, but also what is not said or done. Corporate documents, emails, letters also are a part of the interactions that constitute the organisation.

The theory is called *complex responsive processes of relating* and not *complex adaptive processes of relating* to highlight that these patterns and how we relate to each other are always potentially emergent and transformative as we respond one to the other. We don't just adapt to what is going on. Unlike the agents in the computer model Boids, we are not billiard balls, which when hit by another are not themselves affected but merely displaced in time and space. Instead, as we act and interact; we are responsive to and affected by what others do and say. We may feel included or excluded. We may be moved to anger, to laughter, to sadness. We may be prompted to understand what is going on in a new light, or we may be confirmed in our previous opinions. All these are just some examples of how we may emerge from our interactions different in some way. This will affect not only us but also our colleagues with whom we interact and, in turn, those with whom they interact in a never-ending cascading of effect. Thus, in contrast with the billiard balls, when we interact with one another, we are changed in some way. We are formed, and at the same time, we affect and form others and the patterning of our interactions. In the result, the whole, is not necessarily the sum of its parts.

While we tend to draw imaginary lines around organisations to denote who is inside or outside the organisation, practically, those lines are permeable or fuzzy. An author can write a book on how to solve a problem. Someone who works in the organisation picks it up and reads it and decides to incorporate it into the approaches used in their workplace. That interaction can thus affect the patterning of the intentions, choices, and actions of the employees of the organisation. The fact that the author never met or interacted with them in person or that they may not even know the organisation exists does not necessarily matter.

Imagine you are walking to work, and you bump into an old friend. You share the rest of the walk with them until one or the other arrives at their workplace and you part. Let's assume that you end up chatting about a problem that you are agonising over. As often happens when a different perspective is introduced, they make a comment, and the proverbial light goes on for you. Suddenly you have a better idea of how to manage the issue. In that interaction they, although not a colleague or an employee of your company, were part of the interactions affecting the patterning of how you work with colleagues. This means that while determining that someone is inside or outside an organisation may well have legal consequences or implications for identity (status and who they think they are), aspirations, and perceptions, it is not necessarily relevant in thinking about what is happening with the complex patterning of relationships affecting individuals and groups within the organisation.

Our social processes of working together are different from the complex adaptive systems that we encountered in Chapter 1. Organisations are not systems. They don't have effective boundaries (other than the legal kind) in terms of how they operate and develop. This is very different from Boids or the other complex adaptive systems in which there are a discrete number of agents and while new ones might be created or old ones die, they are still limited, and their numbers determined by the operation of the computer program. In contrast, our societies, our communities, our organisations, and groups are not limited wholes with boundaries.

Norbert Elias suggested that societies are always more or less incomplete, remaining open in time as a continuous flow. For him, it was a question of what he called *figurations*, a particular patterning of power relations and how we relate to one another.[3] They thus cannot be thought of as systems as that would require that they were complete in and of themselves and somehow hived off from the rest of the world.[4]

This is more than just an interesting intellectual distinction. It helps to explain why our work together is so complex. We don't get to just limit our area of concern to those few people with whom we interact directly. Or perhaps throw in a few clients. When we are interacting with these individuals, we are also interacting with everyone they know or have met—ever. Every book that they have read or movie that they have seen that affects how they understand the world and their place in it potentially comes into play. And, of course, in this time of the internet and social media, the potential influences are virtually unlimited.

Instead of thinking of our organisations as systems therefore, many scholars are of the view that it is more helpful to think of them as relational or temporal processes, which leads us to a consideration of time.

A Consideration of Time

Complexity theorist, Doug Griffin, one of the early scholars in the development of the perspective of *complex responsive processes of relating*, wrote on the relationship between the present, past, and the future. He proposed that

> Knowing what one is doing immediately incorporates anticipation and expectation into the action of the present and it also immediately incorporates reconstructions of actions past, or memory, all as the basis of acting in the present. Anticipations and expectations affect what we remember at any point and what we remember at any point affects expectation and anticipation.[5]

This concept is referred to as the *living present*. We act in the present—in the now—based upon our expectations of what is going to happen in the future. We work on the problems we encounter with the intent (or hope) that they will not be problems in the future. Our understanding of what is going on in the present and our anticipation and expectations of the future are based on our memories of our histories and experiences of the past.

These histories and experiences have, or at least our memories of them have, led to how we understand our reality. What we expect in the future is affected by what we remember about the past. As we learn more about the future, it may cause us to revise our understanding of what went on in the past and, in turn, may affect how we anticipate the future. Again, it is not possible to separate one from the other, and our perceptions of what is going on in the present, what will occur in the future, and what occurred in the past are continually evolving and changing in the emerging and dynamic complexity of our existence. And thus, history matters in that the past can be a guide for us. It is not, however, and cannot be, a hitching post! This counters what Griffin described more colloquially as being the "blinding power of our habit of excluding the future and past from our understanding of the present."[6]

Take an example where you are going to meet with someone to negotiate a contract. Based on your experience with this individual, you anticipate that this will be an easy one to conclude. But as the discussion proceeds, it becomes evident that this is, in fact, going to be much more difficult than anticipated. You start to rethink your past dealings with this person and what you thought you had known about them. You remember a little incident from a few months before and perhaps some gossip in the industry about the company in question. That is to say, you begin to revise your understanding of the past and thus your expectations for what is possible for the future. The more the future becomes the present, the more the past is revised and updated, and the more that your expectations change. This is important for us as complexity thinkers because it departs from a more static or linear view of time, instead showing it as an ever-evolving dynamic in which the past, present, and future are interrelated.

A related concept to the *living present* in complexity science is referred to as path dependence or sensitivity to initial conditions, in which prior choices may constrain and determine our future options. As the noted sociologist Robert Putnam said, "where you can get to depends on where you're coming from, and some destinations you simply cannot get to from here."[7] And thus, in the opening words of the influential economic historian and economist Douglass North's book, *Institutions Institutional Change, and Economic Performance*, "history matters."[8]

A Unique Fusion of Natural and Social Sciences

The discussion to date has focused on what we have learned from complexity research. However, it can clearly be seen that the social sciences are also an important part of this puzzle. Ralph Stacey and colleagues drew heavily upon group dynamics, pragmatic philosophy, and what is known as process or figurational sociology.

Group dynamics is obvious. What is going on is as the result of the inter-actions of many interdependent individuals out of which patterns of how we relate to one another emerge. Thus, by definition, we need to go beyond the consideration of the individual or psychological to examine groups and how they function and how individuals relate to one another.

Process, or figurational, sociology is a field of research that investigates the workings of groups (figurations), of evolving networks of interdepend-ent individuals. Process sociologists attempt to look at the process through which a particular social feature or behaviour has emerged and evolved to more fully understand how it functions in the present. The German-born sociologist Norbert Elias, usually considered to be an early and key prac-titioner as the result of his ground-breaking work, *The Civilizing Process*,[9] wrote extensively on how social processes were derived from the inter-weaving of the aggregates of individual acts, a perspective which mirrors research coming out of the complexity sciences.

Pragmatism as a philosophical tradition became dominant in the United States in the early 20th century. Early scholars in this field included phi-losophers Charles Sanders Peirce, William James, John Dewey, and George Herbert Mead. This way of thinking is founded on the principle that the usefulness, workability, and practicality of ideas, policies, and proposals are what determine their merit and that the pursuit of perfection is unhelp-ful. Action is preferred over theory and experience over fixed principles. Or as John Dewey said, effectively dismissing generalities and abstractions: "There is no such thing as conduct in general; conduct is what and where and when and how to the last inch."[10] Every detail about conduct makes a difference in terms of what happens because of our actions. For example, in a discussion between two co-workers, it is not only the words that are used, but also the tone of voice, physical posture, facial expressions, and even the timing of comments that may determine how the conversation affects the relationship or work project.

Coming Attractions

As we delve further into the question of how complexity affects us in our role as managers, you will notice the influence of these traditions of thought. Chapters 3 through 6 examine key implications for managers that flow from taking complexity seriously. Chapters 7 and 8 explore in greater detail the implications of taking this perspective for our conversations in the workplace by considering the use of metrics and our formal meetings. Each of these chapters concludes with implications for your practice that flow from the con-cepts addressed in that section. Chapter 9 pulls the discussion together and concludes with a reflection on the role of leadership and a challenge to man-agers and leaders to move to a new, more sustainable, way of management.

Before moving on, however, the following is an overview of the key concepts you will be exploring in more depth in the chapters to come:

We Need To Be Both Emotionally Involved and Detached

This chapter addresses a common admonition that our decision-making should be objective and rational and that we should put our emotions, lived experiences, and views aside. Instead, we need to be both emotionally involved and detached at the same time.

Our emotions and cognition are physiologically intertwined, making it impossible to separate them. We need to be both emotionally involved and detached (or rational) at the same time. Emotions can affect our perceptions and cause us to depart from our habits and what we have taken for granted and can lead to significant innovation. The chapter also addresses some of the ways in which emotions can get in the way of our work to make meaning together.

Likewise, our lived histories, experiences, values, emotions, and beliefs are inextricably part of how we understand the world and what is going on. We are involved in the interactions that constitute the patterning of our relating with one another and cannot therefore be fully objective. What is determined to be objective, rational, and a good decision is often a product of who makes the judgement and when they make it.

The concept of *phronesis*, practical judgement and wisdom, essential in complexity management, is explored.

We Are Interdependent

Traditional management approaches often focus on an individualistic approach to leadership and performance management, rewards and incentives, resourcing and finding the right person for the job. Instead, Chapter 4 explores the inherent dilemma or paradox that we, as interdependent individuals, cannot exist without each other and, in turn, society (the organisation) does not exist without us as individuals. We are inseparable and interdependent. Neurological, psychological, and anthropological research confirms that we are fundamentally social; we are who we are because of our interactions and relationships with others. When both the individual and the community are valued, both are stronger.

At the same time as we perform as individuals, we also perform as a group. It is thus imperative that we keep group dynamics in mind as managers. The chapter considers the dynamics of insiders and outsiders and the tendency for "us versus them" thinking in the workplace.

Managers need to be conscious of the needs of others (*groupmindedness*) and responsible for how they relate to others and to groups as well as their role as champions and enablers of the group. The way we work together is likely to affect how we *will* work together.

The Key Element of Trust

The chapter discusses how *trust* can be understood from a complexity perspective. Trust is a patterning of how we relate to one another and is defined as a felt confidence that an individual and/or group will meet our expectations about a particular outcome. Trust is both cognitive and emotional and highly fragile because a single instance of untrustworthy behaviour can break our trust. Trust and respect are interconnected; and the reciprocal nature of trust means that if you don't trust me, then I am unlikely to trust you and vice versa.

Trust can reduce transaction costs and make us more efficient. In times of anxiety and uncertainty, it can also enable us to manage our fear of uncertainty and allow us to explore *productive doubt*, which is fundamental to innovation, creativity, and meaning-making.

Trust can also hinder the exploration of productive doubt. Processes of inclusion and exclusion are often affected or determined by who we trust and who we don't, which can create or strengthen *in-groups* and *out-groups* and lead to *us versus them* thinking. Strong trust relationships can also lead to problems such as *groupthink*, where maintaining inclusion in a group becomes more important than surfacing a different perspective.

The Way We Do Things Around Here

Chapter 6 explores one of the fundamental responsibilities of managers, which is to seek to understand what is going on in the workplace and what that means in terms of how we will be able to work together productively. In other words, the culture, or what scholars have referred to as the *habitus* of our organisations. This represents our agreements and understandings of the "way we do things around here." Our habits, values, and beliefs. The language we use. The stories that we tell ourselves and each other and the symbols that have special meaning and/or emotional connections for us. All of these affect the groups that we belong to and our identities as well as what we take for granted and what and how we understand and perceive what is going on.

The chapter introduces the concept of *value slogans*, a subset of values used as branding or motivational slogans, and an exploration of how they can affect how we work together.

In Metrics We Trust

An example of a value slogan is the expression "evidence-based." Evidence is something that proves or disproves something and upon which we seek to rely. We can draw on both quantitative and qualitative research, each of which have their advantages and limitations. However, often evidence is either not available or imperfect or what we need to know cannot be measured.

Claims of being evidence-based are often biased towards the use of quantitative data or metrics. They are perceived to be certain, rational, objective, and unable to be argued with and thus provide the decision-maker with the ability to demonstrate that they have made the right decision.

The chapter explores the limitations of quantitative research and metrics. Metrics which depend on averages or approximation or which are constructed as an index can cause important information to be lost or obscured. They often improperly infer linear cause and effect. Metrics can be socially determined including by whether they align with social narratives. What is acceptable evidence is often determined by who has power and status.

Metrics convey information but not understanding, may prematurely close the exploration of productive doubt down, affect what we focus on, and displace practical knowledge.

Meetings, Meetings, Bloody Meetings

Our work together is difficult as it is almost impossible to solve a complex problem. Nothing stays the same and tasks are never done. Discussions are often conflict laden and identity challenging. The inability to predict or determine results creates anxiety and challenges our need to control and to be right. Additionally, our histories and past experiences of interactions with each other have a long tail in that they affect how we will relate to each other in the future. The importance of *friction competence* is explored.

This chapter considers the lessons learned from a government department's experiences during the Covid-19 pandemic. The dangers of empty rituals in our meetings are explored with a consideration of how agendas and PowerPoint presentations can negatively affect our ability to make meaning together.

In determining whether our meetings are successful or not, we should look for what is a good enough step to take together for now, acknowledging that in the future we may face a completely different set of problems.

The chapter concludes with a discussion of ways to make meetings more successful in our complex and uncertain environment.

Our Fear of Uncertainty

Before closing off this chapter, a few words on one of the fundamental themes of this book as context for the chapters to come.

In my work experience, I have often found the activity of *sensemaking* to be exciting, a coming together of the team and affirmation of our collective identities, as we seek to find a way to go on together. The process can be rewarding as we feel we have instituted an agreed-upon order to the puzzlement of our existence. There is no better feeling than the high-fives all around that you get when your team has thoroughly nailed it! Indeed, the great American pragmatist, John Dewey suggested that the disciplined mind would delight in and enjoy the doubtful, or as he termed it "operations of infinite inquiry."[11]

The German philosopher Hans-Georg Gadamer once said that every experience worth its name thwarts an expectation.[12] While this can be positive and exciting, in a complex world where we can neither predict nor control what will happen, such surprises can often be anxiety creating and unwelcome. Something may have gone wrong and/or disrupted our expectations[13] contrary to what was supposed to happen. Our plans and hopes for success are thus undermined, and we may doubt our capacity to know what is going on, and ultimately to be successful. All of this is difficult, conflictual, and destabilising and can challenge our very identities as careful and competent managers.

Because we are intelligent people, we fear uncertainty. I have, many times, heard department heads say categorically that we were in a "no surprises" environment, and it was our job to keep it that way. We needed to be "in control" and "on top of what was going on." In the alternative, there was always the prospect of second guessing and blame laying, destabilising the team and threatening both our organisations and our careers. Regardless of how difficult these surprises can be for us, however, Gadamer argued that there is a fundamental link between negative occurrences and insight, which he termed part of the ultimate vocation of human kind.[14]

Conflict is also a necessary part of our work to make meaning and figure things out, as the issue we are addressing often comes to light due to some breakdown or failure to achieve our expectations. Frequently in complex environments, we are called upon to balance conflicting and seemingly irresolvable and deeply felt interests, values, and understandings of what is good and what is to be avoided. We are required to make value determinations which can be challenging—and often disputed. Often, there is no satisfactory answer.

In fact, not only is conflict inevitable, but difference and dissent are necessary for innovation and creativity and the necessary exploration of the diversity of our perspectives. There is no innovation if we are all in agreement. Despite this, we tend to avoid conflict because we need to work together, and conflict is difficult, uncomfortable, and unpredictable. We need to find ways to explore how we can manage conflict so that we are able to stay in relation with each other despite our differences.

Finally, in the give and take of sensemaking, our identities, values, and assumptions as to what we know are right and true are often challenged. As already mentioned in Chapter 2, process sociologist Norbert Elias suggests we continually renegotiate our identities as we form and, in turn, are formed by the reactions and actions of others. Sensemaking can be challenging because it challenges us by *changing who we are* both as individuals and as groups, and how we relate to each other. Neither the individual nor the group emerges unchanged from our work to make sense together. Canadian philosopher Charles Taylor similarly argued that as we come to understand each other, it necessarily leads to a changed understanding of ourselves.[15] Our very sense of our self and our sense of each other is, therefore, continually challenged in our work to figure things out. This can be particularly difficult for individuals or groups who are highly involved (and invested) in a system and are thus often afraid of changes to their accepted reality or status.[16]

Thus, whether prompted by a breakdown in our expectations, by the challenge to our identities or through the conflict that it engenders, anxiety is inevitable in our work together. Our fears of uncertainty, rational although they may be, can lead to coping mechanisms which may exacerbate a difficult situation, even increasing the complexity that we collectively and individually face. Emotions may cause us to engage in defensive behaviours and create unhelpful group dynamics, thus impeding our ability to work together as a team. The desire to make the problem go away can also drive managers and groups to rush to conclusions so that they can have certainty, fix the problem, declare victory, and move on.

While I may be perceived to have accused John Dewey of idealising the joy and delight of the process of inquiry, in fact he wrote eloquently on the challenging nature of problem-solving. His book titled *Quest for Certainty*[17] considers how this continual quest is driven by our anxieties and fears of risk and uncertainty. This is understandable. What we as managers need to do, therefore, is to find ways to deal with our fears of uncertainty in a way that does not make things worse—and hopefully makes them better. Sometimes this just means managing one's own reaction. Ralph Stacey was known to say that sometimes the best leader was the one that was the most able to manage their anxiety. As uncomfortable as it might be, sometimes, as Chris Mowles said to me once, it is just necessary to remain in the fires of uncertainty a little longer to allow a more in-depth exploration of the issue at hand. This work can, however, also include being conscious of the anxieties of others and making them feel safe enough to sit in those fires with you. In the chapters to follow, we will be examining several concepts and implications to support you in doing just that.

Summing Up and the "It Depends" Rule

The theory of complex responsive processes of relating is a radically different way of describing what is going on in our work together which is inspired by complexity science and draws upon social theory. It helps by giving us a starting point to try and understand what is happening. We can then use that understanding to better navigate the shoals and reefs of our shared coexistence and mutual ventures. This way of considering complexity takes us beyond the usual discussions about culture, change management, individual leadership competencies and tools and techniques and focuses on an inquiry into what is going on and the practice of the manager. This perspective places a premium on how we are relating to each other and how that will affect our ability to make meaning in our work together.

As noted previously, this does not come with the security blanket of certainty. There are no guarantees and no answers in our dynamic, ever-changing, interdependent, and unpredictable world. No recipes or tools or techniques will ensure we get the result(s) we are seeking and then allow us to successfully replicate the process elsewhere. In fact, as unsatisfying as it may be, the answer that is likely to always be correct is "it depends"; but just try giving that response to your boss or shareholders!

Despite its limitations, however, this theory does give us a way of looking at what is going on and helps us to make sense of our experience, which is generally a better plan than adopting comforting, although likely to be false, certainties and rules. While we need to accept that we cannot know for sure what is happening now or what will occur in the future, we can increase our understanding of what is going on which, in turn, will help us to work better together. Taking complexity seriously, transforms the way that we work and lead in a way that is profoundly more effective. It allows us to engage in an exploration of different perspectives and enables a more respectful, sustainable, and innovative way of working together in a complex environment. It may also help us to manage our fear of uncertainty so that we are collectively able to do a better job—despite the pressures of the situation.

As you will see, achieving this type of understanding places a premium on the notion of *reflexivity*. By this we mean being aware of the impact upon how we think of both our own personal history and experiences as well as the traditions of thought and history of colleagues and our communities. This will be a theme throughout and is a skillset or competence that demands that we adopt a thoughtful consideration of what is going on in the workplace. What is the nature of the interactions and patterning of how we are relating to each other? What am I doing and why? What are others doing—and again, why? How am I affecting others? How are they affecting me? This can be a highly challenging and sometimes humbling exploration but still one required of managers if they seek to be effective in a complex environment.

Let's Get Started

This chapter has been an attempt to summarise the concept of *complex responsive processes of relating* and to draw out some of the implications of taking such a perspective on how we work together. The next chapters will explore in more detail this theory and its implications, starting with the concepts of objectivity and rationality.

Notes

1 See Patricia Shaw's book, *Changing Conversations in Organizations: A Complexity Approach to Change*, p. 124; also see Doug Griffin's book, *The Emergence of Leadership: Linking Self-Organization and Ethics*, p. 212.
2 See Deirdre Boden, *The Business of Talk: Organizations in Action*, p. 14.
3 Norbert Elias, *The Society of Individuals*.
4 The French sociologist Pierre Bourdieu also argued that societies could not be systems. He used the idea of a *field* which is a domain where specific power relationships and conflict over capital took place.
5 Douglas Griffin, *The Emergence of Leadership — Linking Self-Organization and Ethics*, p. 184.
6 Ibid., p. 184.
7 Robert Putnam, *Making Democracy Work: Civic Traditions in Modern Italy*, p. 179.
8 Douglass C. North, *Institutions, Institutional Change, and Economic Performance*.
9 Norbert Elias, *The Civilizing Process*, 1939/1994.
10 John Dewey, *Moral Theory and Practice*, p. 191.
11 John Dewey, *The Quest for Certainty: The Later Works, 1925–1953*, p. 182.
12 Hans-Georg Gadamer, *Truth and Method*, pp. 364–365.
13 See Andrew D. Brown, Ian Colville and Annie Pie, *Making Sense of Sensemaking in Organization Studies*, p. 266; Karl Weick, *Sensemaking in Organizations*, pp. 4–6, Karen Filbee-Dexter et al., *Ecological Surprise: Concept, Synthesis, and Social Dimensions*.
14 Hans-Georg Gadamer, *Truth and Method*, pp. 364–536.
15 In Jeff Malpas, Ulrich Arnswald and Jens Kertscher, eds., *Gadamer's Century: Essays in Honor of Hans-Georg Gadamer*, p. 295.
16 Norbert Elias, *Involvement and Detachment*, p. xxv.
17 John Dewey, *The Quest for Certainty*.

Bibliography

Boden, D. (1994). *The Business of Talk: Organizations in Action*. Cambridge, UK: Polity Press.

Brown, A.D., Colville, I., & Pye, A. (2015). Making Sense of Sensemaking in Organization Studies. *Organization Studies*, 36(2), 265–277. https://doi-org.ezproxy.herts.ac.uk/10.1177/0170840614559259.

Dewey, J. (1891). Moral Theory and Practice. *International Journal of Ethics*, 1(2), 186–203. www.jstor.org.ezproxy.herts.ac.uk/stable/2375407.

Dewey, J. (1929/1984). *The Quest for Certainty: The Later Works, 1925–1953*. Carbondale, IL: Southern Illinois University Press.

Elias, N. (1983/1987). *Involvement and Detachment*. Oxford, UK: Basil Blackwell Ltd.

Elias, N. (1987/1991). *The Society of Individuals*. Oxford, UK: Basil Blackwell Ltd.

Elias, N. (1994). *The Civilizing Process*. Oxford: Blackwell.

Filbee-Dexter, K., Pittman, J., Haig, H.A., Alexander, S.M., Symons, C.C., & Burke, M.J. (2017). Ecological Surprise: Concept, Synthesis, and Social Dimensions. *Ecosphere, 8*(12). doi:10.1002/ecs2.2005.

Gadamer, H.G. (1960/2013). *Truth and Method*. New York, NY: Bloomsbury Academic.

Griffin, D. (2006). *The Emergence of Leadership: Linking Self-Organization and Ethics*. New York, NY: Routledge.

Malpas, J., Arnswald, U., & Kertscher, J. (Eds.). (2002). *Gadamer's Century: Essays in Honor of Hans-Georg Gadamer*. Cambridge, MA: MIT Press.

North, D.C. (1990). *Institutions, Institutional Change, and Economic Performance*. New York: Cambridge University Press, 1990.

Putnam, R.D. (with Leonardi, R., & Nanetti, R.Y.). (1993). *Making Democracy Work: Civic Traditions in Modern Italy*. Princeton, NJ: Princeton University Press.

Shaw, P. (2002). *Changing Conversations in Organizations: A Complexity Approach to Change*. New York, NY: Routledge.

Weick, K.E. (1995). *Sensemaking in Organizations*. Los Angeles, CA: SAGE Publishing.

Part 2

Key Implications of Complexity Management

Chapter 3

We Need To Be Both Emotionally Involved and Detached

Pierre's Rant

It was just nine days after the declaration of the global pandemic of Covid-19 that Pierre lost his cool in one of our senior management meetings.

Our department was responsible for the delivery of most of the federal government services and benefits to Canadians, most notably employment insurance, Canada Pension and Disability, Old Age Security, Passports, and the Social Insurance Number. Most of us by this time were already working from home. A few—very few—were still going into the office. In place of our normal governance processes, we met every morning at 8:30 am Eastern Time for a half hour in what had become called the "Stand up" meeting, a quick round of updates as to what had happened overnight and what was on for the day to come. Later in the afternoon, around 1:00 pm Eastern, the Departmental Crisis Management Team met. Both meetings were almost entirely virtual. For the most part both meetings included all four department heads, assistant department heads such as Pierre and I, and a few key director generals. The department head who was the chief operating officer of the service delivery part of the organisation chaired. Only a couple of the department heads together with about two or three of the assistant department heads and maybe one or two other support folks would attend in a large meeting room which looked unusually empty. The rest of us were online, mostly from our homes. Pre-pandemic, when the meeting room was full, only a few of us in the regions were online, and we often had to wave our arms wildly like a windmill to get anyone's attention. And even that didn't work half the time. Now, however, more were in "Windmill Land" than in the room.

While these were early days, we had already settled into a routine. The chair would open the meeting. The head of integrity and security operations for the department (responsible for our emergency operations and preparedness) would then report on Covid-19 case numbers in Canada, the US, and the world. This particular day, she announced in a matter-of-fact way

DOI: 10.4324/9781003319528-6

that over 200,000 claims for benefits had been filed in the last three days. This volume eclipsed by a mile (or two) our usual claim rate. She finished up her presentation with a collegial nod to Pierre, the assistant department head responsible for benefits delivery, offering whatever help he needed to deal with this large workload.

Following the report from the policy side of the department, it was Pierre's turn to update the table. With a face like a thundercloud, he said that he didn't need anyone's goddamn help, and he was sick and tired of people offering it to him! According to him, we were way beyond that. No one could help him. He continued in this unusually passionate way to say that we were in deep trouble. Because of the pandemic and thus the increased need for income and other supports, the number of new claims was over seven times the number in the equivalent three-day period the previous year, and the rate was by no means slowing down. The call rate to our call centres was through the roof with most not getting through. Those who did were often waiting on the phone for three to six hours before getting an answer. We needed radical new thinking and to reconsider all our rules and guidelines if we were to have a hope of coping with the deluge. Otherwise, people would not be getting their claims paid for months, which in a pandemic was a recipe for disaster!

When Pierre drew breath, the lead deputy minister quickly jumped in. He asked Pierre to work with his folks to scope out a workable proposal that could be implemented immediately. He recognised that we might need new legislation and a complete rethink of our delivery protocols but that in the circumstances, such extraordinary actions were necessary. After the meeting broke up, the deputy went to the minister who in turn spoke with the prime minister briefing him on the situation. The following day at Stand Up, the deputy reported that since Pierre had put us on what he referred to as a "war footing" the previous day, matters had moved very quickly. At 8:00 am the previous day, the minister knew nothing of the situation, by 10:00 am he was being briefed on options, and that afternoon our recommendations were going to Cabinet for approval of the drastic authority we needed to make all this happen. Thus, what would normally take months (and in some cases years) was now happening in a few days; a pace which none of us had ever seen before. And it all started with an angry rant!

So, What Does This All Mean?

In the workplace as a rule, displays of emotion are frowned upon. As managers, we are expected to be dispassionate, rational, and objective and to put our personal feelings and issues to one side when we are at work. As public servants, we pride ourselves on doing just that. However, these circumstances were unprecedented. The situation Pierre and all of us faced as we confronted Covid-19 had overnight taken us from business-as-usual mode to a state in which everything felt like it was upside down. We had seen nothing like this pandemic before. We didn't know what to expect nor did we understand the likely consequences of what was going on. We typically prided ourselves on making reasoned decisions based upon data and analysis. And yet, in this moment, not only was there little data and analysis because of how fast everything was happening (and the accuracy and reliability of what we had was doubtful), but we didn't even know the questions we should be asking. Nobody around the world did. We were all struggling with ambiguity as science raced to catch up with this new virus. Our very identity and pride in the work we were doing for Canadians was jeopardised as we faced the very real prospect that we would be letting down the country just when it had the most need of what we had to offer.

While unbridled displays of emotion are not recommended as a general tactic, in this case, Pierre's outburst was prompted by his feelings of fear and worry about our situation. This was exactly what we needed, and his sudden eruption galvanised an entire department—and a government—into necessary and quick action. Perhaps a measured response might have sufficed to make the case for a new way of doing things, but the outburst made it clear that normal processes were inadequate and in fact would be disastrous. We needed an urgent response and one that was very different from the norm. Pierre's demeanour brooked no dissent, and we were all shocked out of our customary ways of doing things, to the country's benefit. And all of us who were at that meeting will never forget what we all there-after referred to as "Pierre's rant."

Let's Keep Our Emotions Out of It!

One of the mantras of good decision-making is that we must keep our emotions out of it. One of the early writers on organisational structures was German sociologist and philosopher Max Weber. In his view, bureaucracies were the most technically superior organisational format for large, complicated operations that require highly specialised expert workers to carry out specialised administrative functions according to purely "objective" considerations.[1] He suggested that these organisations would be perfectly developed if all "purely personal, irrational, and emotional elements" could be eliminated from their operations.[2]

Clearly that didn't happen in the meeting at the beginning of the pandemic, which, in retrospect, was a good thing. Was it the exception that proves the rule? Or was it just an exceptional case? While clearly, everything about the pandemic was exceptional, it was neither. It turns out that we cannot keep emotion out of our work to make sense of what is going on because it is just not possible to do so.

Ian Burkitt is Emeritus Professor in the Sociology and Criminology division of the University of Bradford in the UK and an expert on social identity and emotions. His studies suggest that it is impossible to separate mind from body and emotions from the cognitive or rational and that there is no "neutral, non-personal, unemotional way of engaging with the world."[3] Emotion is central to the way that we relate to and engage with one another and woven into the very fabric of our interactions.[4] Our feelings and cognition cannot, therefore, be separated. Each is integral to and interrelated with the other, and we cannot experience one without the other.

The thinking of social scientists writing on the role of emotion is backed up by recent discoveries in the field of cognitive science. The Portuguese American neuroscientist Antonio Damasio is a neurobiologist, which means he studies neural systems underlying decision-making, emotion, language, memory, and consciousness. Much of his work has been informed by the effects of brain lesion studies and has led him to argue that the rational and emotional are physiologically intertwined, making it impossible to consider that one can be present without the other.[5]

In fact, the current thinking of researchers in psychology and the neuroscience of emotion is that feelings are a highly dynamic and interacting combination of autonomic bodily responses and actions, subjective feelings, cognitive processing functions such as perception, attention, memory, and decision-making, the firing and projecting of neural circuits, verbal reports, and communicative signals such as facial expressions.[6] In other words, an interdependent network of functions and actions that includes both what we think of as emotion and our cognitive capacity.

Thus, for example, it has been shown that our emotional state may colour how we form opinions about others[7] and may affect our perceptions of what is going on.[8] Our micro emotions, which are our rapid, and often unconscious emotions that trigger micromovements such as facial micro expressions or muscle tension produce physiological reactions which can influence, or orient, our thoughts in a variety of ways. They may subtly activate our emotions, distract or redirect our attention, and/or facilitate the retrieval of certain memories related to a triggering perception or an idea, thus affecting how we think and process information.[9]

Our feelings can also affect our memories, which are important in terms of how we make sense of the world. Lisa Feldman Barrett, a professor of psychology at Northeastern University, writes that the "human mind is constructed by a brain in constant conversation, moment by unique moment, with a body and the outside world." When we remember, we are recreating bits and pieces from our past and, in her words, assembling or constructing our memory in different ways each time we remember based upon internal and external sensory data as well as our experience and histories, and thus necessarily our emotions.[10] In effect, our memories are assembled. What we experience as our reality is constructed by us more than it is received or discovered by us.[11] We never approach something new with a clean slate but process what is going on based on previously established habits, perceptions, and understandings.

Other research confirms that those who engage with their intuitions and emotions fare better in their personal and professional lives. A study by British researchers provided a fascinating look at how emotions influenced the decision-making of investment traders in four City of London banks. Traditionally, banks are a setting in which it is assumed that the work will be dominated by rational analysis. Instead, traders who engaged with their intuitions and emotions on a proactive basis performed noticeably better. The scholars attributed these traders' success to their ability to combine analysis with emotional cues in arriving at intuitive judgements. They were able to regulate their emotions more effectively and to use them as information or signals that might illuminate risks and better understand how others might experience (and thus react to) what was going on.[12]

Clearly then, we cannot separate our emotions from our cognition. Even Weber seemed to recognise the inevitability of our emotions as he famously warned that the more perfect the ability to remove "all personal, irrational and emotional elements," the more that bureaucracies were dehumanised—and dehumanising. He also suggested that the downside of bureaucracies was their ability to become like an iron cage, trapping individuals through their systems of efficiency, rational controls, and calculation.[13]

In the story at the beginning of this chapter, emotion prompted us as a department to depart from our habits and what we had taken for granted in terms of how we operated, paving the way for significant innovation in service to Canadians. This is not to suggest that we idealise emotions or say that their influence on our work together is always helpful. Emotions may lead to aggressive or defensive behaviours that make it more difficult to establish collaborative working relationships and reduce our capacity as a group to explore an issue. Our feelings can also cause us to resist knowledge that challenges what we accept as our reality. Often the more we are involved in a certain way of knowing, the more likely we will be afraid of changes to it as greater emotional involvement can come with a decreased ability to understand and control events. Norbert Elias suggested that the greater the anger and passion involved, the less likely we would be capable of more realistic, less fantasy-laden thought.[14]

Often our fear of uncertainty and the need to be seen as taking prompt action to resolve the problem at hand, can push managers and groups to prematurely close the discussion down by jumping on the first viable solution. This rush to conclusions terminates the exploration of the issue prematurely, leading to a superficial analysis of the issue in question. As a result, we fail to inquire into or even permit others to surface doubts or to bring different perceptions to the table.

This is no small thing. We are all limited in terms of our understanding and perspective as we are a product of our history. We thus depend on bringing a variety of perspectives into the debate to try and ensure that we have as much information as possible. The great pragmatist, John Dewey was known to praise what he referred to as "the productive use of doubt,"[15] reflecting the importance of doubting, of inquiring into what might otherwise be considered as settled fact. In our complex and uncertain world where one of our greatest fears should be what we don't know, the rush to action can be extremely damaging to our ability to figure things out. Indeed, a large part of our work together involves weighing the appropriateness of our goals and values as noted earlier. These efforts can have significant consequences for the reputation and functioning of an organisation, meaning that these discussions are essential and moreover, that we need to engage those with dissenting opinions. The ability to tolerate ambiguity and uncertainty, or in the words of Chris Mowles, to "sit in the fires of uncertainty," may allow managers and their teams the time they need to properly consider the situation and its implications.

Managing the pressures of the moment during the pandemic was extremely difficult. In many ways, what we were dealing with was what business scholars Jeanne Mengis, Davide Nicolini, and Jacky Swan call *epistemic breakdowns*.[16] These are disruptions of expectations which are deeply unsettling both cognitively and emotionally because previous ways of understanding and addressing a problem turn out to be unworkable. In the early days of Covid, our very identities as competent public servants were threatened in this world in which the unthinkable was happening daily. We were trying to make sense of ambiguity and facing high uncertainty which provoked emotions and messiness in a culture in which we were supposed to be "in control and decisive."[17] Thankfully we don't face existential dilemmas every day; however, our feelings are always a fundamental part of who we are and thus an inevitable part of our work together.

Let's Be Objective About This

We have seen how emotions and cognition cannot be separated, but surely, we can be objective and thus rational about our decisions? After all, one of the many ways that we cope with our fears of uncertainty and the anxiety that sensemaking can engender, is to seek information and data as evidence for our decisions so that we can keep our emotions out of it and can make a judgement grounded in facts. In fact, one of the key assumptions of scientific management is that there is an objective reality which can be known through rigorous observation, recording, measurement, and analysis of resulting data. The analysis presumes that the whole is the sum of its parts and that reductionist analysis, reducing what is being studied to its component parts, will allow us to do a proper scientific analysis of the subject. That way we can find the right answer and the best options based upon authoritative, rational, and objective analysis and be certain that our conclusions will be defensible! This too is not as straightforward as we often think.

The concept of objectivity means that observations that are made are independent of the person making them. According to this view, the observer stands outside the situation and is not influenced by personal feelings or opinions in considering and representing the facts. The universal or general rules must be adhered to regardless of the specifics of the situation. Neutrality, detachment, efficiency, and depersonalisation and an avoidance of politics, will ensure that we take the appropriate approach, which is to say the rational and scientific one.[18] The opposite of rational is portrayed as subjective or pejoratively, anything goes, where everything is relative, dominated by specific interests and by those who have an agenda and the power to accomplish it.

But is it even possible to be objective as we have defined it? In our uncertain and nonlinear world, the simple answer is no. The American political scientist and Nobel laureate in economics, Herbert A. Simon, considered this problem. He coined the term *bounded rationality* to refer to the idea that the perfect rationality of decision-making proposed by mathematical and neoclassical economics is not truly rational but limited by virtue of our inability to access all needed information and by our cognitive capacities.[19] Because of this, we cannot be perfectly rational in our processes and seek optimal results but are limited to making decisions that are satisfactory in the circumstances.

You can see how bounded rationality makes sense as it is very difficult and may not even be possible to reduce the complexity of what is going on into numbers and quantities that can be measured. Not everything is capable of measurement by a long shot, which means that important information will almost always be missing. The whole is very definitely not the sum of its parts, as the outcome is not necessarily predictable from the inputs.

However, the difficulties with being fully rational and objective go beyond the limitations on available information and our intellectual capabilities. If we take complexity seriously, then we understand that what is going on is based on the interweaving and interplay of the interactions of the many, many interdependent individuals interacting with each other, out of which, patterns of how we relate to one another emerge. We cannot stand outside what is going on because we are *part* of the very process of interactions, actions, and reactions and therefore necessarily impact, and are affected by, what is being explored.[20] It is impossible to be objective because we are involved in what is going on. We cannot *not* be involved. We are participants, not observers. And in our role as participants, we affect in some way, large or small, what is happening at the same time as it affects us. Even if we just watch from a distance or receive reports from others, the fact of our doing so is likely to affect the dynamics of the situation.

We cannot separate ourselves from our experiences. What and how we understand what is going on is, essentially, determined by our history[21] As Philosopher Thomas Nagel wrote, there is "no view from nowhere" because we see the world through our own perspective which influences how we understand the world to be.[22]

An increasing volume of research in the natural sciences confirms and expands upon the concept of bounded rationality and the lessons from the complexity sciences by showing how our perceptions and other factors affect how we understand the world around us. The Israeli-American psychologist, economist, and Nobel laureate Daniel Kahneman together with Amos Tversky, a cognitive and mathematical psychologist, are known for their work on the psychology of judgement and decision-making as well as behavioural economics,[23] what the Lebanese-American mathematical statistician, former options trader and risk analyst Nicholas Taleb, author of the books *The Black Swan, Antifragile* and *Fooled by Randomness*, referred to as irrational behaviour under uncertainty.[24] Based on extensive empirical work, Kahneman and Tversky challenged the prevalent assumption of human rationality in modern economic theory by showing how factors such as mood, stress, fatigue, group dynamics, heuristics, and cognitive biases and differences in skill all significantly affect our perception and decision-making.[25] Or as the pragmatic philosopher John Dewey expressed it, "the ways in which we believe and expect have a tremendous affect upon what we believe and expect."[26]

During the pandemic, it was impossible for us to be perfectly objective. This went way beyond the fact that there was limited authoritative data available as at least at the beginning, the science just wasn't there. We were in it up to our necks. Our regular working world had been tossed out the window along with our regular expectations and routines. And at home, all of us, in both big and small ways, were dealing with our own fears and anxieties related to the pandemic. The pretence of being objective and uninvolved was fantastical in the extreme.

This begs the question then of what can take the place of objectivity if it is indeed not possible, at least as classically understood. After all, we still have an obligation to make the best decisions that we can in the circumstances and to do so in a way that is as fair and even handed as possible. This is not an argument for self-interest or for the injection of private interests and concerns into the decision-making process.

Firstly, there is a distinction between being rational (in the objective, non-emotional sense) and being reasonable, a distinction made by Stephen Toulmin in his book *Return to Reason*. Being critical of rationality is not the same as advocating abandoning reason and the systematic consideration of our situation, assumptions, and investments.[27] This is still an important part of how we solve problems and make meaning together.

Secondly, knowing that we are always hostage to our history and perceptions is important as it means that we must continually examine and be prepared to be open about the meanings, assumptions and values which we rely upon in our decisions[28] as they will affect both our understanding of what is going on and our perspective on what to do about it. We need to acknowledge the limitations of our perceptions and resulting blind spots and actively engage diverse perspectives in the exploration of what is happening, what we know about it, and what we might do about it.

We also need to keep in mind that what is the *good* or the *right* way inevitably depends on who is making the assessment, their perspectives, and values and when they are making the decision. These determinations often involve negotiating between different understandings of what is right or desirable in terms of competing values and goals, which are subjective considerations and thus cannot be arrived at in an objectively rational manner. Thus, in our ever-evolving world, what can be called a triumph and a good decision one day may be considered a debacle the next. What I think is a great idea may be exactly what someone else would immediately dismiss.

The American pragmatist G.H. Mead proposed that the question is not whether there is a right value or a wrong value at stake, but that "it is a question of finding the possibility of acting so as to take into account as far as possible all the values involved."[29] Rather than searching for the right answer, we must, as complexity theorist Chris Mowles counsels, take a more pragmatic approach and see *right* as the best we can do in the circumstances in which we find ourselves today and seek out a *good enough* step to take together *for now*, acknowledging that in the future "we may be facing a completely different set of problems."[30]

In this chapter we have been exploring the accepted wisdom that we must be rational and objective and that emotions have no place in the working world. We have shown how in fact it is impossible to be objective; that we bring to our interactions with each other our histories, traditions, experiences, and yes, our emotions. We have examined some of the research that confirms that emotions are physiologically inseparable from our cognition and thus always a factor in our working together.

Pierre's rant was fundamentally important in getting us on a war footing promptly in the early days of the pandemic. His fear and anxiety about loss of control and inability to meet the needs of Canadians prompted the development of a whole new approach for our department to the emergency response benefits. He knew viscerally that we were in big trouble and that our usual responses wouldn't get us to where we wanted to be. His emotional reaction was invaluable in bringing us together in the required concerted effort.

Rather than suggesting we must be objective and rational and keep our emotions out of the workplace (which we now know is not possible), the approach proposed by sociologist Norbert Elias is a way of thinking about this dilemma. He argues that one needs to be *both* involved and detached emotionally to understand social life. He proposed that we think of it by using the metaphor of an airman and a swimmer. It is only from the perspective of the airman that we can gain some detachment, a relatively undistorted view of what is going on and how we have arrived at our decision. However, only by adopting the perspective of the swimmer, who is obliged to act in the moment itself, is it possible to see how varied are the different pressures that affect us. Only then are we able to identify opportunities to bring about different outcomes[31] in the processes in which we find ourselves participating. We need to be *both* detached and focused on what is often called the big picture or universal principles *and* involved emotionally and with the details of what is going on to function effectively.

This brings us to the concept of *phronesis*, a form of knowing that is also referred to as practical judgement or wisdom.

A Fancy Word for Practical Judgement

Imagine someone coming into an office to apply for a passport. His documentation is properly filled out. He satisfactorily answers all the questions that the passport officer poses, and he is polite. Nothing stands out as a problem. And yet . . . .

The officer concludes the meeting with the client and temporarily closing her wicket, goes to her supervisor. She tells her that she has just received this application and while everything looks fine, there is something just not right about it. She cannot point to anything in particular, but her years of experience are telling her to investigate this case in more detail. The supervisor agrees and the documents are checked even more thoroughly than usual and additional inquiries made. Turns out this client was a wanted fugitive from Florida, USA who was attempting to get clean documentation in Canada. Instead, when he came to pick up his passport, he was met by uniformed police officers who led him off in handcuffs.

There was no reason to do the extra due diligence on this client. Nothing was evidently wrong. From a perfectly rational and objective perspective, this should have gone through easily, but it didn't. What was going on here?

What was going on was a demonstration of what ancient Greek philosophers called *phronesis*, practical judgement or wisdom. *Phronesis* is one of three types of knowledge identified by the Greek philosopher Aristotle: *episteme* (abstract universal knowledge), *techne* (technology associated with production, e.g., applied) and *phronesis* (practical wisdom and good judgement associated with *praxis* or what we would call practice or experience).

To think about this more we might turn to James C. Scott, a political scientist and anthropologist. His book, *Seeing Like a State: How Certain Schemes to Improve the Human Condition Have Failed* examined failed cases of large-scale plans, arguing that centrally managed social plans fail when they impose solutions that disregard the complex interdependencies that are at play. He argued that "a wide array of practical skills and acquired intelligence in responding to a constantly changing natural and human environment"[32] is particularly important in complex and "non-repeatable" environments where "formal procedures of rational decision making are impossible to apply."[33]

This is what is referred to as *phronesis*.[34] It comes from experience and reflection on experience and consequently develops over time. It is a capacity that is gained over the years with all the ups and downs, trial and error, and learning from mistakes as well as the emotional baggage that comes with experience. While someone with this practical wisdom or judgement will also draw upon the relevant episteme or techne, it is a form of knowledge that goes beyond the theoretical or technical types of knowing.

Phronesis is knowing how to do things well. It is not based on certainty but is non-universal and based in the now. It is like feeling that you have seen the movie before, and that you may know how it ends. As was demonstrated by the bank traders in the story earlier in this chapter, practical judgement or wisdom allows us to have a better feel for the relationships and events that are going on around us and the emotions that are affecting us and others. There is no book page on which the answer will be found. Instead, it is our spidery sense, our gut feeling, our judgement that guides us. It is our embodied emotions that, based upon our experience, indicates that all is not as it should be. It is know-how knowledge rather than know-that knowledge.[35]

Phronesis is as much an emotional reaction or feeling as it is intellectual. Our passport officer did not know why she reacted as she did to this passport application. The feelings that are experienced when something unexpected happens have been studied by sensemaking scholars Karl Weick and Kathleen Sutcliffe. Their research documented reactions of surprise, puzzlement, agitation, anxiety, and feeling unsettled, frustrated, or even startled. Aviators call these feelings *leemers* (probably from *leery*), the feeling that "something is not quite right, but you can't put your finger on it."[36] And while there is no 100% guarantee, these feelings and practical wisdom are often as good as it gets in a complex environment.

There is a great demonstration of *phronesis* in the movie rendition of Arthur Hailey's book, *Airport*. Joe Patroni, the tough and practical head of maintenance operations for the airport in which the film is set, is faced with moving a disabled aircraft. It is blocking a runway that is urgently needed for an emergency landing. If this cannot be done, the aircraft will be pushed out of the way by snowploughs that are standing by with their engines running. In true Hollywood style, at the last minute he is successful. When one of his colleagues gushes to him that the textbook said it couldn't be done, his gruff response is that that was why he didn't read the textbooks!

Phronesis is important to us in our complex environment because individuals and the issues and situations that arise in the patterning of their relating to one another are infinitely variable and ever-changing. Our rules, generalisations, best practices, scientific theories, and metrics that guide us in making sense of what is going on and what is to be done about it can only take us so far. We know that what is going on is because of the patterning that emerges from our interactions. We cannot say with certainty what will happen because these patterns are not predictive, but with experience, we may be able to recognise certain patterns and what feels right.

In today's business world, we have increasingly bought into the importance of credentialled experts who are expected to be able to come into any workplace and solve our most difficult problems despite not knowing the people, the history, the culture and sometimes even the business. Our world has also become more and more quantified and financialised, and we are continually confronted with the need to pay attention to the bottom line and to have goals, indicators, and results that can be measured and reported. This reduces meaning to these targets and indicators, and often dismisses the practical judgement of the experienced manager and worker—and robs employees of being valued for their know-how.

In fact, one could argue that it is novices that take the textbook approach to solving problems. The real experts are those with practical knowledge. They are the ones with lived experience that have seen it, done it, and been there before![37] This is not to say that those with *phronesis* are not also conversant with the theories and requirements of their work, but an expert practitioner brings experience with both theory and practice as tested and tried and experienced over a lengthy period of time so that they can sense when something is off or doesn't make sense. Paradoxically, the quality that often marks an expert is what the Zen Master Shunru Suzuki calls the "beginner's mind." This is a capacity and confidence that knows what they don't know or is prepared to call into question what they do know.

John Dewey was seized with this conundrum. In his book, *The Quest for Certainty* he wrote about the denigration of practice and the high value placed on theory and abstractions which stems from the desire to pursue certainty in an uncertain world. He saw the "exaltation of pure intellect and its activity above practical affairs" as being fundamentally connected with our search for absolute and unshakeable certainty despite the reality that one cannot eliminate uncertainty in our daily existence and practice.[38] In his view, generalities and abstractions are limited in their usefulness as our duty is always to respond to the nature of the actual demands made upon us and the particulars of the situation in question.[39]

Summing Up and Conclusion

In this chapter we address the common admonition that our decision-making should be objective and rational and that we should put our emotions and our lived experiences and views aside. While on its face this is quite logical, it is not possible.

We cannot be objective as we are in it up to our proverbial necks. We are participants and affect and are affected by what is going on. What is determined to be objective, rational, and even a good decision is often a product of who makes the judgement and when they make it. As the philosopher Thomas Nagel said there is "no view from nowhere." We cannot divorce ourselves from our perceptions, habits, feelings, and histories. We bring all of these to our work and our collaboration with colleagues. Our perceptions tailor or affect what we pay attention to, what we observe, and what we perceive. What we have learned or come to value and appreciate influences what we prioritise and worry about, and in fact, even how we determine which questions are important to ask.

It is also impossible to separate knowledge from context or feelings from cognition. Our lived histories, experiences, values, emotions, and beliefs are inextricably part of how we understand the world and what is happening. How we understand what is going on is predicated on our take on the situation, on our perspective and prior experience as well as the thoughts and feelings that are evoked for us. Our emotions are not severable from our cognition and cannot be put to one side while we go about our daily business. They are both part of who we are and affect what we see, what we value, and what we don't.

This does not mean that irrational or highly emotional behaviour should be an ideal or even the norm, but that both cognition and emotion are always present. We cannot be truly objective, and complete rationality is impossible. And as the last section of this chapter suggested, it is our feelings, perceptions, habits, and histories that can also bring value and insight to our endeavours through practical judgement or *phronesis*.

We need to be *both* involved and detached emotionally to understand what is going on in the workplace. In the words of Norbert Elias, we need to be both an airman and a swimmer. We do need to be concerned about the big picture or universal principles, but it is only by also adopting the perspective of the swimmer, in the weeds of it all and involved emotionally with the details of what is going on that we can function effectively.

As managers, we need to be thoughtful about how this affects our working together. This brings us back to Ralph Stacey's advice to us that sometimes the best leaders and managers are those who are the most able to manage their anxiety so that they can resist the temptation to grasp for the first and most obvious solution, to put an end to the emotional discomfort and angst of anxiety and put the issue to bed. Not only must they be conscious of, and manage, their own anxiety, but they must consider what is going on for others.

In the previous chapter, we saw how the competence of *reflexivity* is fundamentally important for us in the workplace. Reflexive thinking is not only cognitive but highly relational and emotional.[40] Managers need to ask what is going on here? What does this issue evoke for each of us? What makes it challenging? How am I affecting others? How are others feeling? How can we make our environment safe for us as colleagues to engage in the necessary exploration of our differences? Of productive doubt? How can I ensure that I and others don't prematurely shut down the conversations that we need to have? What perspectives are missing around the table?

These questions remind us of the importance of thinking about our interactions and how we are relating to one another. This goes beyond an individualistic approach to the workplace and requires that we consider the collective and thus the social dynamics. This is what the next chapter will explore.

Implications for Your Practice

1. It is not possible to be fully objective because we are involved in what is going on and therefore necessarily impact and are affected by what is being explored. What and how we understand what is going on is determined by our experience. How can you be open to a diversity of perspectives and include them in your problem-solving? You might be wise to assume that you and colleagues all have your own biases and assumptions and that they may differ. How can you provide safe spaces for these differences to be discussed?

2. Cognition and emotion are physiologically interwoven, and thus emotions are always involved in our work. How can you as a manager respectfully inquire into what may be going on for others and how it may be affecting them at the same time as you consider how your own feelings are affecting your actions and reactions?

3. Try to resist the urge to prematurely close discussions down in a rush to find certainty and resolve a problem quickly. Sitting in the "fires of

uncertainty" while uncomfortable, can allow for the productive exploration of doubt and additional perspectives, reduce blind spots, and increase the information available for the group.

4. How can you actively give permission to team members to speak up when they have concerns or take a different view on what is going on. I always struck a deal with colleagues, including those that reported to me, that required them to let me know when I was missing something or was otherwise making a mistake. While it didn't mean I always agreed, I did more often than not, and it saved us many a stubbed toe!

5. Consider Elias' suggestion of the airman and the swimmer in terms of your management practice. This requires that you be both detached and aware of the big picture and emotionally involved and in the weeds of what is going on. Where you feel that you will be practically unable to juggle both perspectives because of scale and scope of your position, how can you be open to and enable others to bring both perspectives to your work discussions?

6. How can you engage and actively listen to those with practical judgement, *phronesis*, in your work of decision-making?

7. Consider how you can develop your own capacity for reflexivity. This means being aware of the impact upon how you think of both your own personal history and experiences as well as the traditions of thought and history of colleagues and your communities. How can you support your team in doing the same in their work?

8. In problem-solving, the question is not whether there is a right or a wrong value, but of finding the possibility of acting so as to take into account as far as possible all the values involved. Rather than searching for the right answer, be prepared to take a more pragmatic approach and see *right* as the best we can do in the circumstances in which we find ourselves today and seek out a *good enough* step to take together *for now*, acknowledging that in the future we may be facing a completely different set of problems.

Notes

1 Max Weber, *Economy and Society: An Outline of Interpretive Sociology*, p. 973.
2 Ibid., p. 975.
3 Ian Burkitt, *Bodies of Thought: Embodiment, Identity & Modernity*, 1999, pp. 2–12; also see his book titled *Emotions and Social Relations*, p. 21.
4 Ian Burkitt, *Emotional Reflexivity: Feeling, Emotion and Imagination in Reflexive Dialogues*, p. 459; see also Margaret Wetherell in *Affect and Emotion: A New Social Science of Understanding*, p. 24; John Baldwin's article in the journal *Sociological Perspectives* titled "Habit, Emotion and Self-Conscious Action," pp. 52–53; and Laurajane Smith, Margaret Wetherell and Gary Campbell's book, *Emotion, Affective Practices, and the Past in the Present*, p. 1.
5 Antonio Damasio, *Descartes' Error: Emotion, Reason and the Human Brain*.

6 Margaret Wetherell, *Affect and Emotion: A New Social Science of Understanding*, 2014, p. 62.
7 Gareth Jones and Jennifer George, *The Experience and Evolution of Trust: Implications for Cooperation and Teamwork*, p. 534.
8 See Ted Cadsby, *Closing the Mind Gap: Making Smarter Decisions in a Hypercomplex World*, p. 61.
9 Francois Richer, *Where Our Thoughts Come from: How Microemotions Affect Spontaneous Thought*, https://theconversation.com/where-our-thoughts-come-from-how-microemotions-affect-spontaneous-thought-177241.
10 Lisa Feldman Barrett, *This Is How Your Brain Makes Your Mind*, p. 1.
11 See Ted Cadsby's, *Closing the Mind Gap: Making Smarter Decisions in a Hypercomplex World*, pp. 43–44.
12 Mark Fenton-O'Creevy, Emma Soane, Nigel Nicholson and Paul Willman, *Thinking, Feeling and Deciding: The Influence of Emotions on the Decision Making and Performance of Traders*, in the *Journal of Organizational Behavior*, pp. 1044–1061.
13 Max Weber, *Economy and Society: An Outline of Interpretive Sociology*, 1905/2002, p. 123; also, *The Protestant Ethic and the Spirit of Capitalism*, 1922/1978, p. 975.
14 Ibid., pp. 66–67; also, Norbert Elias's book, *What Is Sociology?*, p. 22.
15 Dewey, *Experience and Nature*, p. 182.
16 Jeanne Mengis, Davide Nicolini and Jacky Swan, *Integrating Knowledge in the Face of Epistemic Uncertainty: Dialogically Drawing Distinctions*, p. 607.
17 Karl Weick, *Sensemaking in Organizations*, p. 186.
18 See Barbara Townley, *Reason's Neglect*, pp. 70–86.
19 Herbert A. Simon, *On the Concept of Organizational Goal*; also see Herbert A. Simon, *Bounded Rationality and Organizational Learning*.
20 See Chris Mowles, *Complexity: A Key Idea for Business and Society*, chapter 6 starting at p. 103.
21 Hans-Georg Gadamer, *Truth and Method*, p. 310.
22 Thomas Nagel, *The View from Nowhere*.
23 While Tversky died six years before the awarding of the Nobel prize in 2002, Kahneman always viewed it as a joint prize due to their intense and lengthy collaboration.
24 Nassim Taleb, *Fooled by Randomness: The Hidden Role of Chance in Life and in the Markets*, p. 38.
25 For additional discussion of some of these concepts, see Phaedra Daipha, *Masters of Uncertainty: Weather Forecasters and the Quest for Ground Truth*; also Filippo Menczer and Thomas Hills' article in Scientific American, December 2020 titled *The Attention Economy: Understanding How Algorithms and Manipulators Exploit Our Cognitive Vulnerabilities Empowers Us to Fight Back*; *Closing the Mind Gap: Making Smarter Decisions in a Hypercomplex World* by Ted Cadsby and Hugo Mercier and Dan Sperber's, *The Enigma of Reason*.
26 John Dewey, *The Quest for Certainty: The Later Works, 1925–1953*, p. 14.
27 See Stephen Toulmin, *Return to Reason*, 2001.
28 Hans-Georg Gadamer, *Truth and Method*, p. 280.
29 George Herbert Mead, *The Philosophy of the Act*, p. 465.
30 Chris Mowles, *Managing in Uncertainty: Complexity and the Paradoxes of Everyday Organizational Life*, p. 144.
31 Norbert Elias, *The Society of Individuals*.
32 James C. Scott, *Seeing Like a State: How Certain Schemes to Improve the Human Condition Have Failed*, p. 313.

33 Ibid., p. 316.
34 James C. Scott used a similar Greek term, *mētis*, distinguishing it from *phronesis* because the latter incorporates an ethical dimension of conscience and care, while the former is secular and ethically neutral. The term "cunning" is sometimes associated with *mētis*, but Scott suggested it also describes the knack that comes with an experience encountered frequently. Despite this, as he pointed out, we are actually talking about the same thing whether we refer to *mētis* or *phronesis* (Scott, personal communication, December 26, 2018).
35 For commentary on this see Ralph Stacey and Chris Mowles', *Strategic Management and Organisational Dynamics: The Challenge of Complexity to Ways of Thinking about Organisations* (7th ed.), pp. 512–513; also see Barbara Townley's book, *Reason's Neglect: Rationality and Organizing*, pp. 213–217; Chris Mowles, *Complexity: A Key Idea for Business and Society*, pp. 89–90, 95–98, and 117–120.
36 Karl Weick and Kathleen Sutcliffe, *Managing the Unexpected: Assuring High Performance in an Age of Complexity*, p. 41.
37 Commentary from lecture by social scientist Davide Nicolini at June 2022 Complexity and Management Centre Conference, Roffey Park, UK.
38 John Dewey, *Quest for Certainty*, pp. 5–6.
39 Ibid., pp. 199–200.
40 Svend Brinkmann, *John Dewey: Science for a Changing World*, p. 107.

Bibliography

Baldwin, J.D. (1988). Habit, Emotion and Self-Conscious Action. *Sociological Perspectives, 31*(1), 35–58. https://doi.org/10.2307/1388950.

Brinkmann, S. (2017). *John Dewey: Science for a Changing World*. London, UK: Routledge.

Burkitt, I. (1999). *Bodies of Thought: Embodiment, Identity & Modernity*. London, UK: SAGE Publishing.

Burkitt, I. (2012). Emotional Reflexivity: Feeling, Emotion and Imagination in Reflexive Dialogues. *Sociology, 46*(3), 458–472. https://doi-org.ezproxy.herts.ac.uk/10.1177/0038038511422587.

Burkitt, I. (2014). *Emotions and Social Relations*. Los Angeles, CA: SAGE Publishing.

Cadsby, T. (2014). *Closing the Mind Gap: Making Smarter Decisions in a Hypercomplex World*. Toronto: BPS Books.

Daipha, P. (2015). *Masters of Uncertainty: Weather Forecasters and the Quest for Ground Truth*. Chicago: University of Chicago Press.

Damasio, A.R. (1994). *Descartes' Error: Emotion, Reason and the Human Brain*. London: Picador.

Dewey, J. (1929/1984). *The Quest for Certainty: The Later Works, 1925–1953*. Carbondale, IL: Southern Illinois University Press.

Dewey, J. (1929/2015). *Experience and Nature*. New York, NY: Dover Publications, Inc.

Elias, N. (1908/1978). *What Is Sociology?* New York, NY: Columbia University Press.

Elias, N. (1987/1991). *The Society of Individuals*. Oxford, UK: Basil Blackwell Ltd.

Feldman Barrett, L. (August 25, 2021). *This Is How Your Brain Makes Your Mind*. www.technologyreview.com/2021/08/25/1031432/what-is-mind-brain-body-connection/, accessed April 10, 2023.

Fenton-O'Creevy, M., Soane, E., Nicholson, N., & Willman, P. (November 2011). Thinking, Feeling and Deciding: The Influence of Emotions on the Decision Making and Performance of Traders. *Journal of Organizational Behavior, 32*(8), 1044–1061.

Gadamer, H.G. (1960/2013). *Truth and Method*. New York, NY: Bloomsbury Academic.

Jones, G.T., & George, J.M. (1998). The Experience and Evolution of Trust: Implications for Cooperation and Teamwork. *The Academy of Management Review, 23*(3), 531–546. doi:10.5465/amr.1998.926625.

Mead, G.H. (1938). *The Philosophy of the Act*. Chicago, IL: University of Chicago Press.

Menczer, F., & Hills, T. (December 2020). The Attention Economy: Understanding How Algorithms and Manipulators Exploit Our Cognitive Vulnerabilities Empowers Us to Fight Back. *Scientific American, 323*(6), 54–61.

Mengis, J., Nicolini, D., & Swan, J. (2018). Integrating Knowledge in the Face of Epistemic Uncertainty: Dialogically Drawing Distinctions. *Management Learning, 49*(5), 595–612. https://doi-org.ezproxy.herts.ac.uk/10.1177/1350507618797216.

Mercier, H., & Sperber, D. (2017). *The Enigma of Reason*. Cambridge, MA: Harvard University Press.

Mowles, C. (2015). *Managing in Uncertainty: Complexity and the Paradoxes of Everyday Organizational Life*. London, UK: Routledge.

Mowles, C. (2022). *Complexity: A Key Idea for Business and Society*. London, UK: Routledge.

Nagel, T. (1989). *The View from Nowhere*. Oxford, US: Oxford University Press.

Richer, F. *Where Our Thoughts Come from: How Microemotions Affect Spontaneous Thought*. https://theconversation.com/where-our-thoughts-come-from-how-microemotions-affect-spontaneous-thought-177241, accessed April 10, 2023.

Scott, J.C. (1998). *Seeing Like a State: How Certain Schemes to Improve the Human Condition Have Failed*. Durham, NC: Yale Agrarian Studies Series.

Simon, H.A. (1964). On the Concept of Organizational Goal. *Administrative Science Quarterly, 9*(1), 1. doi:10.2307/2391519.

Simon, H.A. (1991). Bounded Rationality and Organizational Learning. *Organization Science, 2*(1), 125–134. www-jstor-org.ezproxy.herts.ac.uk/stable/2634943.

Smith, L., Wetherell, M., & Campbell, G. (2018). *Emotion, Affective Practices, and the Past in the Present*. New York, NY: Routledge.

Stacey, R.D., & Mowles, C. (2016). *Strategic Management and Organisational Dynamics: The Challenge of Complexity to Ways of Thinking about Organisations* (7th ed.). London, UK: Pearson Education.

Taleb, N.N. (2004). *Fooled by Randomness: The Hidden Role of Chance in Life and in the Markets*. New York: Random House Trade Paperbacks.

Toulmin, S. (2001). *Return to Reason*. Cambridge, MA: Harvard University Press, 2001.

Townley, B. (2008). *Reason's Neglect: Rationality and Organizing*. New York, NY: Oxford University Press.

Weber, M. (1905/2002). *The Protestant Ethic and the Spirit of Capitalism*. London, UK: Routledge Classics.

Weber, M. (1922/1978). *Economy and Society: An Outline of Interpretive Sociology*. Los Angeles, CA: University of California Press.

Weick, K.E. (1995). *Sensemaking in Organizations*. Los Angeles, CA: SAGE Publishing.

Weick, K.E., & Sutcliffe, K.M. (2001). *Managing the Unexpected: Assuring High Performance in an Age of Complexity*. San Francisco, CA: Jossey-Bass.

Wetherell, M. (2014). *Affect and Emotion: A New Social Science of Understanding*. Los Angeles, CA: SAGE Publishing.

Chapter 4

Interdependence Changes Everything

Introduction

On April 9, 2017, on United Express Flight 3411, Dr David Dao Duy Anh, a Vietnamese American pulmonologist (and folk musician) boarded a flight to Kentucky at the Chicago O'Hare Airport in the United States. The aircraft was full, however, and at the last minute, an announcement asked for four volunteers to take a later flight to accommodate the staff needed for another aircraft. No one volunteered, and they finally identified four passengers (supposedly by computer), who were asked to leave the aircraft and wait for the next flight. Three complied but the fourth, Dr Anh, who needed to see a patient the next day, refused to disembark. Shortly thereafter, he was forcefully removed from the aircraft by three Chicago Aviation Security Officers from the Chicago Department of Aviation. In the process, Dao's face struck an armrest, and he was pulled, apparently unconscious, by his arms along the aircraft aisle past rows of shocked (and in some cases filming) passengers. These videos went viral after the incident, leading to public outrage.

Then United CEO, Oscar Munoz at first apologised for having to "re-accommodate" the customers in question (a phrase which was widely ridiculed in social media) and later defended staff for following established procedures, blaming Dao for being disruptive and belligerent. It was later announced that Munoz was no longer in line to become chairman of the company. Following an inquiry, the aviation security officers involved were disciplined, and the Department of Aviation decertified as a police agency. Others blamed the airline supervisor for her tone and demeanour in the way she had asked for volunteers.[1]

A consultant in change management once said that no one (well, almost no one) gets up in the morning with the avowed intent of being a jerk or of causing harm to others. Instead, they repeat the behaviours that they believe have worked for them in the past. This raises an important question. What was it about the experience of being an employee of this airline and

DOI: 10.4324/9781003319528-7

the Department of Aviation, and how they interacted, were rewarded, and recognised, that led to these individuals believing that this was an appropriate way to treat customers? Or as Doug Griffin, one of the original scholars involved in the development of the theory of complex responsive processes of relating used to say, what had led them to become this way?

Beyond an Individualistic Approach

In the previous chapters we looked at three models of change (magical-mystical, scientific management, and a complexity sciences theory of management). Each differs depending upon the underlying interpretation of the relationship between the individual and society or group.[2] We live in a world with a propensity to take an individualistic approach to understanding events and interactions and so, not surprisingly, the first two focus on managing from an individualistic perspective. The third theory, however, inspired by complexity, takes a social view of our work as managers, and considers the interactions of interdependent individuals *and* the groups to which they belong. This rather paradoxical relationship has significant implications for how we do our work together.[3]

Individualism is the promotion of the goals, interests, and desires of the individual over that of the group or society and the veneration of independence and self-reliance. A significant factor in this sense of ourselves is thinking about the individual as separate and closed off from others versus interdependent and inseparable from the group. This individualistic approach has come to dominate societal mores in the last 60 or so years, including management theory and practice. There have been many that have contributed to the development of this individualistic patterning of how we relate to one another. One of the most influential scholars on the subject, was Nobel prize winner Frederick Hayek, who came to dominate thinking on this issue in the latter part of the 20th century.

Hayek took a radical individualistic perspective and wrote that the individual was sovereign, and their interests were never to be subsumed by the collective. He apparently was even suspicious of the word "social" as he believed it to be something created by intellectuals to advance the workings of the collective. Former Prime Minister Maggie Thatcher became a well-known proponent of this approach to life when she famously observed,

> and who is society? There is no such thing! There are individual men and women and there are families and no government can do anything except through people and people look to themselves first.[4]

However, if we take complexity seriously, we know that what is going on is the result of the patterning that emerges and evolves based upon the results of the very many interactions of people and groups and not just the actions of any one autonomous individual. It is therefore challenging to lay the blame on any one person for what occurred on United Express Flight 3411. Obviously, each is responsible individually for their actions, but in this narrative, several people were involved in what unfolded. It wasn't just one maverick that dragged Dr Anh off the plane. No one from the airlines or the security company attempted to intervene or to prevent what was happening. It is possible that other staff didn't agree with the actions but felt that they could or should not intervene. Or that they did indeed believe that this was an appropriate response to the situation. Certainly, the initial reaction of the chairman of the airline to blame Dr Anh conveyed a supportive message to staff who had taken part in this incident, which also suggests that this approach to customers was not new.

While this may be an extreme case, a similar dynamic happens all the time in our work. We act and react to each other's actions and omissions and what goes on is the result of all our efforts. Whether we think what happens is a good, mixed, or bad result, there are always many cooks in the kitchen! We or colleagues might be influenced by an author or perhaps a relative or a passing stranger who makes what we think is a prescient comment. Thus, if we really want to understand what led to that highly regrettable incident on United Flight 3411, we cannot point fingers at any one individual without also considering what else was going on in the social interactions and relationships of all involved. We need to consider the history and the patterning of how individuals in that workplace related to one another. What was rewarded and what was reinforced? Only then, might we begin to understand why several employees thought that dragging a passenger off a plane was acceptable; and why the CEO reacted in the way he did. It is mindbogglingly complex, of course, but we need to consider what had led them to become that way.

To better understand the nature of our social interactions and the implications for how we work together, an examination of the extensive psychological, anthropological, and neurological research into our development as social beings is necessary. This is what we will now turn to.

The Need for Attachment

Humans are often described as a social animal, for whom both the ability to cooperate and collaborate in large numbers and the nature and quality of our relationships have been essential to our development and to our survival, well-being, and reproductive success.[5] A particularly powerful area of research pioneered by British psychologist John Bowlby speaks directly to our social natures. His work on the concept of attachment originated with his studies of maternal deprivation[6] and human infant development which show that our attempts to figure things out, to develop meanings, and to understand and hopefully control uncertainty start at least from birth.

This suggests that humans have evolved to have a physiological need to attach to other human beings and to belong to groups.

Attachment refers to the bond that forms with the caretaker present at a crucial stage of development of the infant, usually in the second half of their first year of life. The bond is strongest for about the first three years. Researchers believe, however, that the impact on personality development is such that the experience of attachment during infancy has a far-reaching impact upon the individual and how they develop and sets the context for interpreting future experiences and attachment opportunities.

This behaviour has been observed systematically in several different human societies despite differences in their child rearing and family life practices. It has also been noted in other species, particularly apes who are closely related to us. Studies have found that the interaction between the child and the caregiver shapes the development of the brain, and at the same time, the developing brain is involved in the shaping of these interactions. Research into the opioid processes of the brain which involve endogenous neuropeptides such as endorphins shows that they are morphine-like and give rise to soothing feelings of control and calm. Other neurochemicals (e.g., norepinephrine) are related to the arousal processes and produce feelings of excitement, fear, and anxiety. It appears that this chemical regulation system which mediates between feelings of arousal and contentment cannot develop in isolation from other bodies.[7]

Those who do not have the experience of attachment within the first two years of life have great difficulty throughout their development. Many researchers believe that our very sense of self and of security and approach to future attachments and relationships continues to be fundamentally predicated upon our early experiences. Those without the experience of attachment, for example, often have difficulty developing healthy relationships later in life. It is also through these attachment relationships that we first learn how to understand order and control,[8] and how to get things done through and with other people, which will affect how we deal with issues of power and control and uncertainty throughout our lives.[9] In other words, we cannot separate ourselves as individuals and our development from our social relationships because our social nature is fundamental to who we are.

We Are Interdependent

Noted sociologist Norbert Elias wrote extensively on the nature of the relationship between individuals and groups. He differed from many of his colleagues who focused either on the behaviour of large numbers of individuals using statistics or on societal structures. Instead, he argued that we need to think differently about the nature of the relationship between the individual and society and that what is going on is happening because of people communicating and interacting with each other.[10]

Norbert Elias strongly advocated that we as individuals are who we are because of society. Sigmund Henry Foulkes, the German-British psychiatrist and psychoanalyst who developed a theory of group behaviour that led to his founding of group analysis, a variant of group therapy, agreed, saying that we are social through and through.[11] We do not exist without society. Attachment theory confirms that we depend on others for our very existence and our development. Starting with our attachment behaviours, we become the individual that we are because of all those with whom we have interacted and the groups we have belonged to. Our very sense of self is historically formed and alterations in our social context and development lead to changes in the sense of who we are. The development of our identity is a dynamic, evolutionary, and social undertaking.[12]

At the same time, society does not exist without the individual. And as the nature of the interactions between individuals changes, our social context is also affected. We are not like the billiard balls earlier referred to; we don't just bounce off one another and alter direction when we interact but remain otherwise unchanged. Instead, we change in some large or small way through each interaction, and those with whom we interact do the same. Over time these experiences shape who we are and our identity, as we, in turn, affect others through our interactions.

In other words, the two, society and the individual, "mutually co-constitute each other."[13] There is a paradoxical relationship between the individual and society, somewhat akin to the conundrum, What came first the chicken or the egg? The "I" and the "we," according to Elias, are two sides of the same coin.[14] There is no "we" without the "I" and vice versa. One cannot exist without the other. Neither is more important than the other; they are inextricably intertwined.

One of the implications of looking at the world this way is that we need to accept that we are not closed off from each other, but we are instead, interdependent. Elias argued that in a very complex society we depend upon many others for the fulfilment of our needs. We don't all grow our own food, make our own clothes, or build our own cars. The many products and functions that we need to sustain our life and to maintain our safety, health, and ability to live what we consider to be a good life, means that each of us depends on many others both at home and around the globe every day of our lives. Similarly, for each of us to get our jobs done, we are permanently and functionally dependent upon one another. Just as others depend on us to do their work, we also are not atomistic individuals performing tasks in a vacuum. And it is impossible to know which of our actions are more or less important if we consider the nonlinear nature of our existence. As the smallest of events or interventions can lead to significant changes and results, it can be the tiniest of commissions or omissions (perhaps by someone on the other side of the world!) that can determine the ultimate success of our efforts. Thus, any consideration of how we work together cannot be based upon the concept of the individualistic, atomistic individual. It is so much more complex than that.

Our interdependence as individuals and a species is stronger than ever today. Norbert Elias's historical review of processes of civilisation in societies,[15] demonstrated that the more highly differentiated the society or group, the more its members are interdependent.[16] As tasks become more specialised, we rely even more upon the efforts of others to be successful, and the ability to collaborate becomes even more necessary. Just how interdependent and highly differentiated our world has become was made very evident during the pandemic. Three years on and we are still experiencing significant disruptions of our supply chains, essential and health care services, and the labour market (to mention just three).

The same goes for our organisations. The larger and the more differentiated they are, the more their employees are interdependent both with each other, but just as importantly with suppliers, clients, or competitors. Even those outside the organisation may have a significant influence upon the complex patterning of relationships affecting individuals and groups. Looking back to the work of Dr. Stuart Kauffman, the American medical doctor, theoretical biologist and complex systems researcher in Chapter 1, the amount of complexity is determined by the number and strength of the connections between involved entities. Thus, we can easily see how the size of an organisation and increase in differentiation of tasks exacerbate the complexity of our management practice.

In the case of the United Airlines story, we cannot know for certain what types of actions and inactions of those involved led to the patterning of how they worked together and ultimately to the rather brutal deplaning of Dr Anh. What was it about the way that they worked together that led them to think that this type of action was appropriate? Or even one that they could contemplate? Had they done this before? What did they think they were accomplishing? And for those that did have misgivings about what was going on, why didn't they do something to prevent it? Had they tried before and been unsuccessful and perhaps been punished by being told that they were not on message or one of the team? Were they dependent upon their colleagues for approval or even their ability to do their jobs well, necessitating that they keep their heads down and go along with what was happening? You can imagine that given their necessary interdependence, some, or all of this was going on.

Now, while fascinating, this may seem like a far cry from the issues and challenges you face as a manager in the workplace. Interesting as these theories are, they don't exactly help you to solve the problem du jour that is making you lose sleep. However, it reminds us that what is going on is as a result of our many interactions and the resulting patterns of how we relate to each other as we enable and constrain each other and negotiate how we will go on together. These patterns affect how we will behave and interact with each other in the future. Thus, how we work together today may affect how we will work together tomorrow. Our work is indeed a collective enterprise. We are interdependent, and no one of us achieves (or fails) by themselves.

So far in this chapter we have explored our highly social nature, how we are interdependent with each other and the extent to which the individual cannot be separated from society. If we are serious about complexity in the workplace, we accordingly need to think not only about managing from the individual perspective but in a way that considers group dynamics. This is the subject of the next section of this chapter.

On Groups

As humans are social animals, understanding the dynamics of groups is fundamentally important to a manager. Our work to make sense of what is going on and to make meaning, is a social process as it is through our interactions that we accomplish our work. This is the very essence of interdependence.[17] We are always working directly or indirectly, with others and thus by definition, in groups. In fact, some studies have suggested that we use information about the crowd that we are in to infer what are appropriate actions to take in a situation.[18]

This is pretty obvious when you think about it. At work you meet to discuss and hopefully resolve a mutual issue. You hold conferences (virtual or otherwise). You brainstorm together, you survey your employees. You talk it through. We interact our organisations into being. It is through our interactions that the moments, the stories and myths, the *habitus*, and over time, the structure of the organisation are constituted.[19]

Our ability to collaborate, to work together, and to form groups is a key element of the human experience and has over the ages supported our evolutionary successes. In fact, some studies suggest that our social nature is not only learned but has become part of our genetic inheritance. Researchers Brian Hare, professor of evolutionary anthropology and Vanessa Woods investigated why it was *homo sapiens* who became the last surviving human species. Their theory? That we were the friendliest in comparison with other human species and had the capacity for cooperative communication. We could work together with others and communicate even with someone we

had never met before. They (together with anthropologist Richard Wrang-
ham of Harvard University and psychologist Michael Tomasello of Duke
University) proposed that humans were self-domesticators in terms of the
evolution of the species over many years in which the capacity for friendli-
ness was favoured. Here they use the term "domestication" in the sense
that is used when a species becomes domesticated by humans. They note
that in addition to becoming friendlier and more receptive to human con-
tact, this also involved changes to face shape, pigmentation changes, and
changes to hormones, the nervous system, and reproductive cycles.[20] For
example, the larger the typical group size, the more neocortex is needed
to cope with the complexities of social life as social interaction is mentally
very demanding.[21]

The importance of groups and group membership is confirmed by recent
research on synchrony. Doing things synchronously is shown to build
greater social ties and a sense of well-being, as well as to increase gener-
osity, trust, and tolerance towards others. A series of experiments has also
confirmed that it can heighten an individual's threshold for pain through
the production of endorphins—over and above what has been referred to
as the *runner's high*. Whether the activity is line dancing, singing in a choir,
being on a rowing team, marching or even clapping in time, these types of
synchronous activities have all been proved to boost a sense of belonging
and improve positive group feelings. Scientists attribute this effect to a combination of neurohormonal, cognitive, and perceptual factors. There may,
however, also be a genetic component as research on very young children
(14 months old) also confirmed that in-unison bouncing compared with
non-synchronous bouncing led to an increase in helpful behaviours. This
was measured by the likelihood of an infant picking up a ball that one of the
adults participating in the bouncing activity had dropped.[22]

One of the ways in which *homo sapiens* is thought to be different from
other species is that we have a different concept of who is or is not a stranger
to us. Our evolutionary cousins recognise strangers based only on famili-
arity, e.g., someone that lives with them in their territory. Otherwise, they
are a stranger. Instead, humans can define the groups that they belong to,
based upon their language, their appearance, or even their beliefs. We can
recognise people who are like us even if we have never met them before,
which allows us to expand our social network far beyond that of any other
species.[23]

The intent here is not to idealise groups and group formation as clearly
this preference for those that are like us has led to the infliction of untold
misery and suffering upon each other (and the planet) over the ages. As
always in the world of complexity whether something is good or bad
depends upon who is making the judgement and when they are making it.
However, groups are an inevitable part of the way we are together. The next

section explores some of the implications of the relationship between the individual and groups for us as managers.

Both the Individual and the Group Come First

Why do we need to think about this? Well, it turns out it matters a great deal both in terms of our status and how we are valued in the groups that we belong to. But first a personal story.

I live in a small village. A couple of years ago, I was driving through a busy intersection in the neighbouring city and noticed a woman probably in her 50s or 60s waiting to cross the road at the lights. No one special here went through my mind. I didn't know her and started to dismiss her. And yet it hit me that she looked very much like Jean, a member of my community (it wasn't her). It occurred to me that while I found it easy to dismiss this individual, I would never pass Jean on the street back home without a wave or a smile because of how important she is to me as part of the village. This is not to say that she is a close friend, but she is an avid bicyclist and friendly face at the local café. She is a good singer and plays a mean accordion. She is a mainstay of the French Club that we have formed. She is an important part of the fabric of my hometown and for that reason, is a special person to me.

Organisational behaviour expert Kenwyn Smith from the Penn Social Policy and Practice Faculty at the University of Pennsylvania and organisational psychologist David Berg from the Yale School of Medicine have written a fascinating book titled the *Paradoxes of Life, Understanding Conflict, Paralysis, and Movement in Group Dynamics*, which can help us to understand what happened that day on the street corner. They consider group and intergroup relations from a paradoxical perspective and examine the question of whether the group exists for the individuals or the individual exists for the group. As it is a paradox, of course, both are true. In their words, however, this question disappears "only when members accept their groupness and groups accept [the] importance of the individual." Later in the book, they propose a paradox of individuality and suggest that a group can only become a group when its members are able to express and fully develop their individuality while the only way for individuals to do so is to accept and develop how they connect to the group. The group gains solidarity as individuality is legitimated while the individuality of the members is established when the primacy of the group is accepted. They go on to say that

> The paradoxical perspective emphasizes that the group exists, grows, and becomes strong and resourceful only if the individuality of its members can be expressed. At the same time that a group requires connections, conformity, and similarity for its existence, it also requires discontinuities

and differences. . . . The paradoxical struggle is again within the individual *and* within the group, to live with the tensions that emanate from the group's dependency on the individuality of its members and the individual's dependency on the commonality of the group.[24]

This statement highlights the importance of the individuality of a group's members, but in the context that *both* the individual *and* the group are important versus one subsuming or outranking the other. It is not either-or but both-and. In the previous chapter we discussed the importance of different perspectives which come about because of our different histories and experiences as we collectively seek to make sense of what is going on. The Jean's of this world who are strong and valued for who they are and what they bring to the party bring richness to and strengthen the groups that they belong to. And at the same time, the importance of the group means that individuals like Jean are also valued.

Insiders and Outsiders

Of course, where there are groups, there are necessarily those that are not in them. For every "we" there is a "they." Just as we need to think about what is going on in interactions and relationships between individuals, we need to be thinking about the interactions between individuals and groups and between the various groups themselves. While there will be a company or organisation culture[25] in terms of expected behaviours and beliefs, norms and values, there will also be various groups with their own evolving way of doing things. Many groups, in the boundaryless world of complex existence, will include individuals from outside the company paywall! All bringing different identities and world views to the discussion.

Different cultures and a feeling of "us" versus "them" can easily develop. When I was practising law, I saw it firsthand. We had run out of office space in our traditional location on Bedford Row in downtown Halifax, Nova Scotia, and took an additional suite of offices in a building down the street, about three buildings down from the main location. I was one of the lawyers that moved there, and very quickly Sackville Place developed its own identity and perspectives. Winter in Nova Scotia is a messy business, and the support and central functions were still in the firm's primary location. This was in the days of physical pay checks, and they always arrived later (along with the mail) if you were at Sackville Place—that is if you weren't prepared to don boots and winter coats and brave the trek to Bedford Row—all one hundred steps of it.

We began to view our status as second class, although in retrospect there was no real difference in our prospects or reputations. But we no longer bumped into the same people or were part of the gossip around the coffee pot as we had been before. We had our own coffee pot, and it was a different subset of partners and staff that hung out together and constructed stories about what was going on and why and who was doing what to whom. These stories affected how those of us at Sackville Place felt about our colleagues in the Bedford Row location and in turn impacted how we interacted with them.

Clearly, we were all still part of the same firm. But there were in-jokes and shared grudges (such as getting our pay checks so much later in the day than our colleagues) no matter how small or imagined, specific to both locations. We also got to know those with whom we shared our different spaces more than we did those that worked only those few steps down Bedford Row, meaning that our relationships were affected as well. A sense of rivalry, luckily enough a relatively friendly one, developed and much was made of successes that showed the superiority of one location over the other. This is clearly a minor example, but it does show how easily and almost inevitably we construct or create groups based on sometimes the most minor of differences. All affecting in larger and smaller ways how the groups relate to and work with each other.

Norbert Elias teamed up with his postgraduate student, John L. Scotson, to write an excellent book, *The Established and the Outsiders* in which they examined the differences in power and rank between two very similar working-class groups in a local community in the early 1960s. In effect, the only real difference between the two groups was the duration of residence in the village they called Winston Parva. However, even trivial differences were used to establish different membership categories or groups. These differences meant that there were certain expectations and demands placed upon individuals which enabled and/or constrained what they could or could not do or say if they wanted to stay a member of the group or groups that were important to them. The question of group membership and the processes which determine who is included and excluded, therefore, were very much a function of the power relationships between these groupings.

Power for Elias and Scotson was based upon our relationships with each other and whether someone was more or less powerful than another was a function of the nature of the interdependencies between them. Elias wrote that interpreting the word "power" to mean that a person does or does not have it, was a relic of magical-mythical thinking and famously said that "power is not an amulet possessed by one person and not by another; it is a structural characteristic of human relationships."[26] In other words, it is not something that is possessed, but part of all human interactions, reflecting how we are interdependent and enable and constrain each other based upon *need* for each other. Whether the need is for love, money, status, or something else, when we need others more than they need us, they have power over us. These power relations are dynamic and as needs shift, so does the locus of power.

Simply stated, if I have something or can do something for you that you need, I have power over you. Thus, it is not necessarily a question of hierarchy (although of course it often is) whether positional or status wise. It is a matter of who needs whom the most.

Elias and Scotson wrote extensively about the processes of inclusion and exclusion. In their work in Winston Parva, they observed how failure to meet expectations could lead to the threat of exclusion from a group, and the prospect of disgrace, humiliation, and shame.[27] These feelings assure compliance with societal/group norms and values. Studies show how significant these enforcement mechanisms are. Being excluded has been shown to involve the same areas of the brain as is stimulated by physical pain.[28] The direct connection between attachment-separation behaviours and opioid-arousal functions within bodies means that being included as part of the "we" prompts the experience of attachment and physiological calming. Being excluded on the other hand, is linked to a threat to our "we" identity which leads to physiological arousal felt as anxiety.[29] It can also lead to some of the same impacts as opioid withdrawal,[30] providing a powerful incentive to maintain membership in the group, in the "us," versus becoming one of "them"![31]

Thus, the threat of being socially excluded from the groups that we seek to belong to is both physiologically and emotionally significant and a powerful example of how we constrain each other to ensure our individual and collective maintenance of group norms and values. The assurance that you are one of us is highly consequential and a powerful enforcer of desired group behaviours.

Managers need to be aware of this tendency to revert to "us versus them" type of thinking in our complex world where we are so interdependent. There will of course be groups and others that stand in opposition to our collective goals. However, within the group of those sharing the same objectives, the concept of "us versus them" can be unnecessarily divisive and thus interfere with our ability to go on together productively. Thus, as Chris Mowles put it, "We might think of one of the responsibilities of contemporary managers as being the custodian of the idea of interdependence, becoming entrepreneurial in finding ways of bringing people into relation with one another."[32]

The "So What" of the Paradox of the Individual and the Society

The implications of the paradoxical relation between the individual and society are significant. We need to extend our scope of concern and questioning beyond a focus on optimising individual performers in the workplace. Instead, we need to also consider what is going on for the group or groups that are involved, what is important to them, and how we can best support them. In other words, we need to focus both on the "we" and the "I" of our colleagues. Complexity theorist Chris Mowles refers to this as *groupmindedness*, a process of keeping the group *and* the individual in mind at the same time.

This is where the competency of *reflexivity* which was first introduced in Chapter 2 comes in. We need to seek to understand the workplace dynamic, by inquiring into what is going on and how that is impacting ourselves and others. While historical context is an important consideration, in the *living present*, the patterning of how we relate to one another that emerges is also dynamic. We need to think about why we are acting and reacting as we are. How are we affecting each other? What patterns are we noticing and how might they be the same or different from those previously encountered? What do each of us as individuals and groups need from one another? What do we expect of each other? How are desired behaviours being rewarded or reinforced by both managers and the group?

This places a premium on deliberation and contestation, on how we allow ourselves to raise, address, and discuss our different perspectives. We need to make it safe, including when it might otherwise feel unsafe, to have a different view even if it is contrary to the orthodoxy of the workplace.[33] How do we deal with others who have different interests and needs from us? How can we find common grounds for collaboration when our goals and constraints may be very different?

We also need to look to both the individual talents of our employees and managers and to the combination of expertise and know-how that they bring and how they work together. If we accept that employees are interdependent, then their individual talents alone are insufficient. It is not exclusively the super stars that will determine and sustain the success of the company but how effectively they work together.[34] We see this in the sports world when the dream team doesn't necessarily triumph. Called the "Miracle on Ice," a team composed of young hockey players trounced the four-time gold medal Soviet Union squad at the 1980 Olympics. Similarly, the 2014 German soccer team which was considered to have no super stars was able to trounce Brazil's five-time World Cup winning team on the latter's home turf. Yes, there is a benefit to having highly talented players. However, because of the significance of the interdependence between these individuals, it is also necessary to have a team that knows how to play and to win together.[35]

As managers we need to be concerned with how competition features in the workplace. One of the challenges of taking an individualistic approach to leadership is that it generally engenders unhelpful competitive behaviours as optimised individuals compete for status and rewards. This may be built into the ways in which their performance is managed through ranking systems, pay for performance, and other ways of comparing one to another. This is not to say that some measure of friendly competition is unhelpful or that one can remove competition from the environment. However, unnecessary, or even aggressive competitive behaviours, can undermine the social reciprocity that we depend upon in our workplaces. In other words, we can no longer rely upon others to be helpful colleagues because they are pursuing their own separate objectives. The less group members concern themselves with meeting the expectations and needs of others, the less trustworthy they will be seen to be. Our inability to rely upon them or to take them at their word, in turn, will increase the uncertainty and complexity of the working environment and increase the transaction costs of dealing with each other. As we react to this doubt about their trustworthiness, we are also less likely to be trusted. This can result in a vicious cycle that reinforces an increasingly competitive struggle to the detriment of our collaborative efforts.

There is much to be learned from other species than *homo sapiens*, species that are also trying to survive in a complex and uncertain environment. The botanist, Dr. Robin Kimmerer, observes that

> when conditions are harsh and life is tenuous, it takes a team sworn to reciprocity to keep life going forward. In a world of scarcity, interconnection and mutual aid become critical for survival.[36]

In times of high stress and/or reduced resources, our interconnection and mutual aid becomes more important than ever. In a crisis or during a time of tight budgets and cutbacks, our ability to draw on the resources and synergies of others and their organisations becomes essential to our success. While our interdependence is a continuing theme, during difficult times, our ability to bring people together and to leverage their talents and our mutual efforts and resources becomes even more important. Our capacity to do so will depend upon the nature of our relationships with each other which developed during the good times. It is important to develop relationships with colleagues both within and outside the organisation *before* things go to hell in a hand basket. In times of crisis, a call for help from someone that previously treated you with respect is likely to be answered much more quickly than from an individual who previously had no interest in or time for you.

We also need to take care as managers not to increase the uncertainty of our working relationships. Many of our management practices foster competition between employees and groups for increased compensation and resources or promotional opportunities. As noted previously, this can undermine the very social reciprocity that fosters collaboration. Why should I help you when ultimately if you succeed it may be at my expense?

We have also discussed how we need to be able to sit in the "fires of uncertainty" and to manage the anxiety of problem-solving. Too often, managers pride themselves on being action-oriented and in control and are unable to allow the possibly uncomfortable exploration of what is going on that is needed to have a better sense of the situation. When you consider that in our social world problems do not come with labels on them, the inability to debate and discuss what is happening has real consequences in terms of what we are trying to do. We may grasp at short-term solutions to make the pain go away quickly, thus likely creating even more issues in the longer term. Or if nothing else can be thought of, in our haste to be seen as a competent and decisive manager and to demonstrate that we have a plan, our anxiety can drive us to launch new initiatives or to reorganise, downsize, or otherwise to rearrange the deck chairs on the Titanic (an expression which refers to occupying oneself with some trivial activity while ignoring something significantly more important). All of this is likely to unnecessarily increase the stress and burden on employees, both individually and collectively, and to adversely affect their ability to work together collaboratively. Our actions can prompt unanticipated results in our nonlinear world and serve to increase the uncertainty that we are trying to deal with, and thus the complexity of the environment.

Summing Up and Conclusion

This chapter introduces important questions for all of us in organisations. What is going on in our interactions? How are we affecting each other? What is at play? What patterns are affecting how we go about things? Who are we becoming?

Traditional theories of management (and indeed Western society) have, however, taken a more individualistic approach to understanding what goes on in the workplace. While we may talk a pretty good line of inclusiveness and the importance of the collective activity of the organisation, most practices are heavily weighted towards the individual. We recruit, manage, reward, and reinforce people as individuals. When we consider what is going on from the perspective of complexity, however, we understand that both the individual and the group are important. The individual does not exist without the group and vice versa. The "I" and the "we" are two sides of the same coin. In fact, the more we investigate it, including recent neurological, psychological, and anthropological research, the clearer it is that we are social animals and that the individual and the collective are inseparable and interdependent. If we understand that what is going on is as the result of the many interactions in which we are formed by others and society as at the same time we impact and form others and society, then it is clear our work together is both a social and collective endeavour as well as an individual one. Our approach to management and leadership must reflect this reality.

We then considered what it means to be inside or outside a group, how the social behaviours of inclusion and exclusion are used to enforce adherence to the norms, values, rules, and assumptions of the group and thus the preconditions for inclusion in the group. In other words, what determines what is considered to be successful or appropriate behaviour. Often the relationship between different groups can develop into an "us versus them" type of dynamic which can lead to a failure to explore productive middle ground because of our repudiation of the interests and concerns of those who are not like us. Factions within organisations and/or with key stakeholders can become difficult to work with because they have conflicting or different objectives, beliefs, and priorities, even though they are supposedly working towards the same goals. As well, whether we are inside or outside of a group can affect how we understand what is going on, its significance, and even our ability to perceive an issue.

The implications of what we have discussed in this chapter leads us to the need to keep both the group(s) and the individuals in mind. Both are important and interdependent. We cannot have one without the other. It is a both-and situation, where each is stronger if the other is valued and respected. Keeping the other(s) in mind, or what is referred to as *group-mindedness*, is fundamental to being an effective manager or team member. Managers have the role of being champions and enablers of the group and need to focus on the nature and health of relationships in the organisation and with stakeholders. They also need to be conscious of the needs of others and be responsible for how they relate to and affect them. Failure to operate in this way can even lead to an increase in the uncertainty and complexity of the environment.

We have examined the relationship between the individual and society in this chapter, keeping complexity in mind. The next chapter considers how trust both enables and constrains our efforts to work together.

Implications for Your Practice

1. Remember that we are, at all times and in all ways, social animals. The individual and the group/society are inseparable. We are interdependent, and we perform successfully or not as a collective. The Lone Ranger might have made for a good TV series, but in the long run, he/she will not add value to your team.

2. Try to be mindful of what is going on in, and what matters to, the group(s). How can you develop your capacity for *groupmindedness* which supports your ability to keep both the group *and* the individual in mind at the same time?

3. When seeking to understand a workplace dynamic, it is important to be reflexive and to inquire into what is going on. Why are we acting and reacting as we are? Why is this behaviour repeated? Does this differ from one group to another? What and who are you rewarding? Reinforcing? What patterns are we encountering, and how are we affecting them?

4. Consider the agreements that you have made in your groups. What are the assumptions and preconditions that you adhere to in order to belong? To succeed?

5. Think about the "we" and the "they" groups, the different factions, both in your organisation and among your key stakeholders. Are they able to work together, or do they have conflicting or different objectives? Do those differences of perceptions and understandings add value in terms of bringing other important perspectives to the table? Or do they create a zero-sum game that gets in the way of sustainable long-term collaboration and relationships?

6. Understand the individuals and groups that are important and, perhaps more importantly, that *might* become important to your organisation and group. Consider how you can foster collaborative relationships with them *before* you need them.

7. Remember that the way we work together today may affect the way we *will* work together. What is going on for us and how we work together is formed by history. It is dynamic and ever evolving, and thus we always need to ask ourselves: "Who are we, what are we doing and who are we becoming?"

Notes

1 Daniel Victor and Matt Stevens, *United Airlines Passenger Is Dragged from an Overbooked Flight*, April 10, 2017, The New York Times.

2 In this discussion, we use both the words "group" and "society." Both connote individuals who are in ongoing, cooperating, and ever-evolving networks of interdependent relationships with each other. When the intent is to refer to larger communities, nations, or broad groupings of people who have common traditions, institutions, and collective activities and interests, we will refer to society. The word "groups" is used to refer to smaller subsets or groupings of individuals.

3 For further discussion see Chris Mowles' book, *Complexity: A Key Idea for Business and Society*, starting at p. 49.

4 Margaret Thatcher, *Interview for "Woman's Own" ("No Such Thing as Society")*. *Margaret Thatcher Foundation: Speeches, Interviews and Other Statements*.

5 Yuval Noah Harari, *Sapiens: A Brief History of Humankind*, p. 26; also see his book *Homo Deus: A Brief History of Tomorrow*, p. 153; Richard Wilkinson and

Kate Pickett, *The Inner Level: How More Equal Societies Reduce Stress, Restore Sanity and Improve Everyone's Well-Being*, p. 125.

6 See Peter Marris' book, *The Politics of Uncertainty: Attachment in Private and Public Life* starting at p. 40.

7 Ralph Stacey and Chris Mowles, *Strategic Management and Organizational Dynamics*, pp. 102–103, 129.

8 Peter Marris, *The Politics of Uncertainty: Attachment in Private and Public Life*, p. 160.

9 Chris Mowles, *Complexity: A Key Idea for Business and Society*, pp. 62–64.

10 Patricia Shaw, *Changing Conversations in Organizations: A Complexity Approach to Change*, p. 72.

11 Also see the work of Sigmund Foulkes, *Therapeutic Group Analysis*, 1948.

12 Chris Mowles, *Complexity: A Key Idea for Business and Society*, pp. 61–64; also, Peter Marris, *The Politics of Uncertainty: Attachment in Private and Public Life*, pp. 61–65.

13 Ibid., p. 7.

14 Norbert Elias, *The Society of Individuals*, pp. 153–237.

15 Norbert Elias, *The Civilizing Process*.

16 Norbert Elias, *The Society of Individuals*, pp. 66–67.

17 Karl Weick and Kathleen Sutcliffe, *Managing the Unexpected: Assuring High Performance in an Age of Complexity*, pp. 89–90.

18 Filippo Menczer and Thomas Hills, *The Attention Economy: Understanding How Algorithms and Manipulators Exploit Our Cognitive Vulnerabilities Empowers Us to Fight Back*, December 2020, p. 58.

19 Deirdre Boden, *The Business of Talk: Organizations in Action*, p. 8.

20 Brian Hare and Vanessa Woods, *Survival of the Friendliest*, August 2020, Scientific American.

21 Richard Wilkinson and Kate Pickett, *The Spirit Level: Why Equality Is Better for Everyone*, pp. 205–206; Richard Wilkinson and Kate Pickett, *The Inner Level: How More Equal Societies Reduce Stress, Restore Sanity and Improve Everyone's Well-Being*, p. 124.

22 Marta Zaraska, *All Together Now* in October 2020 edition of Scientific American, p. 64.

23 Research Brian Hare, professor of evolutionary anthropology and Vanessa Woods, research scientist, featured in the August 2020 issue of Scientific American, *Survival of the Friendliest*, at p. 62, refer to this expanded concept of stranger as the *intragroup stranger*.

24 Kenwyn Smith and David Berg, *Paradoxes of Life: Understanding Conflict, Paralysis, and Movement in Group Dynamics*, pp. 99–102.

25 For a more in-depth discussion of culture (or *habitus* as referred to in this book), see Chapter 6.

26 Norbert Elias, *What Is Sociology*, p. 74.

27 Elias was, in fact, of the view that shame, including self-disgust, inhibition, isolation, and fear was fundamental to the development of civilization and was produced by any transgression against society's rules.

28 Richard Wilkinson and Kate Pickett, *The Spirit Level: Why Equality Is Better for Everyone*, p. 214.

29 Ralph Stacey, *Complexity and Group Processes: A Radically Social Understanding of Individuals*, pp. 129–130.

30 Anthony L. Suchman, *Organizations as Machines, Organizations as Conversations: Two Core Metaphors and Their Consequences*.

31 See Ralph Stacey, *Complexity and Group Processes: A Radically Social Under-standing of Individuals*, p. 127; and also, Richard Wilkinson and Kate Pickett, *The Inner Level: How More Equal Societies Reduce Stress, Restore Sanity and Improve Everyone's Well-Being*, p. 122.

32 Chris Mowles, *Managing in Uncertainty: Complexity and the Paradoxes of Everyday Organizational Life*, p. 78.

33 Often, as James C. Scott discusses in his book *Domination and the Arts of Resistance*, starting at p. 45, positional power is used to determine what is acceptable to say or not. Thus, it is up to the manager to establish an environment in which uncomfortable truths can be spoken—whether in the group or in a one-on-one setting. The irony of the expression of speaking truth to power is that very often those in power know all too well what is being said but have been careful to suppress its voicing.

34 Richard Wilkinson and Kate Pickett, *The Inner Level: How More Equal Societies Reduce Stress, Restore Sanity and Improve Everyone's Well-Being*, p. 262.

35 Satyam Mukherjee, Yun Huang, Julia Neidhardt, Brian Uzzi and Noshir Contractor, *For Teams, What Matters More: Raw Talent or a History of Success Together?*

36 Robin Wall Kimmerer, *Braiding Sweetgrass: Indigenous Wisdom, Scientific Knowledge, and the Teachings of Plants*, p. 272.

Bibliography

Boden, D. (1994). *The Business of Talk: Organizations in Action*. Cambridge, UK: Polity Press.

Elias, N. (1908/1978). *What Is Sociology?* New York, NY: Columbia University Press.

Elias, N. (1987/1991). *The Society of Individuals*. Oxford, UK: Basil Blackwell Ltd.

Elias, N. (1994). *The Civilizing Process*. Oxford: Blackwell.

Foulkes, S.H. (1964). *Therapeutic Group Analysis*. London: George Allen & Unwin.

Harari, Y.N. (2014/2016). *Sapiens: A Brief History of Humankind*. Toronto: McClelland & Stewart.

Harari, Y.N. (2015). *Homo Deus: A Brief History of Tomorrow*. Toronto: McClelland and Stewart.

Hare, B., & Woods, V. (August 2020). Survival of the Friendliest. *Scientific American*, *323*(2).

Kimmerer, R.W. (2013). *Braiding Sweetgrass: Indigenous Wisdom, Scientific Knowledge, and the Teachings of Plants*. Minneapolis, MN: Milkweed Editions.

Marris, P. (1996/2009). *The Politics of Uncertainty: Attachment in Private and Public Life*. New York: Routledge, Taylor & Francis Group.

Menczer, F., & Hills, T. (December 2020). The Attention Economy: Understanding How Algorithms and Manipulators Exploit Our Cognitive Vulnerabilities Empowers Us to Fight Back. *Scientific American*, *323*(6), 54–61.

Mowles, C. (2015). *Managing in Uncertainty: Complexity and the Paradoxes of Everyday Organizational Life*. London, UK: Routledge.

Mowles, C. (2022). *Complexity: A Key Idea for Business and Society*. London, UK: Routledge.

Mukherjee, et al. For Teams, What Matters More: Raw Talent or a History of Success Together? *Kellogg Insight*. Kellogg School of Management at Northwestern

University. https://insight.kellogg.northwestern.edu/article/talent-versus-teamwork-for-successful-teams, accessed June 17, 2022.

Scott, J.C. (1990). *Domination and the Arts of Resistance*. New Haven, CT: Yale University Press.

Shaw, P. (2002). *Changing Conversations in Organizations: A Complexity Approach to Change*. New York, NY: Routledge.

Smith, K.K., & Berg, D.N. (1997). *Paradoxes of Life: Understanding Conflict, Paralysis, and Movement in Group Dynamics*. San Francisco, CA: Jossey-Bass.

Stacey, R.D. (2003/2010). *Complexity and Group Processes: A Radically Social Understanding of Individuals*. New York: Routledge.

Stacey, R.D., & Mowles, C. (2016). *Strategic Management and Organisational Dynamics: The Challenge of Complexity to Ways of Thinking about Organisations* (7th ed.). London, UK: Pearson Education.

Suchman, A.L. (2011). Organizations as Machines, Organizations as Conversations: Two Core Metaphors and Their Consequences. *Medical Care, 49*(12, Suppl. 1), S43–S48. doi:10.1097/MLR.0b013e3181d55a05.

The Sunday Times. (October 31, 1987). Interview for 'Woman's Own' ('No Such Thing as Society'). *Margaret Thatcher Foundation: Speeches, Interviews and Other Statements*. https://briandeer.com/social/thatcher-society.htm, accessed April 25, 2023.

Victor, D., & Stevens, M. (April 10, 2017). United Airlines Passenger Is Dragged from an Overbooked Flight. *The New York Times*.

Weick, K.E., & Sutcliffe, K.M. (2001). *Managing the Unexpected: Assuring High Performance in an Age of Complexity*. San Francisco, CA: Jossey-Bass.

Wilkinson, R., & Pickett, K. (2009/2010). *The Spirit Level: Why Equality Is Better for Everyone*. London: Penguin Books.

Wilkinson, R., & Pickett, K. (2018). *The Inner Level: How More Equal Societies Reduce Stress, Restore Sanity and Improve Everyone's Well-Being*. New York: Penguin Books.

Zaraska, M. (October 2020). All Together Now. *Scientific American, 323*(4), 64–69.

Chapter 5

Trust and Consequences

Introduction

Trust is an example of one type of patterning of how we relate to each other that can be both helpful and unhelpful as we work together to try and make sense of what is going on, to manage risk and to solve the many problems facing us at work. Trust is always fundamental to how we collaborate, our ability to inquire into productive doubt and to be innovative and creative, particularly in high stress situations.

To provide some context for this exploration, the following are two different experiences in which we were trying to make sense of an issue. Both stories relate to minor little incidents that in the scheme of things would not have stood out as being particularly eventful. However, in a complex world with nonlinear relationships, such events, of which there are many during a workday, can have a significance out of proportion to their size. These were two such instances.

Productivity Woes

Our department was responsible for processing, in other words, receiving and deciding upon the applications of citizens for certain benefit programmes. This work was done in various locations across the country and was the responsibility of the heads of the four regions who report directly to the chief operating officer of the organisation. We were dealing with higher inventories than usual and in many cases, the inability to meet our delivery standards, a situation that none of us were happy with.

The COO, Robert, was concerned about recent numbers purporting to measure productivity of our processing operations. At a previous meeting that I had been unable to attend, officials working in the headquarters' policy and programme development section had introduced metrics that they claimed demonstrated that only 63% of regional staff were 100% productive. Robert described this revelation as a moment when the top of his

DOI: 10.4324/9781003319528-8

head had blown off. He had demanded site-by-site numbers for comparison to explain what was going on in the processing centres. Who was doing a good job and who was not? Those numbers had been assembled and a follow-up national meeting was convened, including Robert and both headquarters and regional direct reports to consider them.

The night before, we had been given the information which consisted of complex, formula-based tables. I and the other regional colleagues had received a hurried brief from our staff shortly prior to the meeting which was scheduled first thing in the morning.

Measuring productivity is not easy. The numbers, which purported to measure the time it took to process applications were derived from work site records used by local managers to evaluate individual staff performance. Also included was the cost per work item so we could assess how well we were managing our finances. The numbers were gathered manually on a site-by-site basis and did not necessarily use the same criteria or methodology, making it difficult to compare the data between sites. They were significant, untested, potentially open to gaming, and more importantly, different assumptions (e.g., from site to site) were buried in them. Certain types of necessary work were not reflected, thereby understating staff effort. Quality of work, fundamental to sustainable excellence in service delivery, was considered separately. The efforts of staff from other parts of the department can significantly affect the service delivery experience and effectiveness of operations, but they were not incorporated in any way. Finally, budgets available for processing used in calculating work item costs were treated differently across regions, thus over or understating costs on a relative basis.

None of this mattered when these numbers were used to manage individual performance by managers at a site as managers were able to apply their judgement and awareness of individual situations to better understand what was going on. For example, if the information suggested that an individual was underperforming, their boss would generally know if there was a justifiable reason or if it was a continuation of a problematic pattern. As a final judgement on productivity of the workforce and to compare work sites across the country, however, the usefulness of these numbers was limited.

The meeting started and Sonia, the executive responsible for the team that had prepared the numbers, took us through the document. When she was finished, Robert asked for comments. I responded with the usual compliments about their good work and then referred to the first discussion question, labelled "How to resolve the productivity problem?" I suggested it might be premature to conclude there was such a problem. I further noted that it was not yet clear that the numbers and the methodology with which they were developed were sufficiently robust and reliable to determine what the issue was or to be used for comparison purposes. Based on my experience, I was hesitant to document as fact something that might not be correct and, more importantly, might lead to a rush to conclusions and prevent a deeper exploration about what was going on.

Robert responded immediately. Looking directly at me and holding up the report, he said that the numbers were indisputable proof of a productivity problem. He looked to Sonia for confirmation, who quickly repeated his statement, almost word for word. Everyone else remained quiet.

I was completely taken aback. I had assumed we all recognised that the numbers were questionable but were a good starting point for us to explore our concerns about our inventory levels and failure to meet delivery standards. Instead, it appeared Robert and Sonia had already decided that this data was reliable and suitable for purpose and saw further discussion as unnecessary. A rush of anxiety washed over me, and I wanted to disappear. I instantly regretted having spoken and feared Robert would presume I was not on top of my areas of responsibility and was being naïve and obstructive. I was concerned I was at risk of not being considered part of the team because I was not singing from the same song sheet.

In retrospect, I might have stood my ground and questioned the basis for Sonia's assertion that the productivity problem was indisputable. I could have tried to convince them of the need to investigate the issue further. However, I realised that to do so I would have to be critical about my colleagues' work and might thereby be perceived as throwing them under the bus. This is never a good career move and particularly ill-advised when these colleagues have significantly more political capital than I. Robert and I already had a rocky relationship, and I believed he didn't have much faith in my abilities.

In that moment, I was highly anxious and neither trusted my ability to convince him of anything nor that it would be *safe* to even try. I sought to find a way to retract my comments. I agreed there was an issue and went on to say that because it was early days and the numbers were still unreliable, we couldn't fully know what they might be telling us. The conversation continued for a few minutes longer as I attempted to undo the damage I felt my remarks had caused and to negotiate myself back into the group and my boss's good graces. I was relieved when he redirected his attention to Sonia and my colleagues, and the discussion turned to what we could do to solve this indisputable problem of productivity.

Equity Differences

On another occasion, the senior management of my region was meeting to discuss the work of the diversity and equity committee, which Peter, one of my team, led. Our group worked well together, and I looked forward to our meetings. Most of us had known each other for many years, and there was an atmosphere of trust, accompanied by lots of teasing and laughter. When opinions conflicted, there was sparring between individuals, but this was generally addressed collegially through both group and informal one-on-one conversations.

On this day, we were considering the representation of minority groups in the employee population. Peter commented that we needed to balance competence and skills with equity requirements. He noted that we were responsible for finding the best person for the job, and thus *merit* must always be our primary concern. This statement resonated with me given the importance we placed on hiring decisions.

At this point, another team lead, Colleen, who is of African-Nova Scotian descent, jumped into the discussion. She spoke forcefully, critiquing Peter's comments. She observed that whenever we had these types of discussions, someone almost always raised the need to protect merit as a criterion for employment. To her it implied that equity hiring meant the lowering of standards or that equity hires might not otherwise be qualified. There was an awkward silence. Peter responded that he had not meant to suggest equity hires were not competent, and repeated that we must be careful to hire on merit.

After a few minutes, Colleen said that she felt this was going to be too difficult a conversation and perhaps we should move on. My immediate reaction was to agree, but I hesitated. In what felt like forever, but was probably only a few seconds, several thoughts raced through my mind. I experienced significant discomfort and nervousness about where further discussion might take us. I worried that I might be shamed in front of my team as a racist because of my initial reaction to Peter's views. There were risks both if we talked about it and if we did not. I was proud of the way the team worked together, their ability to disagree and challenge each other and yet to maintain their mutual affection, caring, and respect and did not want to lose this spirit of respectful collaboration. I realised however, that the issue was already on the table, and while it might be more comfortable to leave it, the lasting impact of what had already been said would be even more harmful if not addressed. On balance I felt the team was up to having the discussion. I felt safe in what was potentially an unsafe situation and trusted that we would be able to handle this together. I acknowledged that it was likely to be a difficult conversation but said that if Colleen was okay with having it, I thought it was important to do so.

Colleen was willing to continue and for the next half hour we explored her concerns. We were ultimately able to move on—certainly not to a perfect place but having had a sharing of different perspectives. Colleen later said that this had been the first time she had participated in such an honest and difficult exchange with colleagues. Despite feeling a bit raw from having participated in a professional and emotionally charged exchange about her racial identity, she was proud of the team for staying in the tough conversation and felt more understood. She also believed that we were in a better place as a team, with a shared understanding of where we were on the issue considering our respective experiences, histories, and identities. She commented that we were often too polite or otherwise reluctant to share our feelings, which then surfaced in unhelpful ways in our interactions. Colleen later told me that she believes we are more alike than different, but that in that moment her colleagues heard her voice and recognised her selfness.

Trust Patterns

These two stories illustrate how different patterns in how individuals and groups relate to each other can lead to very different results and affect our ability to engage in important conversations and explore *productive doubt*, a concept of John Dewey's mentioned in Chapter 3. Both meetings took place in person and evoked significant anxiety and emotional responses. In the section, *Productivity Woes*, for reasons pertaining to my relationship with my boss, I felt that it was not safe to continue with what I thought was an important conversation. I did not believe that my views would be listened to or appreciated and that all I would accomplish was to further harm my reputation with the COO. In *Equity Differences*, despite it being even more emotionally charged, I felt that we could—and should—explore what was going on for all of us because I believed we had sufficient regard for one another and cared for and valued each other's perspectives.

When trying to understand what had been going on and the difference between how these two narratives turned out, the words that came to mind were respect (or the lack of it), feeling unsafe, and trust. Would my colleagues listen to me? Believe in me? Respect me? Give me the benefit of the doubt? And did I dare intervene despite being in what felt like a very unsafe situation? The bottom line was whether I trusted my colleagues and myself to engage in an emotionally charged, meaning-making process.

What Is Trust?

The word trust is a challenging one to define as it is frequently used in our everyday speech as well as in both academic and popular literature. Making it even more difficult to pin down, there are many ways that the word can be used. The *Canadian Oxford Dictionary*, for example, identifies ten meanings of the noun trust, but it can also be a verb, an adjective, or an adverb![1]

Although my doctoral thesis was on trust, I will spare you the riveting academic discussion of the meaning of this term. If you are starved for sleep some night, you will find the online reference to my thesis in the endnotes,[2] and I commend it to you to solve your insomnia problem. For our purposes, however, trust will be defined as being a "felt confidence"[3] that an individual and/or group will meet our expectations about a particular outcome.[4]

Early scholars understood trust on an individualistic or one-on-one basis. If we take complexity seriously, however, we accept that patterns of relating emerge from the many interactions of individuals and groups which then organise our experience together. Trust is an example of such a patterning and affects how we relate to and understand each other.

The early scholars weren't necessarily wrong about the nature of trust. You could see in the case studies at the beginning of the chapter, just how situationally specific and individually felt trust is. Behavioural scientist and expert on trust, Robert F. Hurley,[5] described trust as individual A trusting B in matter X, in context C. I (A) may trust my neighbour (B) to drive my car (X) in my local community, but not in the big city (C), for example. The persons involved, both the person trusting and the person being trusted, what they are being trusted to do, and the context are all important. This makes trust very situationally specific. At the same time, it is also influenced and affected by the relationships among those involved. In other words, we need to understand that *trust* is both a social patterning of how we relate to each other *and* is also individually experienced and particularised at the same time.

Trust relates to more than just the personal and individual relationships such as between you and your boss or your employees. This type of relationship has the benefit of direct knowledge and experience of how the other will act and react and rests upon interpersonal connections that are strong and frequent. Well-known American political scientist and Harvard professor Robert Putnam has referred to this as "thick trust." But the importance of the concept of trust in the workplace (and indeed in our communities) extends to less direct relationships than the one-to-one and beyond the roster of people we can know personally. This Putnam called "thin trust" because it is based on a background of shared social networks and more generalised expectations of reciprocity, the phenomenon that we treat others in the same way that others have treated us in the past.[6] This is even more useful in terms of enabling larger numbers of individuals to collaborate and band together to achieve common goals. And particularly key for our ability to work together to solve problems across an organisation or community.

In both narratives, the patterning of our different histories, experiences, capabilities, reputations, and emotions shaped our experience of being together. We individually and collectively made determinations as to what was and was not right and whom we should believe, what we expected from one another, and whom we could trust. What was going on was paradoxically both the product of the generalised patterns of relating and situationally specific to the individuals and circumstances at hand.

Three Key Points About Trust

There are three particularly significant aspects of trust: it is both cognitive and emotional, fragile, and reciprocal. Each of these has implications for how we work together.

Trust Is Both Cognitive and Emotional

As we have already discussed, it is impossible to separate the mind from the body and the rational or cognitive from the emotional. We can only engage with the world in a personal, engaged, and emotional way. This applies to trust as well. How our colleagues, bosses, and those that report to us relate to us and more importantly, whether they feel they can trust us or not (and vice versa), will not be just a product of rational consideration and reasoning.[7] Instead, it will include how they feel about us. Do they feel confident that we can be relied upon? Logically, everything you are saying may add up, but if they don't feel comfortable with you, or if they feel more comfortable with someone else, your perspective and insights may fall on deaf ears.

It's not "just the facts, ma'am" as Joe Friday in the 1950s TV series Dragnet allegedly[8] used to say. It is the version of the facts from someone that I trust, ma'am.

Trust Is Fragile

One of the consequences of trust being both rational and emotional at the same time is that it is slow to develop and easily lost. An old Dutch proverb states that trust arrives on foot and leaves on horseback.[9] Former Governor of the Bank of England and the Bank of Canada, Mark Carney, wrote that "trust takes years to build, seconds to break and forever to repair."[10] Trust can take varying amounts of time and investment to develop, reflecting how it arrives slowly on foot as in the Dutch saying. On the other hand, if something happens to challenge the expectations upon which our trust is based, we immediately experience a disruption of the patterning that we had previously relied upon, and the horse bolts.

Think of it this way. Trust in many ways is a form of risk management. When we are determining whether we trust one another, we are assessing the risk of relying upon them. The felt risk of trusting can weigh heavily and a single negative experience is likely to outweigh several—or even many—positive experiences. Even one breaking of trust introduces uncertainty into a relationship that was not there before. No matter how many times everything went as expected, that one surprise is proof that we cannot necessarily be counted on. History has a long tail—memories of our experience in previous interactions linger, and trust is a stitching with fine thread, easily broken and undone.

It is a real question as to whether and how trust can be rebuilt. If it is possible, it certainly doesn't happen overnight. Like a healing process it takes time and effort. Effectively, to repair or rebuild trust, others need to not only think but feel that the break in trust was an aberration that will not reoccur. It's a very steep hill to climb. Too often, managers dismiss the impact of the loss of trust. They may not understand how it can be so important in the workplace. Surely, with their positional power, it doesn't matter if they are trusted or not. If managers do address the issue, they often do so via a carefully airbrushed communication piece. However, the burden is on the one(s) that lost the trust to show that they can be trusted again. In my experience, it often requires a demonstration of genuine humility and vulnerability to start the rebuilding process, and actions speak louder than words.[11]

The fragility of trust and its impact on how we will work together is a continual balancing act. We need to be aware of the impact on others of our behaviour and words—a careless email, an overreaction, a misinterpreted remark, a raised eyebrow—all can be destructive of trust depending upon the strength of the trust relations among those involved.

This is one of the aspects of trust that can be particularly challenging for managers as vertical networks and hierarchies can make it difficult to sustain social trust and cooperation. For one thing, sanctions are less easily (if at all) imposed upwards, weakening employees' confidence that managers will meet their expectations as they feel that there is no way to punish a breach of trust.[12]

As trust scholar Russell Hardin stated,

> Substantial power differences virtually wreck the possibility and meaningfulness of trust. The more powerful agent need not trust the less powerful, who may have little choice but to do what the more powerful wants. And the less powerful cannot trust the more powerful because there is likely no reason to believe the more powerful party encapsulates the interest of the less powerful.[13]

Trust is so very fragile that it is very easy to lose or damage the confidence that others have in how we will behave. There is generally much more going on in the workplace than can be shared with all involved, and while your actions may seem to be thoroughly reasonable, necessary, or even inevitable to you given the circumstances, your decisions may cause a loss of trust. Maintenance of trust where we as managers are highly constrained or regulated in terms of what we can and cannot do for others can be particularly challenging. Extreme care must be taken when making commitments, as we may not be able to honour them with negative repercussions for our relationships.

Before we leave our exploration of the fragility of trust in the workplace, it is appropriate to spend a few minutes on the issue of virtual working. During the Covid pandemic, many had to work from home. While this by no means was a universal benefit, in many instances this was experienced by workers as a positive development (not the pandemic but the acceptance of virtual working and thus the implied trusting of the worker to do their work remotely). As we work to resume our lives post-Covid (or with Covid as endemic), in many industries there is significant pressure to retain this way of working, and in planning for a post-pandemic world, there is much discussion about flexible workplaces and hybrid models.

Managers need to think through the differences between telework and face-to-face working. Virtual is generally less spontaneous or synergistic. We don't get the chance to have a sandwich together or an impromptu chat around the water cooler. Sociologist Robert Putnam has suggested that widespread use of computer-mediated communication will require *more frequent face-to-face* encounters and that an extensive, deep, and robust network of social relationships must exist so that those using the electronic media will have a full understanding of what others are communicating to them.[14]

All of this affects the patterning of our interactions with each other and thus the development—or not—of trust. Managers in a hybrid workplace will need to consider how individuals will have the opportunity to develop (and maintain) trusting relationships in the new ways of working through an intentional incorporation of opportunities for social interaction to replace those that develop in an in-person workplace.

Trust Is Reciprocal

Trust is reciprocal in nature. If I trust you, then you in return are more likely to trust me. And the reverse is true as well. If I don't trust you, then you are well advised to not trust me. The expectation of reciprocity plays an important role in determining how or if we trust one another.

Several scholars have recognised the importance of reciprocity in understanding trust. Political scientist Robert Putnam referred to it as a "norm of generalised reciprocity." He explained this as our understanding of how we reconcile our own self-interest with our obligations to support and help our colleagues. He saw reciprocity as a combination of short-term altruism and long-term self-interest: I will help you out now based on the (probably unenforceable) expectation that you (even though I may not know you) will reciprocate by helping me out in the future.[15] This ability to work cooperatively is essential in the cooperative management of uncertainty[16] and limits the disruptiveness of competitive behaviours which often preempt the ability to collaborate for the common good.[17]

In the second narrative, I felt—even in the throes of my anxiety—that I could rely upon my colleagues and that they would have confidence in me as we negotiated a difficult conversation. Our trust in each other was reciprocal and mutually reinforcing. In the first narrative, when considering whether to pursue or retreat from my questions about the numbers, I was concerned that Robert had no confidence in me. This weakened my capacity to trust my own abilities, perhaps reinforcing Robert's view that I was missing the point which would have further undermined his confidence in me. It felt easier and safer for my career to be an obedient civil servant rather than to rock the boat. The potential for a cruel and negative circle is obvious: because you do not trust me, I do not trust you and because I do not trust you, you do not trust me.

The reciprocal nature of trust can pose challenges in managing large populations where the risks posed by a small percent of wrongdoers can be significant. We often make the mistake of treating most employees who are trustworthy like the very small percent that are not. The message from this leadership style is that all are not trusted, often resulting in increased levels of distrust of managers and leaders. Similarly, command-and-control leadership practices can be experienced as a lack of trust by those being managed as the directive type of style conveys the message that the employee cannot be counted on either to know or to do their job. According to neuroscientist Henning Beck, neurobiology research shows that those who try and control others end up losing both their trust—and their ability to perform.[18] American political economist, Gary J. Miller refers to it as the control paradox.[19] Again, there are obviously instances where this may be appropriate; however, any workplace where this approach predominates is likely to be one in which there are low levels of trust between colleagues and in managers.

Why Should We Care About Trust?

The real question is what does trust mean for us in the workplace?

Trust Can Make Us More Efficient

Stanford University professor and American political scientist and economist, Francis Fukuyama, writes that if the institutions of capitalism and democracy are to function effectively, and be stable and prosperous, they need more than law, contracts, and economic rationality. There must be "reciprocity, moral obligation, duty toward community, and trust, which are based upon habit rather than rational calculation."[20] The very same can be said about our work in organisations. Not everything is cut and dried and can be covered in advance through the promulgation of rules, laws, and contracts. As we have already seen, in a complex world, you cannot predict what is going to happen. You might have a good idea based upon experience or upon the commitments that others have made, but you cannot know that it is going to turn out as anticipated.

Fukuyama also pointed out that societies with a high degree of communal solidarity and shared moral values are often more economically efficient than their more individualistic counterparts. Needing to reduce everything to writing or to a hard and fast rule means high transaction costs and resulting inefficiency. And even then, what is put in writing or stated as a rule needs to be interpreted by those attempting to implement or enforce it. Given our different perspectives and experiences, we cannot expect everyone to understand laws, rules, and contracts the same way.

Trust Can Increase Our Ability to Deal With Our Fear of Uncertainty

Our work to figure things out is dynamic, and we are always adapting, problem-solving, and negotiating how to go on together. We don't know what we don't know and are slaves to our own perceptions. We need to be able to explore a diversity of opinions and perceptions in our highly complex world. Patterns of trust relating can help us to make sense of what is going on by supporting us to stay in relation with one another despite our anxieties and emotions. This allows us to plumb the depths of our differences, thus enhancing our ability to engage with productive doubt.

If we are unable to engage in an exploration of difference because we seek unity and conformity, we cannot expect to see novelty and creativity.[21] Disincentives to raising different views can obstruct different ways of looking at issues and, therefore, negatively affect not only our ability to innovate but the engagement of our workforce—both goals that figure prominently in much corporate literature. This was well put by Raghuram Rajan, Indian economist and former governor of the Reserve Bank of India who wrote that "people innovate when they are confident that they can question, when they are free to make radical changes, and when they do not fear reprisal for it."[22]

Failure to be open to different ways of understanding what is happening can have consequences. In *Productivity Woes*, there were clearly significant issues that we needed to address. We needed to better understand what was going on to cause the backlog and service standard issues we were observing. Once it had been decided that we had a lack of worker productivity, a whole range of options was ruled out and others became relevant. This can be efficient if we have done a good enough job of exploring the issue. If we haven't, however, we can end up not addressing what is going on and introducing additional and unnecessary disruptions into the environment, which only serve to increase the uncertainty and complexity we face. In this case, we ended up in a perpetual loop of decrying the lack of productivity and yet not being able to have the conversations we needed to understand what was causing the problem.

Admittedly my intervention may have puzzled my boss and my colleagues as it was directly counter to what everyone else around the table seemed to have bought into. A respectful reaction from Robert would have been to note that I obviously had a very different perspective on what was going on and to ask why I saw it so differently. Such a response would have shown that I was a trusted team member and allowed me to share my views in the meeting.

We thus need to try to take as many perspectives into account as we can—both in defining the problem and in determining what we need to do about it. Where an individual doesn't feel safe to make such an intervention because either they don't trust others—particularly those with more power—or they don't feel trusted themselves, it is unreasonable to expect them to speak up. Asking a question or offering information that might not be considered relevant or appropriate can feel risky in terms of being excluded from the group and/or being judged to be off the mark, making it safer to stay silent. We saw this during the first narrative in this chapter. We often hear the admonition to keep your head down and go with the flow. So often the cry from the corner office is "Why did no one tell me?" as they attempt to deflect responsibility for having missed an important issue that is now seriously affecting the organisation.

The Downside to Trust

Trust is often idealised in the sense that managers decry the lack of trust in their organisation or society. Consultants and authors promise that they can help to instil trust or restore trust, as if trust was some sort of engine that just needs the right part. Headlines such as "All you need is trust" convey the message that trust is an unalloyed benefit for a government or an organisation.[23] As usual the reality is a trifle more nuanced than that. We are, once again, in the *It Depends* zone. While trust can be both helpful and unhelpful in our working together, it is neither a panacea nor a magic formula or guarantee of success. And in fact, our trusting patterns can get us into deep trouble.

An excellent example of the negative effects of too much trust is what psychologist Irving Janis[24] called "groupthink." He coined this term in his study of the Bay of Pigs and other high-profile disasters in American public policy to describe how contradictory views can be prevented from being expressed and evaluated. A factor that potentially leads to groupthink in organisations is a strong patterning of trusting relationships that, rather than assisting, prevents productive exploration of the issues at hand through a blind acceptance of *people like us* and their views. For example, studies have shown that we are more likely to accept information from those that we trust.[25] Where *groupthink* reigns, contradictory perspectives, which challenge our group and *we-identities* and commonly accepted assumptions and values, are not likely to be expressed and evaluated, as they might jeopardise relationships with colleagues and lead to exclusion from the group. In such cases, maintaining inclusion in a group becomes more important than surfacing a different perspective, with a corresponding lessening of our ability to inquire into what is going on.

Who is considered an insider or an outsider is often affected or determined by who we trust and who we don't. Thus, the presence or absence of trusting relationships can create or strengthen *in-groups* and *out-groups*. Rather than helping us to manage the anxiety and conflict of meaning-making, the resulting us versus them thinking can tend to strengthen and increase the competitive or polarising conflict we experience, making it even more difficult to collaborate.

In the first narrative, the boss and the experts had all labelled the problem as a workforce productivity one, and this became the only basis for exploration of the issue. The experts were trusted to know what was going on, and it was their numbers that had generated the discussion and supported the conclusion about the lack of productivity. If they had it wrong, then we really were in a difficult situation. Our patterning of trust relationships supported their authority and credentials to make this determination and any view to the contrary was not credible and a waste of time when we needed to get on with solving the problem.

Summing Up

In this chapter we have examined a specific patterning of our relationships called trust, a "felt confidence" that an individual and/or group will meet our expectations about a particular outcome. While trust is generalised, it is at the same time highly specific to an individual situation, and its fragile and reciprocal nature can pose challenges for managers.

We are always negotiating how to go on together. We act and react to each other informed by both our emotions and our cognition, and in the process, our expectations and understandings of the other develop. Relationships of trust or distrust among individuals and groups are strengthened or weakened or even destroyed, as we form and are formed by our interactions. As we work together, our experiences will affect how we anticipate our future interactions and how we make sense of what went on in the past as we reinterpret our experience in light of current events. How we work together is likely to affect how we *will work* together in that how we deal with one another today will affect our patterns of trust relating and thus how we will relate to each other in the future.

We live in highly contingent and uncertain times. More than ever, we need to be able to collaborate to solve the many and varied problems that face us. Trust and trusting relationships, their presence and absence, have huge implications for how we do this—both positive and negative. They can help us to be more efficient and to manage our fears of uncertainty, or they can reduce our ability to explore productive doubt. Or as described by American historian and political philosopher Hannah Arendt, our capacity to make and keep promises or to meet another's expectations can create covenants that help us to cope with the unpredictable consequences in our work together by throwing "islands of predictability" into the "ocean of uncertainty."[26]

Trust scholar Barbara Miztal said it well in her book *Trust in Modern Societies: The Search for the Bases of Social Order*. She noted that her book was an attempt

> to look at modern societies and their problems from the perspective of the quality of social relationships rather than in terms of goal achievement or performance of the system. . . . Because experience of how societies cooperate and cohere points to the conclusion that it is the relationships that hold us together, trust and the conditions facilitating trustworthy relationships should be at the centre of public attention.[27]

If this is true at the societal level, it can be no less important at the community and organisational levels.

Implications for Your Practice

1. In your workplace, are individuals able to develop trusting relationships, and do you see it in their working together? Or do you see a more competitive and polarising conflict which can interfere with the team's ability to work together effectively? What is going on to cause and/or reinforce these patterns of relating in your organisation?
2. Given that strong trust relationships can sometimes prevent questioning the articles of faith of the group or organisation, how can you make it safer for team members to bring new perspectives to the table?
3. As trust can be highly fragile, how can you cultivate a preparedness within the team to speak truth to your power and to each other when something has gone awry?

4. Can you make an important part of your contract with each of your direct reports that they are expected to deliver the bad news as well as the good? And in turn, that you expect the same dynamic between them and their staff?

5. Could your management practice and style of interaction be seen as conveying a lack of trust in team members, and if so, how can you change your practice to show your trust in colleagues. If there is a lack of trust, can you deal with it directly?

6. When there are the inevitable bumps in the road that cause conflict or disruption, how can you address what is going on with team members so that you can rebuild or restore your ability to trust each other.

Notes

1 Katherine Barber, *Canadian Oxford Dictionary*, 2004.

2 Sara Filbee, *Trust and Its Consequences: A Regional Senior Manager's Experiences of Meaning Making in the Canadian Public Service*, https://uhra.herts.ac.uk/handle/2299/26037.

3 Confidence is a key element to understanding trust. Katie Stockdale, in her excellent book, *Hope Under Oppression*, distinguishes hope and trust, particularly on the presence or absence of confidence. She observes on p. 40, that both "hope and trust are attitudes that we invest in others to behave in ways we think they should. Like hope, trust is an attitude that implies our relative vulnerability and dependence on other people. . . . But unlike hope, trust requires a certain degree of confidence in the person (or group, or institution) in whom one invests trust."

4 While I focus on trust in this book, it is with the recognition that one cannot have trust without distrust (the absence of trust) and vice versa.

5 Robert Hurley, *The Decision to Trust: How Leaders Create High-Trust Organizations*, p. 9.

6 For a discussion on "thick" and "thin" trust, Robert Putnam's book, *Bowling Alone* starting at p. 134 is also a helpful resource.

7 Over and above the inseparability of emotion and cognition, studies confirm that trust is also a matter of our biology. Doses of oxytocin, what is popularly referred to as the trust hormone, makes people more likely to trust one another. Conversely, if individuals are trusted, there is an increase in their production of that hormone. (See *The Spirit Level*, pp. 213–214) Interestingly, oxytocin is also referred to as the momma bear hormone. The levels of this neurotransmitter dramatically increase during pregnancy and postpartum, affecting the parts of the brain that control empathy, anxiety, and social interaction. While this results in feelings of love, trust, and sensitivity to the emotions of others, it also can lead to overprotective and even aggressive behaviours.

8 While attributed to the TV series, Sgt. Joe Friday never really said it. He said something like it, "All we want are the facts, ma'am" and/or "All we know are the facts, ma'am" and Dan Aykroyd later rephrased it as "just the facts, ma'am" in a pseudo-parody movie.

9 There are many versions of this expression. One of my favourites is that trust crawls in and leaves in a Ferrari.

10 See Mark Carney, *Value(s): Building a Better World for All*, p. 107.

11 Mark Carney, in his book, *Value(s): Building a Better World for All*, identifies one of the five essential and universal attributes of leadership as humility (p. 368). To him, it is so important that he dedicated his concluding chapter to it.

12 Robert Putnam, *Making Democracies Work*, starting at p. 172.

13 Russell Hardin, *Trust*, p. 35.

14 Robert Putnam, *Bowling Alone*, pp. 176–177.

15 Robert Putnam, *Making Democracy Work: Civic Traditions in Modern Italy*, p. 172; also see, *Bowling Alone*, p. 134.

16 For further discussion see Chapter 11 of Peter Marris' book, *The Politics of Uncertainty: Attachment in Private and Public Life*.

17 For further discussion of reciprocity, see Polish trust scholar, Piotr Sztompka, *Trust: A Sociological Theory*, pp. 51–52, 69–77 and Chapter 11 of Peter Marris' book, *The Politics of Uncertainty: Attachment in Private and Public Life*.

18 Henning Beck, *How the Mind's Mistakes Make Humans Creative, Innovative, and Successful*, p. 82.

19 Roderick M. Kramer and Karen S. Cook, eds., *Trust and Distrust in Organizations—Dilemmas and Approaches*, p. 12.

20 Francis Fukuyama, *Trust: The Social Virtues and the Creation of Prosperity*, p. 11.

21 Chris Mowles, *Rethinking Management: Radical Insights from the Complexity Sciences*, p. 165.

22 Raghuram Rajan, *The Third Pillar: How Markets and the State Leave the Community Behind*, p. 264.

23 Monica Brezzi of the OECD, *All You Need Is Trust: Informing the Role of Government in the COVID-19 Context*.

24 See the works of Irving Janis, particularly *Victims of Groupthink; a Psychological Study of Foreign-Policy Decisions and Fiascos, 1972*, and *Groupthink: Psychological Studies of Policy Decisions and Fiascos, 1982*.

25 See Filippo Menczer, and Thomas Hills' article in Scientific American, December 2020 titled *The Attention Economy: Understanding How Algorithms and Manipulators Exploit Our Cognitive Vulnerabilities Empowers Us to Fight Back*, p. 56.

26 Hannah Arendt, *The Human Condition*, p. xix.

27 Barbara Misztal, *Trust in Modern Societies: The Search for the Bases of Social Order*, p. 9.

Bibliography

Arendt, H. (1958/1998). *The Human Condition* (2nd. ed.). Chicago: The University of Chicago Press.

Barber, K. (2004). *The Canadian Oxford Dictionary* (2nd ed.). Oxford, UK: Oxford University Press.

Beck, H. (2019). *How the Mind's Mistakes Make Humans Creative, Innovative, and Successful*. Vancouver, Canada: Greystone Books.

Brezzi, M. (2022). *All You Need Is Trust: Informing the Role of Government in the COVID-19 Context*. www.oecd.org/gov/all-you-need-is-trust-statistics-newsletter-12-2020.pdf, accessed August 24, 2022.

Carney, M. (2021). *Value(s): Building a Better World for All*. Toronto: Penguin House Random Canada Limited.

Filbee, S. (2020). *Trust and Its Consequences: A Regional Senior Manager's Experiences of Meaning Making in the Canadian Public Service*. https://uhra.herts.ac.uk/handle/2299/26037.

Fukuyama, F. (1996). *Trust: The Social Virtues and the Creation of Prosperity*. New York, NY: Free Press Paperbacks.

Hardin, R. (2006). *Trust*. Cambridge, UK: Polity Press.

Hurley, R. (2012). *The Decision to Trust: How Leaders Create High-Trust Organizations*. San Francisco, CA: Jossey-Bass.

Janis, I. (1972). *Victims of Groupthink: A Psychological Study of Foreign-Policy Decisions and Fiascos*. Boston, MA: Houghton Mifflin.

Janis, I. (1982). *Groupthink: Psychological Studies of Policy Decisions and Fiascos*. Boston, MA: Houghton Mifflin.

Kramer, R.M., & Cook, K.S. (Eds.). (2004). *Trust and Distrust in Organizations: Dilemmas and Approaches*. New York, NY: Russell SAGE Foundation.

Marris, P. (1996/2009). *The Politics of Uncertainty: Attachment in Private and Public Life*. New York: Routledge, Taylor & Francis Group.

Menczer, F., & Hills, T. (December 2020). The Attention Economy: Understanding How Algorithms and Manipulators Exploit Our Cognitive Vulnerabilities Empowers Us to Fight Back. *Scientific American, 323*(6), 54–61.

Misztal, B.A. (1996). *Trust in Modern Societies: The Search for the Bases of Social Order*. Maldan, MA: Blackwell Publishers.

Mowles, C. (2015). *Rethinking Management: Radical Insights from the Complexity Sciences*. Surrey, UK: Gower Publishing Limited.

Putnam, R.D. (2000). *Bowling Alone: The Collapse and Revival of American Community*. New York, NY: Simon & Schuster.

Putnam, R.D. (with Leonardi, R., & Nanetti, R.Y.). (1993). *Making Democracy Work: Civic Traditions in Modern Italy*. Princeton, NJ: Princeton University Press.

Rajan, R. (2020). *The Third Pillar: How Markets and the State Leave the Community Behind*. London, UK: Penguin Books.

Stockdale, K. (2021). *Hope under Oppression*. New York: Oxford University Press.

Sztompka, P. (2006). *Trust: A Sociological Theory*. New York, NY: Cambridge University Press.

Wilkinson, R., & Pickett, K. (2009/2010). *The Spirit Level: Why Equality Is Better for Everyone*. London: Penguin Books.

Chapter 6

Habitus

The Way We Do Things Around Here

Introduction

A fundamental part of being a manager is developing an understanding of what is going on in the workplace. To this end, we track where we are financially, how our revenues are doing and/or if we are producing what we had said we would. What we need to know, however, is so much more than this.

If we are trying to engage or motivate employees, we need to know what is prized or denigrated and what is important or immaterial to them. If we are launching a new initiative, we might want to have an idea of just how much of a change to habits and routines it will be so we can see how difficult and burdensome implementation might be. If we are trying to achieve a consensus on the path forward, we will want to know if we share a similar understanding of what we have agreed upon. If we are exhorting our staff to be innovative, we must seek out the practices and habits which prevent them from being creative. In other words, to do our job, we need to inquire into the way that we work together, the rules of the road and behaviours that are considered acceptable, as well as the agreements, understandings, and habits that organise how we work together. In short, we need to inquire into the social context.

What we are talking about is what is generally called the culture of the organisation. Another term for this concept, which we will predominantly use in this book, is *habitus*.[1] How to ensure the right kind of culture and if necessary to change or improve it, is extensively discussed in both academic and popular literature and is a key business focus of many consultants. The assumption that this is within the power of any one individual will be doubted by readers who have taken on board the concepts written about so far. However, developing a sense of the culture or *habitus*, is still vitally important if we want to understand how we can effectively work together in an uncertain world.

DOI: 10.4324/9781003319528-9

Before exploring the concept of culture, or *habitus*, let me share a narrative about a human resources meeting in which an intervention was heard differently by almost everyone that was present.

Hearing Versus Understanding

I was in Ottawa for meetings. As the head of a regional sector of the department, I mostly attended national gatherings virtually (even before Covid), but this time I was there in person. The meeting was to discuss certain staffing decisions and other issues related to our human resources practices. One of the topics was a presentation on a new means of tracking improper accesses and transactions in the client database. Security of our client information was a priority for us, and this proposal promised to help us make this data more secure.

This tracking approach had been piloted in my region and was now rolling out across the country. While an important initiative, it was not as simple and unambiguous in practice as might first appear. Some of the now forbidden practices had previously been considered acceptable when used in certain selected circumstances. For example, using your own identification number to access your files while now expressly prohibited, had at one time been the way that new employees were trained in the benefits programmes.

There were also very real issues and implications for this type of heightened enforcement, particularly for smaller communities. One of the rules was that officers were not to conduct transactions or even access files of individuals that were close to them, particularly family members. This is necessary to prevent fraud and/or preferential service. In small rural or remote offices with only one or two staff in the office at any one time, however, this rule was often difficult to implement. Where employees know almost everyone, it can sometimes be impossible to avoid serving relatives and other close contacts. Staff validly felt that clients should not receive a lesser standard of service by virtue of being related to an employee. There were, of course, workarounds to manage this, but they often created extra work and delays in service. Many staff, particularly those with long tenure, took particular pride in solving a client's problem as quickly as possible. While this is a good thing in terms of customer service, it occasionally led to improper accesses because of their desire to help an individual dealing with an urgent issue.

After the update on this new policy, the floor opened for comments, and I weighed in to identify the issues affecting small offices that had been identified in the pilot. While the issue of small offices was not limited to my region, we did have the largest number, proportionately, of such service locations in the country. The only reaction to my comments came from the section head for the programme in question who responded that we needed to be careful about watering down these provisions. It was agreed we would take my perspectives into account and revisit this matter as necessary.

The next day as I was walking to another meeting with my colleague who is responsible for in-person service delivery nationally, he expressed some concern about my remarks the previous day. He had understood me as saying that my region should have special treatment with respect to this policy. I immediately reassured him that that was not the case and clarified that I was looking for us to consider the different situations that small service offices face across the country. He agreed with my concerns, and we parted with a better shared understanding of the issue.

As a result of this exchange, however, I became concerned that there might be others (perhaps everyone) that shared his initial understanding of my comments. Knowing from experience how such misunderstandings can take on a life of their own, I resolved to speak with each person that had been at the meeting to ascertain their take on what I had said and to, where necessary, explain my concerns.

The results were fascinating. For example, the individuals who were involved at the policy level, both in policy development and service delivery both heard me say that we were looking for special treatment for our region. These folk are engaged at the conceptual and not applied level and are not as familiar with the details of the challenges of small offices. The head of integrity for the department had a similar take on my comments. She was protective of the rules and the need to protect security of information and, reasonably given her responsibilities, could not conceive of any approach but the most stringent, applied to all equally. Some weren't quite sure what I had meant, while others completely missed the message or misunderstood me but got my point. Others understood exactly what I was saying and were in complete agreement. Our audit chief, whom I would have expected to take a more stringent approach, concurred wholeheartedly. He came from a private sector background and knew from experience that not everything is as simple in application as it is in theory.

In brief, everyone in the room heard the same thing but understood it in very different ways.

The Power of *Habitus*

How could so many intelligent and good colleagues in the same meeting hear and understand my intervention so differently? Authors Smith and Berg, in trying to explain a similar experience, suggested that a group event can have different meanings for those participating, based upon their different frames of reference.[2] Their explanations "are the products of who they are, as determined by their histories."[3] How individuals see the world and understand its import is partly determined by the patterns that they are used to seeing and experiencing. In short, what they *expect* to see is what they see.

This brings us to the concept of culture or *habitus*. In the early 1950s, psychoanalyst, social scientist, and management consultant Elliott Jaques used the term "culture" to mean the

> customary and traditional way of thinking and doing of things, which is shared to a greater or lesser degree by all its members, and which new members must learn, and at least partially accept, in order to be accepted into service in the firm.[4]

While the term "culture" is the more popular name for this concept, the concept of *habitus* has been with us a lot longer, first appearing in the works of Aristotle. The concept as we understand it today was introduced in the 19th and early 20th centuries by sociologists Marcel Mauss and later Maurice Merleau-Ponty. However, it only became one of the cornerstones of modern sociology through the works of Norbert Elias and, later on, philosopher Pierre Bourdieu in the 20th century.

Norbert Elias, perhaps the preeminent sociologist of the 20th century, is known partly for his work on civilising processes and how the culture of a nation develops over time. His last major work, *Studies on the Germans*, subsequently renamed *The Germans: Power Struggles and the Development of Habitus in the Nineteenth and Twentieth Centuries*,[5] featured a collection of essays studying the evolution of German society and its citizens over time (particularly in the 19th and 20th centuries). An insightful analysis of nationalism, violence and the breakdown of civilisation, his opus shed light on the origins and growth of Nazism and the Holocaust and how the horrific behaviours of Nazi Germany could have happened and been accepted, sustained, and protected.

In *The Germans*, he examined the nature of the group identity or what he called their *we-image*. He described this as deeply anchored in, and indeed inseparable from, individual personalities and thus simultaneously both an integral element of the identity of each person and of the group's common identity. He saw adoption of the *we-image*, or behavioural pattern, as a reliable symbol of a person's belonging to the group and a major part in their understanding of how to behave and what was required to belong to their groups.[6] Elias referred to this concept as *habitus* and described it as our second nature or embodied social learning, which instils a particular world view by determining what is valued and what is not. French sociologist Pierre Bourdieu described it similarly. According to him, *habitus* gives individuals a sense of how to act and respond in the course of their daily lives. It orients their actions and inclinations without strictly determining them. It gives them a "feel for the game," a sense of what is appropriate in the circumstances and what is not, a "practical sense."[7]

One of the many fascinating essays in Elias's book, considered the impact of the practice of duelling on the culture and social mores, or *habitus*, of German society. Elias traced how this practice had led to the adoption and formalisation of violence and had become part of the accepted and indeed expected behaviour in the higher classes.[8] He described duelling as a "symbol of a particular human attitude, a socially regulated fostering of violence"[9] and how it had led to a culture in which "Questions of honour ranked high, moral questions low."[10] Elias referred to this practice as

> a training process for inculcating quite specific values, and a selection process for choosing quite specific personality structures. The selection process favoured the physically strongest, the most agile ruffians and fighting cocks, as is always the case in societies with a warrior ethos.[11]

This had led to a society with pronounced hierarchical inequalities in which those higher in the ranks ostentatiously behaved as if they were superior and better than those lower in the hierarchy, who were denigrated as inferior and weak.

While Elias wrote about nations and not organisations, this way of thinking is equally applicable in our groups and workplaces. Our habits, what is second nature to us as well as how we make our choices as to what it is appropriate and what is not, all flow from our *habitus*. It defines who we are and the parameters of belonging to our groups, what behaviours are expected and rewarded, how we perceive and understand what is going on, what is valued and prioritised, and what is not. It encompasses the stories that we tell each other, the symbols that are important to us and the language we use. Organisational theorist Karl Weick along with his colleague Kathleen Sutcliffe described culture as being both "a way of seeing and a way of not seeing"[12]:

> The trouble starts when I fail to notice that I see only whatever confirms my categories and expectations but nothing else. The trouble deepens even further if I kid myself that seeing is believing. That's wrong. It's the other way around. Believing is seeing. You see what you expect to see. You see what you have the labels to see. You see what you have the skills to manage. Everything else is a blur.[13]

In other words, we see what we expect to see because of our culture. *Habitus* can be either a potential source of blind spots, or a "source of an economical, powerful 'similarity of approach'" because of shared values, norms, and perceptions which enhance our ability to collaborate.[14]

From a complexity perspective, *habitus* is the environment that has developed over time based on our individual and shared histories and the resulting patterns and themes of how we relate to one another. In Elias's words, "the fortunes of a nation over the years become sedimented into the *habitus* of its individual members."[15] While the generally accepted view in the 20th century was that the national character of a country (e.g., its *habitus* or culture), was fixed and static, Elias viewed it as dynamic and evolving over the years as the "fortunes and experiences of a nation (or of its constituent groupings) continue to change and accumulate."[16]

This concept of culture (*habitus*) and how strongly it is held was well described by Canadian anthropologist and ethnobotanist Wade Davis:

> All cultures are ethnocentric, fiercely loyal to their own interpretations of reality. . . . We too are culturally myopic and often forget that we represent not the absolute wave of history but merely a world view, and that modernity—whether you identify it by the monikers *westernization, globalization, capitalism, democracy*, or *free trade*—is but an expression of our cultural values. It is not some objective force removed from the constraints of culture. And it is certainly not the true and only pulse of history. It is merely a constellation of beliefs, convictions, economic paradigms that represent one way of doing things, of going about the complex process of organizing human activities.[17]

Thus, for example, anthropological research shows us that there are cultures in which there is no concept of the past, present, or future, no words for time or notions of linear progression, no goal of improvement or idealisation of the possibility of change.[18] In Borneau, the traditional territory of the Penan, there is no view of work as a burden or separate concept from recreation. Wealth is not material but measured by the strength of social relationships. In fact, they believe that the weakening of these social bonds adversely affects the health and welfare of the whole group. There is no word for thank you as sharing is obligatory and expected. In their culture, a poor man shames them all.[19]

As the *habitus* evolves, we respond by adopting certain behaviours, making assumptions, and developing practices or habits which reflect our understanding of the expectations for how we should act, or in other words, "how we are supposed to do things around here." This, in turn, informs our interactions with others thus affecting our patterns of relating. What we are doing today affects the *habitus* of tomorrow. This brings into focus for us complexity theorist Doug Griffin's question, which Chris Mowles rephrased: "Who are we, what are we doing and who are we becoming?"[20]

Habitus is not something that we can stand outside of or an external force that we can manipulate or fix when we view it as dysfunctional. As leaders and managers, we are inextricably involved in the interactions that have formed the *habitus* and which continue to affect it. We cannot be separated from what is going on. Similarly, a manager cannot change or determine the culture. This is not to say that the *habitus* doesn't change, in fact it is constantly evolving. Managers certainly do have influence over what is going on, however, *habitus* is a patterning of how we relate to each other that has evolved according to our history and experiences and thus cannot be owned or generated by any one person.

There is also no one consistent *habitus* for an entire organisation or society. While one would expect similarities across large organisations, each location is a unique combination of individuals and groups, their histories and experiences and professional affiliations and competencies. Thus, while there are certainly common practices and patterns across an organisation, they may be understood in different ways at the individual and group levels.[21]

All of this means that *habitus* informs how we define who we are, who is like us and the parameters of what is required to belong to a group. This makes the *habitus* fundamental to a manager or leader as they try to project what will work and/or how staff will react to an initiative or some new development. We have all experienced how implementation of new initiatives is rarely straightforward even when we can rationally justify why the change is necessary. I have even heard employees acknowledge that a proposed new practice is better but that they weren't supportive because it was not what they were used to, and they didn't know what to expect. Inquiring into the *habitus*, which helps us to understand the context for our actions, is thus essential.

Why Our Language Is Important

Humankind has been described as a symbol-using animal. Or in the words of American literary theorist, Kenneth Burke, a "symbol using, making and misusing animal." Much of what we consider to be reality has been built up for us through nothing but our symbol systems.[22]

The word "symbol" is generally employed to refer to something that is taken to represent something other than itself. What pragmatist G.H. Mead called "significant symbols" are those that carry a similar meaning for all parties in a communication.[23] They thus become the medium through which we interact and communicate with one another,[24] making possible a shared understanding of our social world and meaning that both particular and general social understandings are incorporated. They are part of our *habitus* and contribute to how we organise ourselves and thus create some form of social order. They can be powerful in creating an emotional bonding with a group or a collective.[25] For example, a flag is just a piece of fabric, and yet, it brings with it very strong emotions both positive and negative depending upon the individual and the context.

Perhaps one of the most powerful of our symbols is language. It too is a social and historical phenomenon that reflects traces of, and helps to reproduce and maintain, our social experience.[26] How we talk about things affects our behaviour.[27] Our language can determine what social groups we belong to and even what is invisible or visible to us through the ideologies or frameworks that we adopt.[28] It can affect our observation and understanding of reality and/or create new ones due to our choice (and use) of language.[29]

A somewhat humorous example of the impact of the symbolic nature of language and how it can affect our understanding comes from the horror movie, *The Shining*. In one scene, Jack Torrance, played by Jack Nicholson is pursuing his wife who has locked herself in the bathroom. He takes an axe to the door and when he has made a big enough hole to get his head through, he shouts, "Heeeeeeeere's Johnny." An incredibly intense scene but one that was leavened a little for North American audiences who were familiar with the Johnny Carson late night television show. This programme always started off with the announcer's "And now, heeeeeeeere's Johnny!" In England, where the show was less well known, this pronouncement by Torrance was experienced as an unalloyed moment of terror. By contrast, on the North American side of the ocean, it was as likely to generate a ripple of relieved laughter and a reduction of the tension of the moment.

Language (and other symbolic devices, such as robes or wigs, respectful references, and other ritual expressions) can affect not only how we perceive what is going on but also can be what is called *performative*. This means that their very use or presence effects a transaction or constitutes the performance of an act. A common example would be the words "I do" in a marriage ceremony which changes the legal status of the relationship between two persons or the ritual expressions that are used in a court that confirm the authority of the speaker and their entitlement to speak.[30] In doing so, these utterances legitimise a certain vision of our social world and its authority structures.[31]

Language can thus have real consequences and can reshape or affect how we view or understand our reality. We measure people, and this affects their status and career potential at work as they are now referred to as under- or high-performing, with all that goes along with that designation. We organise our understanding of our environment and how we relate to and recognise one another into components and groups and name them.

This gives them an existence that they would not otherwise have had in the sense that these concepts or groups now have a meaning and thus a presence for us. This can be highly significant in terms of shaping how we work together.

For example, when I was working in the service delivery world, my area had the largest proportion of small rural offices of all the regions across Canada. Due to lack of economies of scale, these offices are more costly to run but the allocation of funds to pay these expenses had originally been determined as the result of the significant political clout of the regions with much higher populations and proportionately larger offices. While I was heading up the region, the result of this imbalance was that our fixed costs in our in-person service delivery group were over 75% of the income of the unit, as compared with other regions where the ratio ranged from 40 to 60%. Due to this, our region had an ongoing deficit that we were unable to get funding for except as a last resort at the end of each year. This meant that we had to make many decisions that were determined by our funding constraints in the short-term but were often counterproductive in the longer term.

More by good luck than good management, we started using the words "urban, rural, and remote" to describe the three types of offices across the country. Our view was that all of them were important and that all also encountered different challenges based upon which of these categories they fell into. Fairly quickly, this tagline was adopted, and we knew that we had made significant headway when we found that others were bringing it up and making the point about the varying realities in the different offices, including the small ones. For the first time, the challenge of the rural offices started to get traction as all regions could readily understand (and see themselves in) these three categories. While it didn't resolve our financial difficulties overnight, those three words did open the doors to a more informed discussion of the issues faced by different size offices. We had effectively created a way of classifying the in-person offices which then affected how they were seen and the conversations about how they were resourced and supported. These three words had given the rural offices a presence and meaning that would not otherwise have existed.

How Specialised Languages Affect Our Work

It is generally accepted that those with shared expertise often develop a specialised language to enable them to collaborate effectively and efficiently. Thus, certain words may have meanings which are different from common usage. Frameworks for how to think about the world which specify the requisite processes, methodologies, and assumptions for those who aspire to be part of the group are also an integrated part of this shared mode of communication. This terminology can, however, become impregnable jargon which can serve to isolate and exclude those not "in the know," thereby reducing the diversity of perspectives available to us in our problem-solving. These specialised languages and the frameworks of ideas or ideologies that are inherent to them can also prevent any challenge to the accepted orthodoxy of the group.

A common example is the use of abbreviations or acronyms (abbreviations formed by using the first letters of other words, such as NASA or UN or YMCA). While this form of shorthand may allow your colleagues to understand easily and precisely what or who you are referring to, the jargon is likely to exclude others who do not have this knowledge. Anyone who has had the experience of being the only person in a group of professionals, experts, or even employees of an organisation, will understand the challenge of trying to interpret what is being said by others in the room. Acronyms or terms specific to a particular field of expertise can facilitate the exchange of information with those who share the same types of expertise, but at the same time, may also prevent others from understanding what is being said. As very few of our endeavours in an organisation are restricted to a narrow field of specialisation, this exclusionary effect can prevent the inclusion of necessary but different expertise and perspectives.

Specialised languages can also serve as control mechanisms. Pierre Bourdieu commented in *Language and Symbolic Power* that specialised languages are a compromise between censorship caused by the nature of the field in question and the ability to express specific ideas that would not otherwise be possible.[32] We use the universe of meanings that specialised terminology offers us to predict and control but are also controlled by them because to use these meanings, we must conform to the complex and specific rules which are part of the framework of the field in question.

The authoritative nature of the field that establishes the specialised language can make it risky to speak out and to challenge the orthodoxies of a specialisation and the assumptions and ideologies (e.g., the systems of ideas and ideals) that are inherent to these specialised languages, if one wishes to continue to be accepted as a member of the group.[33] Those that diverge from the prescribed practices and ways of thinking, may find themselves excluded.

In the late 1980s at the age of 41, complexity economist Brian Arthur, experienced this firsthand. He held an endowed chair of economics at Stanford, a good nine years earlier than is usual for this type of appointment. He was fascinated with the issue of complexity and instability and saw it everywhere. This had led him to challenge many of the key precepts and assumptions in the field of classical economics, particularly those that pertained to the stability of the marketplace and the balance of supply and demand.

Based on his research, he had proposed the principle of increasing returns, what I would call "them that has gets," rather than the commonly accepted law of diminishing returns. While in his immediate circle, this was well received; elsewhere he encountered significant push back. Journals told him that his articles weren't economics, and at seminars, audiences responded to his proposals with outrage. How dared he suggest that the law of diminishing returns was not a foundational principle? Brian Arthur had chosen to explore other ways of understanding what might be going on based upon his observations and study, and he was being shunned because he challenged the orthodoxy. He wasn't doing economics in the words of the journals because he wasn't following the rules.[34]

What Our Stories Tell Us

Our *habitus* also includes the stories and narratives that tell us who we are and what we stand for. Belief in the same stories can support our ability to collaborate and thus have an important organising effect in our organisations. Emeritus Professor and management scholar at University of St. Andrews, UK, Barbara Townley of the University of St. Andrews suggested that stories document the common law of an organisation or group and serve as the unwritten "rules of the road" for inclusion in the group.[35] These stories can tell us a lot about the type of organisation or community and what is valued or not in that environment. For example, stories about high status individuals often role model the behaviours required for success in a group. Other social narratives can highlight what is considered to be undesirable comportment in an organisation.

Israeli historian Yuval Noah Harari recognised the importance of myths and stories and was known to say that if you rewrite history and the stories and myths that are told, you can change the culture.[36] While stories do evolve, and new ones develop based upon arrivals and departures and the behaviours of members of the group—particularly if they are in influential positions—changing accepted narratives can be incredibly challenging. Myths are incredibly powerful despite their sometimes fictional nature, and it can be pretty difficult for any one person or group to dislodge a strong social narrative. In fact, narratives are held on to and defended the most by those who have benefited by and/or sacrificed for them, which generally includes those at the helm of the organisation.

Back in the 1980s I was very involved with the United Way of Canada. In the city of Winnipeg, 100% of the administrative costs of the local United Way, had for years been paid for out of the proceeds of a local lottery fund. All campaign literature and advertisements as well as speeches and announcements had for years emphasised how this meant that the full amount of any donation went directly to community needs. Despite this, the results of their annual surveys continually showed that one of the strongest objections to giving was the view that administrative fees were too high. No amount of communication, advertising, or discussion had been able to change the firmly held beliefs of the community.

Gossip is a form of narrative and a key means of social control. American political scientist James C. Scott in his book, *Weapons of the Weak*, suggested that it is almost always news that a norm has been broken or a value disregarded.[37] Sociologists Norbert Elias and his colleague John Scotson studied the workings of gossip in a village in England at the end of the 1950s in their seminal work, *The Established and the Outsiders: A Sociological Enquiry into Community Problems*. They were looking at the relationship between two groups, one being well established in the community and the other made up of newcomers (many of whom had escaped from the blitz in London during World War II). While the two groups were demographically very similar, the established group successfully closed ranks to exclude and marginalise new arrivals.[38] Elias and Scotson noted that this group was able to do this because they had stronger social connections and networks, which facilitated the spread of gossip throughout their community.[39]

Elias and Scotson identified both *praise gossip* (designed to reinforce the stories the established wanted repeated about themselves) as well as *blame gossip* (which emphasised the poor behaviours of the outsider group). Their analysis found that praise gossip tended to be modelled on the "minority of the best" and inclined towards idealisation of the more powerful group, confirming their higher status. The image of the "outsiders," the groups with relatively little power tended to be modelled on the "minority of the worst" and was prone to denigration.[40]

Thus, while the behaviours in the two groups were often similar, what was picked up and amplified in the village gossip (or ignored), depended upon whether it conformed with the existing social narratives about the established or the outsiders. In this way, gossip enforces expected norms and values. It can also contribute to the development and maintenance of an us versus them dynamic in our interactions and workplaces which can hinder our ability to cooperate because the other is considered to be of lesser status and thus not a worthy or productive colleague.

We Don't Have Values, Values Have Us

Values,[41] which form part of the patterning of how we relate to each other are yet another aspect of the *habitus*. The philosopher G. H. Mead saw them as arising in the evolution of our organisations and as important for our organisational and societal functions.[42] Effectively they are idealised and shared belief systems that highlight what is important to, and desired by, the group.

For example, we might say that we aspire to be evidence-based, to serve collegially and with integrity, and to focus on excellence. These are statements that describe universal and generally idealised concepts which are not specific to any one situation but can serve to identify the kind of people we are and guide us on the behaviours that are appropriate and expected in the workplace.

Values are compelling and inspiring and constantly evolve as we continually negotiate what we should be doing together. They express who we are and what we hold dear. Values are typically experienced as greater than us as individuals and are compelling because they represent our aspirations. Stacey and Mowles wrote (quoting pragmatist John Dewey) that values, and a commitment to them, often feel as if they come from outside of ourselves.[43] They provide the criteria for who is in and who is out of the group. Adherence to them is to define one's identity as "one of us" while questioning them can often be considered an offence against the whole community.[44] Challenges to these world views and slogans can be threatening as they directly affect our ability to connect with others, our individual and group or we-identities, our views of a desirable future, and even how we construct our own personal hero stories.[45] This view of values led to a saying at the Complexity Management Centre at the University of Hertfordshire that "We don't so much have values, as values have us."[46]

Values can become what Norbert Elias referred to as "self-praising belief systems."[47] We are special because we are a democracy, and we believe in diversity and inclusion or equal opportunity for everyone. They are appealing to the individual as they often derive a sense of enlarged personality from their values, which can thus become a significant part of their identity. In the extreme, individuals can feel that they will be able to overcome all obstacles simply by virtue of their belonging to that group and subscribing to those values.

Managers often originate, reinforce and reward certain values that support their vision of the future of the organisation. These values are then used in prioritising, controlling, or prescribing what is appropriate behaviour. Sometimes they are written down and formalised such as in a strategic plan, but most of the time, they are unwritten. Some values are not meant to be spoken of publicly or shared widely outside the group. They are still, however, powerful drivers of behaviour and attitudes. An example of the latter is the organisation that promotes itself as client centric but instructs its staff to follow processes which will maximise profit regardless of impact upon customer service.

Public or not, the case for values is that they promote alignment and harmony as they ensure that we are all working towards the same thing. As values are abstractions or generalisations, however, we need to negotiate how they apply to a specific situation through our daily interactions as we seek to particularise, or interpret, the general rule.[48] Such values may be understood very differently across the organisation whether determined by location, function, or other criteria. Different interpretations may emphasise one aspect of the desired future over another, again, the interpretation being affected by the perspective of those involved. Production or sales. Policy or service delivery. Legal or marketing. Each function has different concerns, constraints, and objectives which colour their interpretation of the value, all supported by the teachings of the prevalent social narratives or gossip which highlight what is rewarded and recognised as appropriate comportment.

Authors Smith and Berg wrote that conflicts between groups also arise over differences in values and ideologies.[49] Different understandings of important values can also lead to dysfunctional us versus them dynamics with ensuing power struggles which can transform exchanges between groups. In some cases, it can be almost impossible to reconcile one value or understanding with the other when they come into conflict, particularly when they are strongly held. We may also resist the goals and values of others because we feel it is necessary to preserve our own group and individual identities.[50]

This can be even more challenging when values are presented as absolutist or non-negotiable. The requirement to comply with ideals, creeds, principles, or values which are absolute, unyielding, and unalterable can mean that they can be neither questioned nor modified in the light of new experiences or reasoned argument.[51] If one is seen as asking questions about a particular value, it may be interpreted as questioning the value itself, which is something that must not be done if you wish to remain in the group. As a result, members are increasingly silenced in exploring what is meant by them for fear of the threat of being excluded or sidelined because they aren't on message. An inability or unwillingness to inquire into what we mean by our values reduces our ability to find common ground. This led Doug Griffin to refer to absolutist values as "unreflected ideologies."[52] American law professor and philosopher, James Boyd White, likewise warned against slipping "into political cant and slogan" lest the discussion become one in which the discovery and expression of new truths are suppressed.[53]

This can be dangerous as it can prevent us from coming to agreement with colleagues and stakeholders. Just how difficult it can be to even inquire into a value was evident in the narrative in Chapter 5, where despite the generally accepted value that the public service is evidence-based, I was unable to question the basis for the numbers that had been developed on productivity.

Value Slogans

This brings us to *value slogans*. These are values that are adopted by organisations as branding statements or motivational slogans, in other words they are values which are expressly adopted and made public. Again, they can be highly symbolic and provide an idealised view of the future which evokes the sense of belonging to something greater than oneself and becomes an important part of the identity of members of the group. There are no qualifiers as to the constraints or barriers that might lie in the path to this wonderful future. Thus, statements like "We will be number 1" or "We will be the leader in our market" or "We will make our country great again" are idealised promises about the bright future awaiting us as a group if we sign on to these values. Often, *value slogans* are used as shorthand to express a concept or value or to convey a brand. For this reason, they often feature prominently in corporate and planning documents.

While value slogans can be tremendously helpful in helping us to work together, when we are unable to examine and understand them, they can become part of the empty language often used in organisations and a replacement for thinking and understanding. Mats Alvesson and André Spicer's provocatively titled book, *The Stupidity Paradox*, considered the question of why organisations often do stupid things such as "pointless rebranding exercises, ritualistic box-ticking, misguided attempts at vision-ary leadership, thoughtless pursuit of rankings"[54] and so on. The superficial and unreflective use of value slogans is also an example of problematic practices. Many a time, the statement "oh and of course this will be evi-dence-based" is added to a presentation, almost as an afterthought. This is clearly an important value as we as custodians of the public interest need to be seen as doing good work for good reasons, e.g., based on evidence. However, once that box is ticked, the speaker moves on with nary a thought as to the nature of the evidence, whether it is causal or merely correlative, or if the action in question and its results are even measurable. We are evi-dence-based and no further details or explanation are required. If you need to ask questions, it just shows that you don't have a proper understanding of what we are trying to do.

Just how empty this language can be is demonstrated by another story about a government department that delivered services to Canadians. Their public mantra was "More ways to serve you," but behind the scenes, the popular rephrasing of it (including by some senior executives) was "More ways to screw you." What made it even more amusing (albeit sad) was that the stated values of the organisation were pride, respect, integrity, and col-laboration. A most apt acronym!

Alvesson and Spicer suggest that the reason for doing these stupid things is that these behaviours work, albeit in the short-term. By ignoring the many uncertainties and complexities, we allow everything to run smoothly and the job to get done! No need to think as that can just be awkward. From the perspective of employees, it is easier and safer to steer clear of bother-some doubts so that they are seen as positive contributors who don't ask too many annoying questions. Being able to assert that we pursue excellence or are evidence-based puts us in the right immediately. Our resolute certainty shows that we are leadership material. When we declare authoritatively that we pursue excellence, our "decisiveness and conviction will betray no signs of doubt."[55] We are demonstrating an admirable bias for action and commitment to being evidence-based. Defaulting to a slogan is much easier and safer than defining what is meant by excellence or evidence-based as then we might have to demonstrate exactly how we are living up to these value slogans.

Summing Up

This chapter has been about the culture or *habitus* of our organisations. *Habitus* represents our agreements and understandings about the way we do things around here. It affects the groups we belong to and our identities, habits, values, and beliefs. It is what determines the ways in which we and others perceive and understand what is going on in our groups and what is prioritised, valued, and expected. As Weick and Sutcliffe said, *habitus* is a way of seeing and not seeing. Just how strongly held our understandings are about the world we inhabit was noted by the pragmatist philosopher John Dewey who wrote that "It is easier to wean a miser from his hoard, than a man from his deep opinions."[56]

The ideologies we adopt, what is and is not acceptable to do and say, who is an insider and who an outsider and our very observation and understanding of reality are all part of the *habitus*. The stories we tell each other, the symbols and language we use, and the values we aspire to, likewise both form and reinforce the *habitus*.

While there will be common themes, the *habitus* is variable across organisations as the *habitus* will differ in large and small ways from one person or group to another based on their own personal biases, histories, and experiences.

Habitus develops historically, and in the words of Norbert Elias, is "sedimented" into the habits of individuals. This accords with our perspective of complexity which suggests that patterns of how we relate to one another emerge from the very many interactions that are going on all the time. While Elias described *habitus* as sedimented, he also saw it as dynamic and continually evolving, as the themes of our relating to each other are always both affecting our actions and, in turn, being affecting by what we do.

The concepts reviewed in this chapter have significant organising effects that help us to collaborate with one another because they allow us to share an understanding of what is important and expected of us. They can support our work to make sense of what is going on by allowing us to have a common language, understanding, and values. *Habitus* can, however, also be a source of, or exacerbate, intergroup conflict when our understanding of the way we do things around here varies. It can even exclude others or cause us to have different views as to what is a good or desired result. These differences in understanding can significantly compromise our ability to make meaning together and to collectively inquire into productive doubt.

In a perfect world, a manager will take care that there is sufficient openness to exploring the impact of *habitus* and the stories, symbols, language, and values in the workplace. S/he will want to understand its impact on the ability of co-workers to understand each other and to work together productively as well as on what is fundamental to their identities. Such an approach will honour G.H. Mead's advice who suggested that we need to work to find "the possibility of acting so as to take into account as far as possible all the values involved."[57]

This advice is more important than ever before. We are already tackling a daunting array of challenges in our complex and uncertain world. A failure to take our *habitus* into account can lead to an increase in misunderstandings and conflict in our working relationships and serve to magnify the complexity and uncertainties that we face.

Implications for Your Practice

1. Consider the importance of *habitus* as context for your work. What are the agreed-upon rules of the road? What is taken for granted? What are the themes affecting how colleagues relate to one another? What is valued or prioritised? What are the expectations that you have of each other?
2. Where you see unhelpful practices and processes, ask why these behaviours are being repeated? Why do individuals think that they are a good/appropriate way of behaving? Keep in mind that while you as manager may have significant influence on the *habitus*, you cannot control or unilaterally change it. If you are hoping for changes in practices and processes, ask why and how the patterning that reinforces current behaviour has developed.
3. Consider how differences in *habitus* may affect the way different groups react to the same communication or intervention. How can you make it safe or even a required behaviour to address and reconcile these different perceptions? Calling attention to a pattern or an aspect of the *habitus*, and allowing others to do so as well, can open up new ways of understanding what is going on.
4. How is your management style affecting colleagues? What practices are you rewarding and reinforcing and thus making successful? What stories do you tell or are being created about you?
5. How can you make it safe for others to give you direct and candid feedback despite your positional power?
6. How is the language in your area performative in the sense of shaping reality?

7. How might you be welcoming some but excluding others through your use of language? How might different groups understand the same comment or intervention differently?
8. While it is often exceedingly difficult to examine our most prized value slogans, it can be extremely important and informative to do so. How can you make it possible for colleagues to discuss how they understand a value slogan as well as how it applies to their situation?
9. While our *habitus* and our stories, symbols, languages, and values can have powerful effects on our bonding together as groups, they can also be a source of excluding others and lead to an us versus them dynamic, even within an organisation or department. What us versus them tensions might be present? What are you doing to foster these differences or to facilitate productive dialogue?

Notes

1 The concept of culture is explored under the guise of different names, which while they are likely distinguishable from each other technically, are all very similar. In this book, we will mostly use the term *habitus,* although we will also refer to culture. My preference for *habitus* over culture is that the former term expressly considers the inseparable nature of the individual and the group, the always evolving nature of the patterning of how we relate to one another and how these patterns relate to the habits and expected or usual behaviours of individuals, whereas the latter term, culture, has come to be used in ways so vague and general as to be less useful.
2 Kenwyn Smith and David Berg, *Paradoxes of Life: Understanding Conflict, Paralysis, and Movement in Group Dynamics,* p. 55.
3 Ralph Stacey and Chris Mowles, *Strategic Management and Organisational Dynamics: The Challenge of Complexity to Ways of Thinking about Organisations* (7th ed.), p. 35.
4 Elliott Jaques, *The Changing Culture of a Factory,* p. 251.
5 Norbert Elias, *The Germans: Power Struggles and the Development of Habitus in the Nineteenth and Twentieth Centuries.*
6 Ibid., p. 278.
7 Pierre Bourdieu, *Language and Symbolic Power,* p. 13.
8 Norbert Elias, *The Germans: Power Struggles and the Development of Habitus in the Nineteenth and Twentieth Centuries,* p. 101.
9 Ibid., p. 19.
10 Ibid., p. 115.
11 Ibid., p. 101.
12 Karl Weick and Kathleen Sutcliffe, *Managing the Unexpected: Assuring High Performance in an Age of Complexity.*
13 Ibid., p. 46.
14 Ibid., pp. 119–120.
15 Ibid., p. 19.
16 Ibid., pp. ix, 123.
17 Wade Davis, *The Wayfinders: Why Ancient Wisdom Matters in the Modern World,* pp. 193–194.

18 Ibid., pp. 158, 174.
19 Ibid., pp. 171–174.
20 See Chris Mowles, *Rethinking Management: Radical Insights from the Complexity Sciences*, p. 170.
21 While we can argue that the *habitus* is different for everyone in a group in small or big ways, and that it affects our working together, for practical purposes we are focusing on the dynamics of groups.
22 Kenneth Burke, *Language as Symbolic Action*, pp. 3–6 and 47–48.
23 See Chris Mowles, *Complexity: A Key Idea for Business and Society*, p. 85.
24 See Ralph Stacey, *Complexity and Group Processes: A Radically Social Understanding of Individuals*, p. 68.
25 Norbert Elias, *The Germans*, p. 146.
26 Pierre Bourdieu, *Language and Symbolic Power*, pp. 2–4.
27 Mark Carney, *Value(s): Building a Better World for All*, p. 49.
28 John Shotter, *Conversational Realities*, p. 152.
29 Kenneth Burke, *Language as Symbolic Action*, pp. 45–46.
30 Pierre Bourdieu, *Language and Symbolic Power*, p. 9.
31 Ibid., p. 239.
32 Ibid., p. 137.
33 Chris Mowles, *Complexity: A Key Idea for Business and Society*, pp. 110–111.
34 Mitchell Wardrup, *Complexity: The Emerging Science at the Edge of Order and Chaos*, pp. 15–19. Brian Arthur ended up being one of the early researchers involved in the Santa Fe Institute for the Study of Complexity and known for his work in complexity economics.
35 Barbara Townley, *Reasons Neglect*, p. 128. This does not necessarily mean that these stories are objectively true. Barbara Townley referred to them as "rationalised myths" while Yuval Noah Harari, who wrote the best-selling book *Sapiens*, referred to them as "imagined orders." There does, however, need to be a balance between truth and fiction. Narratives are not effective if they are too fictional, and if reality is distorted too much, credibility is lost. See *Homo Deus*, pp. 198–199.
36 See Chapter 2 of Yuval Noah Harari's *Homo Deus*.
37 James C. Scott, *Weapons of the Weak: Everyday Forms of Peasant Resistance*, p. 282.
38 Norbert Elias and John Scotson, *The Established and the Outsiders: A Sociological Enquiry Into Community Problems*.
39 For a more detailed discussion of gossip see ibid. in their chapter on the subject starting at p. 89.
40 Ibid., p. 7.
41 American Pragmatist G.H. Mead described values that are ascribed to an organization or group, as if *it* was an individual rather than a social object or construct and had certain motives or values as *cult values*. The word "cult" is used in the sense of a group bound together by veneration of the same thing, person, or ideal. Norms and values are often mentioned in the same breath. They are, however, different in that norms are constraints that are obligatory and restrict our actions while values are attractive and compelling in a voluntary or committed sense. Because they attract us, values are not experienced as restrictive. From the perspective of complexity thinking, both norms and values are themes that emerge from our interactions and, in turn, affect the patterning of those interactions. For an excellent discussion of *cult values* see Ralph Stacey and Chris Mowles' book, *Strategic Management and Organizational Dynamics*, pp. 391–393.

42 George Herbert Mead, *Scientific Method and the Moral Sciences*, p. 237.
43 See Ralph Stacey and Chris Mowles' book, *Strategic Management and Organizational Dynamics*, p. 395.
44 Chris Mowles, *Complexity: A Key Idea for Business and Society*, p. 134.
45 Thomas Homer-Dixon, *Commanding Hope*, p. 285.
46 It is not clear who first used that expression, but we suspect that it was Doug Griffin, one of the early scholars who collaborated with Ralph Stacey on the development of *complex responsive processes of relating*.
47 Norbert Elias, *The Germans*, p. 150.
48 While we often try to define our core values to ensure we have a common understanding of what we are striving for, that very definition is subject to interpretation, and thus we may find that members of a group or an organization will have different understandings of what is meant by a particular value.
49 Kenwyn K. Smith and David N. Berg, *Paradoxes of Life, Understanding Conflict, Paralysis, and Movement in Group Dynamics*, p. 196.
50 Ibid., pp. 194–196.
51 Norbert Elias, *The Germans*, p. 329.
52 Doug Griffin, *The Emergence of Leadership: Linking Self-Organization and Ethics*, p. 183.
53 James Boyd White, *Living Speech: Resisting the Empire of Force*, p. 45.
54 Mats Alvesson and André Spicer, *The Stupidity Paradox*, p. x; also see Mats Alvesson and André Spicer, *A Stupidity-Based Theory of Organizations*.
55 Ibid., p. 11.
56 John Dewey, *Experience and Nature*, pp. 405–406.
57 George Herbert Mead, *The Philosophy of the Act*, p. 465.

Bibliography

Alvesson, M., & Spicer, A. (2012). A Stupidity-Based Theory of Organizations. *Journal of Management Studies, 49*, 1194–1220. https://doi-org.ezproxy.herts. ac.uk/10.1111/j.1467-6486.2012.01072.x.

Alvesson, M., & Spicer, A. (2017). *The Stupidity Paradox: The Power and Pitfalls of Functional Stupidity at Work*. London: IPS-Profile Books.

Bourdieu, P. (1982/2003). *Language & Symbolic Power*. Cambridge, MA: Harvard University Press.

Burke, K. (1966). *Language as Symbolic Action—Essays on Life, Literature and Method*. Berkeley, CA: University of California Press.

Carney, Mark. (2021). *Value(s): Building a Better World for All*. Toronto: Penguin House Random Canada Limited.

Davis, W. (2009). *The Wayfinders: Why Ancient Wisdom Matters in the Modern World*. Toronto: House of Anansi Press, Inc.

Elias, N. (1989/1996). *The Germans*. New York, NY: Columbia University Press.

Elias, N., & Scotson, J.L. (1965/1994). *The Established and the Outsiders: A Sociological Enquiry into Community Problems* (2nd ed.). London, UK: SAGE Publishing.

Griffin, D. (2006). *The Emergence of Leadership: Linking Self-Organization and Ethics*. New York, NY: Routledge.

Harari, Y.N. (2015). *Homo Deus: A Brief History of Tomorrow*. Toronto: McClelland and Stewart.

Homer-Dixon, T. (2020). *Commanding Hope: The Power We Have to Renew a World in Peril*. Toronto: Penguin Random House Canada Limited.

Jaques, E. (1951). *The Changing Culture of a Factory*. Tavistock Institute of Human Relations. London: Tavistock Publications. ISBN 978-0415264426. OCLC 300631.

Mead, G.H. (1923). Scientific Method and the Moral Sciences. *International Journal of Ethics, 33*, 229–247. www-jstor-org.ezproxy.herts.ac.uk/stable/2377331.

Mead, G.H. (1938). *The Philosophy of the Act*. Chicago, IL: University of Chicago Press.

Mowles, C. (2015). *Rethinking Management: Radical Insights from the Complexity Sciences*. Surrey, UK: Gower Publishing Limited.

Mowles, C. (2022). *Complexity: A Key Idea for Business and Society*. London, UK: Routledge.

Scott, J.C. (1985). *Weapons of the Weak: Everyday Forms of Peasant Resistance*. New Haven, CT: Yale University Press.

Shotter, J. (1994). *Conversational Realities: Constructing Life through Language*. London: SAGE Publications Ltd.

Smith, K.K., & Berg, D.N. (1997). *Paradoxes of Life: Understanding Conflict, Paralysis, and Movement in Group Dynamics*. San Francisco, CA: Jossey-Bass.

Stacey, R.D. (2003/2010). *Complexity and Group Processes: A Radically Social Understanding of Individuals*. New York: Routledge.

Stacey, R.D., & Mowles, C. (2016). *Strategic Management and Organisational Dynamics: The Challenge of Complexity to Ways of Thinking about Organisations* (7th ed.). London, UK: Pearson Education.

Townley, B. (2008). *Reason's Neglect: Rationality and Organizing*. New York, NY: Oxford University Press.

Wardrup, M.M. (1992). *Complexity: The Emerging Science at the Edge of Order and Chaos*. New York, NY: Simon & Schuster Inc.

Weick, K.E., & Sutcliffe, K.M. (2001). *Managing the Unexpected: Assuring High Performance in an Age of Complexity*. San Francisco, CA: Jossey-Bass.

White, J.B. (2006). *Living Speech: Resisting the Empire of Force*. Princeton: Princeton University Press.

Part 3

Into the Weeds With Metrics and Meetings

Chapter 7

Why Metrics Are Not Always Your Friend

Introduction

Robert McNamara[1] was a leader in industry as the first non-Ford family member to be chief executive officer of the Ford Motor Company. He was a long serving secretary of defence under Presidents Kennedy and Johnson and ended his successful career as the head of the World Bank. A graduate of the University of California at Berkeley (Economics) and Harvard (MBA), he is considered by many to be responsible for the adoption of systems analysis in public policy, a discipline which later became known as policy analysis. During his time at Ford, McNamara and his team became known as the Whiz Kids, an epithet which stuck to him throughout his career. He was a key player in the popularisation of scientific management and process optimisation, using both principles to great effect during the Second World War. His photo ended up on the cover of *Time* magazine in 1963, and the cover article referred to him as "perhaps the most efficient, effective Defense Secretary the U.S. has ever had" and the most powerful man in President Kennedy's Cabinet.[2] McNamara was "the model for the rational economic man; a person who put his faith in extensive analysis and a supposedly unbiased focus on making decisions based on a strictly rational analysis of data."[3]

His first major failure happened during the Vietnam war, which many derisively called McNamara's War. His insistence on running what some referred to as a "spreadsheet war" was seen by some as callous and others as strategically short-sighted. His focus on data and logical decision-making and the types of decisions made because of it are, in fact, believed to be one of the main causes of the loss of this war by the United States. Not only were there major questions about the validity of the available data, but there were many key factors that the data, flawed or not, could not measure or assess. For example, McNamara focused on enemy body counts in the Vietnam war as the key measure of success, notwithstanding that the guerilla type warfare in this conflict made this type of measure unhelpful. The

DOI: 10.4324/9781003319528-11

determination of the Vietnamese people was an important element that his spreadsheets could not and did not capture. When McNamara was warned to consider the feelings of the rural Vietnamese people, however, he apparently wrote it down in pencil and then erased it saying that as he could not measure it, it must not be important. This and other examples gave rise to what is called McNamara's, or the quantitative fallacy, which critiques making decisions based only on metrics and quantitative observations and ignoring all others, usually on the basis that they cannot be proved:

> The first step is to measure whatever can be easily measured. This is OK as far as it goes. The second step is to disregard that which can't be easily measured or to give it an arbitrary quantitative value. This is artificial and misleading. The third step is to presume that what can't be measured easily really isn't important. This is blindness. The fourth step is to say that what can't be easily measured really doesn't exist. This is suicide.[4]

Later, Donald Rumsfeld, US Secretary of Defense under George W. Bush similarly became preoccupied with waging wars (particularly the War on Terror) based on better data, clear objectives, and achievable goals, taking the emphasis on quantification to what American author Jon Krakauer referred to as "new heights of fatuity."[5]

One of the deputy ministers I worked with when I was a public servant was asked what kept her up at night. Her response was that she most feared what she didn't know. In a complex world in which we can neither predict nor control what is going to happen, this is a valid concern. In seeking some degree of certainty and ability to defend one's actions in an increasingly complex environment, many organisations have enthusiastically embraced the value slogan that we are evidence-based and thus that we can prove that we have good reasons for our actions. Even where the terms "evidence-based" are not explicitly adopted, whether in the public or private sector or even civil society, anyone suggesting an initiative or investment is generally asked what the business case is or what data they rely upon to justify their proposition.

However, as Robert McNamara ultimately acknowledged, in an uncertain environment, we also need to worry that not only do we not necessarily know what we think we know but that what we do want to know may not be available to us and certainly not in a way that can be incorporated into spreadsheets. We need to be a sophisticated consumer of the many facts and figures—and metrics—that are routinely used in all our organisations. Sometimes, rather than relying on a particular data point, it might be safer to accept that there is a known gap in our knowledge. Particularly when the alternative is an illusion of certainty which turns out to be fallacious and/or misleading and ultimately dangerous. As Mark Twain allegedly said, "It ain't what you don't know that gets you into trouble. It's what you know for sure that just ain't so."[6]

McNamara's fallacy is a good starting point for us to continue the examination of the concept of *value slogans* from Chapter 6. These are the values used publicly in our organisations as branding and motivational statements. When strongly held, these slogans can become absolutist in the sense that they can be neither questioned nor modified, even when new information surfaces. This inability to explore their meaning can lead to such declarations being "unreflected ideologies,"[7] empty language used to brand or motivate but not to engender understanding.

What Does Evidence-Based Mean?

In the highly complex world in which managers operate, we need to be able to demonstrate that we make our decisions prudently and based upon good reasons, and if possible, backed up by evidence. This shows that we are accountable and are properly stewarding the resources of the organisation. It also provides a measure of defensibility when the withering cynical eyes of hindsight take us to task for having made the wrong call. After all, if we took the evidence into account, what more could we have done?

Evidence means something that tends to prove or disprove something, provides grounds for our belief in something, and/or can be considered proof of an assertion. Evidence can be based upon our experience and what we have found to be valid in the past and/or a process of inquiry or research. It can be either quantitative or qualitative, depending upon the question being asked, the resources of the inquirer and the data or information that exists or is available. Some things are measurable and can be quantified. Others, such as experience, cannot.

Quantitative research involves the collection and analysis of data which is numbers-based, countable, and measurable. It is considered objective, rational, and precise and can be analysed and compared using statistical tools. This form of evidence can tell us how many, how much, or how often in calculations.[8]

Qualitative research refers to the collection and analysis of non-numerical data, including text, video, or audio to understand meanings, opinions, concepts, or experiences where the question does not relate to quantity. Three common qualitative methods are in-depth interviews, focus groups, and participant observation. This information can help us to understand why, how, or what happened as well as what may have prompted certain behaviours. It is aimed at gaining a deeper understanding of an experience, specific event, or organisation, rather than a surface description of a large sample of a population. As this form of study involves interpretation by the researcher, it is necessarily subjective and coloured by their perspectives, requiring that scholars be trained to both be aware of and to disclose their biases.

Qualitative and quantitative evidence each have their advantages and disadvantages. In a complex world both can be helpful, although not necessarily sufficient,[9] in allowing us to identify our next steps. One of the legacies of scientific management is that we often default to quantitative evidence and to the spreadsheets that McNamara was so known for. The next section explores this preference.

The Siren Song of Metrics

When we are surprised and trying to resolve an issue, the two questions that need to be answered are "What is going on?" and "What can we do about it?" This work, however, is often difficult, conflictual, and destabilising. We cannot predict or control, and yet we are expected to do just that every day. We are asked for the best or right answer and required to show the evidence that we rely upon. In such an uncertain, high stakes, high stress setting, it is not surprising that we so often default to the use of quantitative research as support for our diagnosis and recommendations. As pragmatist John Dewey suggested, we have a predilection for mathematical objects and

> Gross experience is loaded with the tangled and complex; hence philosophy hurries away from it to search out something so simple that the mind can rest trustfully in it, knowing that it has no surprises in store, that it will not spring anything to make trouble, that it will stay put, having no potentialities in reserve.[10]

Numbers and metrics help us to manage our anxiety and those around us because they appear so obviously rational and objective and thus cannot be argued with. They deliver the certainty we desperately seek and provide us with the means of demonstrating that we have made the right decision, that we are in control, on top of our responsibilities and have solid reasons for our decisions. With metrics and this objective approach, we will be able to demonstrate that we have not presupposed or biased the results or placed our personal interests ahead of those of the public and/or organisation.

Metrics are also valued because we feel they may clarify cause and effect relationships or identify helpful correlations that can help us to understand what is going on. They can provide a common language and increase our capacity to achieve mutual understanding and explore differences leading to increased engagement and innovation. They can also be a tool to make it *safe* for those with less power to bring up puzzling developments for collective exploration and problem-solving. After all, once we have the numbers that have been agreed upon as the relevant and correct ones, it should be easier to surface concerns based upon their analysis.

Science historian Theodore Porter wrote that quantification is particularly appealing where there is an absence of trust in organisations. Often in large bureaucracies, there are limited opportunities for the interactions necessary to develop trusting relationships among co-workers. There may also be requirements and/or corporate directives that constrain managers' ability to act in a manner that meets the expectations of their colleagues and co-workers. As trust is both reciprocal and highly fragile, these constraints on the ability to develop patterns of trust relating can make relying upon numbers which can't be argued with a much more attractive option than depending on our sense of trust in each other.[11]

Why Metrics May Not Be So Scientific

In November 2019, the Global Health Security (GHS) Index was released, which represented the first detailed assessment and benchmarking of 195 countries to prevent, detect, and respond to infectious diseases. They examined several factors, including the total cases and deaths, recovery rates and the total number of tests performed. The United States led the rankings with an overall score of 83.5. The others in the top 5 were the United Kingdom, Netherlands, Australia, and Canada with scores of 77.9, 75.6, 75.5 and 75.3, respectively. In 2021, a second rating was conducted in which the United States continued to rank number 1 with a score of 73.9. Australia was now 2nd at 71.1, and Canada 4th at 69.8. The United Kingdom (67.12) had fallen to 7th while the Netherlands was now ranked 11th at 64.7.

Readers will have varying assessments of how well each of these countries performed during the pandemic. However, a study of the discrepancy between the GHS index ratings and the actual performance of countries during Covid showed an overestimation of the preparedness of some countries scoring highly and an underestimation of the preparedness of others who had had relatively lower scores.[12] Another study found that "the health-related outcomes from the first wave of the pandemic were primarily *negatively correlated* with their expected preparedness."[13] In other words, the preparedness index did not show us how prepared nations were for the global pandemic—and in fact, at times quite the reverse.

Part of the reason for this might be that the methodologies used to generate the data used in the ratings may have differed from one country to another. However, perhaps the most likely is that in a highly uncertain and complex world, life is neither simple nor predictable and thus not amenable to an approach which reduces everything to numbers. Quantitative data, while important, is often not sufficient.[14] We often face what are called wicked problems. These are the kind of dilemmas that have no evident good options; important information is missing, incomplete, or subject to debate. Where social dynamics and concerns are key factors, our inability to measure, know, or describe them can impede our capacity to make an informed decision. The data may not even exist or be available to us. If a situation is the first of its kind, there may be no prior examples to draw upon.

Most importantly, in a nonlinear world, the tiniest deviation or change can alter expected outcomes. Even the advanced science of modelling is based upon the extrapolation of what we already know. Thus the "infinite number of variables, political, social and economic,"[15] makes it impossible to isolate any single process and argue that if one action is taken, then another is a certain result, even if we theoretically have all the data that we need. My somewhat tongue in cheek question to colleagues who fall in love with their numbers and projections is to ask why if they are able to determine what will happen with their metrics, they are still working and not down in the Caribbean on their yachts.

Metrics can also serve to reduce or alter the information available to us. This is because of a fundamental principle called reductionism. To understand something, we reduce what is being studied to smaller components. This is much like taking a motor apart to find out how it works. While reductionism is common in the natural sciences, we are all naturally reductionist in our need to simplify the world around us. We select what we pay attention to; we rely upon models and heuristics and extract signals that fit the patterns that we are used to and what we already believe, and we tell stories. We group like items as we have an easier time remembering them that way. There is just so much going on that we have no choice.

In our quest for certainty and the right answer, however, we can take reductionism too far[16] and in the process lose valuable information. Averages are one example of how information is lost in our need to simplify information. Take for example, the average per capita income of a group. To take a simple situation, there are two people in the group. One making $100 and the other $0. On average the two are each making $50, but of course that is not the case at all. My favourite example is that one hand is on fire and the other frozen in a block of ice. On average, the temperature is quite lovely, but anyone trying to understand the condition of the hand or concerned about the two options of fire and ice, will know that the average temperature is useless information. Thus, while numbers are viewed as scientific and the last word on an issue because they are accurate and certain, they cannot necessarily tell us what we need to know. Instead, when used by the unsophisticated analyst, they are pseudo-scientific tools that promise more than they can deliver.

Challenges with numbers go further than those described so far. In the next section, we will explore how numbers may not be as objective and rational as they are advertised; in other words, how these allegedly certain and indisputable metrics are socially determined.

How Numbers Are Socially Determined

We think of numbers as clear and accurate—or in the words of my boss, Robert, in Chapter 5, indisputable. If the number is 88, then it is not 89 or 87. The benefit of metrics is that they can be precise and because of that they can be compared, ranked, etc. However, this is not completely accurate as metrics are, for the most part, socially formed.

By socially formed or determined we mean that numbers are derived or created based upon the use of social considerations and understandings. A simple example is if you are asked how many mugs are on a table. You will be fairly confident in looking at the array, counting them and proclaiming that there are five (for example). However, you have drawn upon your knowledge of what a mug is or is not, which is an understanding that is socially formed. Thus, you will not have counted the two glasses or three teacups. You may have puzzled over what looks like a mug which doesn't have a handle and yet is made of porcelain and had to decide whether it fell into the category of a mug or a glass. In other words, you had to access your social understanding of what constitutes a mug or a glass to answer the question.

This may seem like an unimportant detail, but it is not. When we use a metric, we need to define what we are counting. We draw upon our understanding which has developed based upon our experience to count and categorise different objects. We also must decide what we will measure and how that will be done. Metrics do not emerge magically from the air. John Dewey suggested that we should not refer to data as "given," but as "taken," as they are "*selected* from . . . original subject-matter"[17] and chosen to provide evidence to define, locate, and hopefully resolve a problem. Thus we select data using our social understanding.

Distinguishing between mugs, glasses, and teacups is fairly easy, provided we share the same culture and understanding of what each of these looks like. However, it is not always possible to put items into categories, or there may be no direct way of measuring something. Instead, we find other ways to get the information we need. For example, something may be a helpful proxy for what we are trying to measure. Thus, we assume that if we measure A, we will know what B is. We may also develop a model, formula, or index that will generate the numerical results that we need to track progress or assess results, based upon certain assumptions or estimations.

In the public domain, examples are the gross domestic product (GDP), inflation figures, or unemployment rates, each of which are constructed in more or less complex ways based upon assumptions. Measures of productivity are an example in the private sector. In developing these indices, we need to determine what gets counted and what is not relevant as well as how the various numbers relate to each other. Economic language tends to dominate this discussion, and social costs and impacts are only rarely part of the conversation because they are hard to measure and quantify.

Constructing indices may also require us to identify the causal relationships that are involved. We don't include X because it is judged different from Y. A causes B but not C. All of this requires assumptions and judgements and depends upon the perspective of who is making the determination and what is taken for granted by them. Data are *selected* and/or *constructed* based upon the needs, interests, perceptions, resources, and capabilities of the inquirer. In other words, there is a social process that is a requisite part of developing these types of metrics. The information is socially formed.

The assumptions and considerations that go into the calculation of indices easily create an oversimplified and incomplete view of what is going on. While some may be explicit, many will not be, and more problematically, may be invisible to us. If we cannot inquire into, or even know what social judgements were made in developing these calculations, we will be unable to know what the analysis is really saying or assess its usefulness.

For example, gross domestic product (GDP) is a standard measure of the value added in an economy through the production of goods and services during a certain period. It originated with the 17th century economist, physician, scientist, and philosopher Sir William Petty who proposed the idea of political arithmetic which would enable rulers to base their policy decisions on metrics. The GDP that we would recognise today was developed further in the 1930s by American economist, statistician, and Nobel laureate Simon Kuznets, and after the Bretton Woods conference in 1944, it became the main tool for measuring the economy and social progress of a country. The trouble is that this tool, according to Simon Kuznets himself, was never designed to measure the welfare of a population and social progress as it takes no account of harm to the environment, human health, the educational status of a population, income distribution, and economic disparity or "the reverse side of income, that is, the intensity and unpleasantness of effort going into the earning of income."[18] And yet, the GDP which makes all these issues invisible is routinely trotted out to measure our progress and thus impliedly the welfare of the nation, as well as to determine, for example, how much national debt is appropriate without providing us any information on the planetary and social costs of our economic system.

Alignment With Social Narratives

Not only are numbers socially determined, but they may also be reinforced or confirmed by social narratives. In one of the government departments in which I worked, its political boss, the minister, had asked how many individuals were being paid a certain social benefit when they were not entitled to receive it. The economic analysts in the department set about calculating the number. They were not familiar with either the details of the programme or the population involved, and so included many individuals that were, in fact, fully entitled to receive the benefit. The final number was significantly overstated: at least 15 to 20 times greater than it should have been. Unfortunately, the results of their analysis were given to the minister before they had been fact checked by those who could have caught the errors, and he began using the numbers publicly.

Once this data had gone public, it was exceedingly problematic to admit that the analysis had been poorly done. The stakes were extremely high for all of us. Misleading a minister is one of the most grievous errors a public servant can make, made worse if the minister has committed him or herself publicly based on that advice. The shame and professional consequences would have affected the credibility of not only the team that developed the numbers, but also the entire department and, perhaps more seriously, the minister and the government. Such a hit to our credibility had the potential of casting doubt on the department's work in the minds of decision-makers and our political masters, particularly when highly regarded executives had been the source of these rather egregious errors. After all, if they erred on this file, where else?

Here is where it gets really interesting. When the numbers were originally developed by my colleagues in headquarters, the resulting storyline was easily accepted because it *reinforced a prevailing social narrative* that there was extensive abuse of this particular social programme in the region. No one questioned whether the data and analysis had been properly done because it was already assumed that the number would be this high. Our attempts to point out the errors in the analysis only resulted in us being labelled as troublemakers and malcontents, and our warnings were brushed aside because we were assumed to be naïve or worse about what was really going on in our region. The problematic inflation of the numbers only became recognized internally when one of our new political bosses came from the region and knew only too well the reality on the ground.

A couple of years later, the auditor general conducted an audit of the programme in question. Two of the auditors were chatting with one of my senior executives in advance of the fieldwork and remarked that it was clear that there was a significant problem in our region. A huge oversampling focusing on the industry (in a general audit) and a compilation of anecdotal evidence later, they released a damning report the conclusions of which were based partly on the legacy of those misreported numbers. One of the department heads spent an uncomfortable couple of hours being grilled by appropriately incensed members of a parliamentary committee. They had no good answer to the many questions as the audit results were partly based upon their own department's numbers. In any event, the results were in accordance with what everyone knows to be true and thus difficult to disprove even if the department head was prepared to own up to their department's errors. Even more recently, this stereotyped view of our region negatively coloured the public response to many of the support programmes during the Covid pandemic.

We have already established that how we interpret our experience is determined by our history, experiences, and socially formed patterns of thinking. John Dewey considered the impact of beliefs on what we both believe and expect to be true and suggested that "The things of primary experience are so arresting and engrossing that we tend to accept them just as they are—the flat earth, the march of the sun from east to west, and its sinking under the earth." He proposed that our beliefs in morals, religion, and politics similarly reflected our social conditions concluding that "the ways in which we believe and expect have a tremendous affect upon what we believe and expect."[19]

Thus, in our selection of what we believe or don't believe, our social narratives serve to confirm that X fact or detail makes sense according to what we already know. What we take for granted and expect is not surprising to us and is easily accepted. This often makes such stories self-sustaining in that these stories produce their own confirmation by creating the conditions that reinforce our beliefs.[20] We saw that in the earlier example, as the belief in the widespread abuse of this programme meant that the analysis was readily accepted with no verification required. Indeed, any attempt to challenge the numbers was actively resisted because everybody *knew* there was a problem with abuse of the programme, and thus any allegation to the contrary was wrongheaded and unfounded. Outside the region, analysts and decision-makers saw what they expected. Even a so-called audit of the programme confirmed the numbers as the auditors *knew* that there was a problem with abuse of the programme before they even started work. They expected it, and they found it, thereby strengthening the social narrative even further. Effectively, the social narrative became *its own confirmation*.

How Power and Status Can Determine Knowledge

Who has power and who does not can also affect what we know. In fact, a key part of having power and status is the ability to determine what is accepted as the truth.[21] In a riff off the old trope that "what interests the boss fascinates the hell out of me," the script for the less powerful is determined by the views of those with power and status. In other words, the question of how truth can be told (and evidence generated) is actually "by what techniques, according to what circumstances etc. is it possible for something to *count* as the truth."[22]

This is often evident in the reaction to any challenge to the orthodoxy. The automatic reaction is to demand evidence for non-status quo proposals regardless of whether the accepted doxa of the organisation has itself been subjected to such study. As an example, the traditional performance management system used in many large private and public sector organisations is based upon older behavioural and motivation research that has since been revised. We now know that the current system of ranking, performance pay and the inherent competitive behaviour that that instils, as well as the inordinately high pay ratios for senior executives all effectively de-motivate and disengage employees.[23] However, that research is not asked for (or even welcome). Instead, evidence is weaponised against any challenges to the accepted orthodoxy and *habitus* of the organisation.

In the aforementioned story, those who had been responsible for generating the erroneous analysis were higher status and had more power than those in the region. In the *habitus* of the department, regions needed the good will of headquarters' colleagues as they were often dependent on the latter for the allocation of financial resources or recognition and success. Policy branches are located at head office and are generally located in the same building as the organisation's senior leaders (bureaucrats and politicians). They generally have more face time with senior management, political leaders, and other key staff, and thus were more trusted and credible than we were.

As a result of this status differential, the departmental leadership generally accepted headquarters colleagues' judgements uncritically, giving them the benefit of the doubt and leaving us less likely to be listened to when there was a difference of opinion. Not only were their views accepted without question, but we were actively prevented from asking questions. Our colleagues had a monopoly over the department's policy process, including access to the data, and thus were able to create and support and defend the data and analysis. We were always brought in at the last minute and not consulted. In effect, it was good work because they said it was.

It is more than a little ironic that quantitative information is trusted because it is considered objective and precise in comparison with other forms of knowledge, while it is itself socially formed. Science historian Theodore Porter suggested that the acceptability of what are presented as impersonal numbers depends on the credibility, whether institutionally or personally derived, of those that produce them.[24] In many ways, this builds on John Dewey's comment that data are *taken* and not *given*, and thus that numbers gain in persuasiveness based on their source and/or where they are published (i.e., if the source or publication is *trusted*). We need to know that an authority has blessed the numbers as otherwise, we cannot safely rely upon the data. The metrics are socially formed and enabled because of our trust in the experts who produce them.

This is problematic; knowledge considered to be objective is meant to be "knowledge that does not depend too much on the particular individuals who author it."[25] And yet, this is precisely what underpins the credibility conferred on many of the metrics we routinely use in our work.

The Downside of Metrics

In addition to the limitations which affect the preciseness or creation of metrics, there are also many implications for our work as managers. We may have the perfect metrics, but for a number of reasons, we may not benefit as much from them as we think we do and thus may not know what we think we know. There are several reasons for this, which this section will explore.

Metrics Convey Information But Not Understanding

Often, as with the meeting on productivity in Chapter 5, we need to know more than the numbers can tell us. We don't need to know what as much as why something is happening. In that narrative (*Productivity Woes*) we were facing large claim backlogs and inventory levels. The numbers and spreadsheets that the policy experts had prepared were an attempt to understand the productivity of employees. Leaving to one side the methodological problems with how the data was generated, what the analysis did not and could not show us was *why* this was happening. Was the issue the way that the employees worked? Was it the processes that they were told to use or the way that we as managers had organised the work? Was the problem due to the working environment? Even if the numbers had been more defensibly developed, they could not and would not tell us why we had such backlogs! We had information but not understanding.

Metrics May Prematurely Close Down Exploration of Productive Doubt

Numbers can also take on a "mantle of incontrovertibility,"[26] as they effectively end our inquiry into productive doubt because by virtue of their indisputable nature, there *is* no doubt. We have determined the evidence that we are going to rely upon in our problem-solving. The problem is clear; we just have to do something about it. We manage our anxiety by prematurely closing the discussion down. We thereby demonstrate our bias for action, show our excellence at decision-making and confirm that we are made of the right management stuff! These sorts of factual assertions which brook no dissent and prevent discussion were referred to by scholar and Professor of Public Administration, Camilla Stivers, as coercive and an exercise of positional power.[27] Regardless, our enthusiastic rush to certainty and conclusions based on numbers can lead to the loss of a rich conversation and reduce the chance to explore other perspectives which might bring new insights to bear on the problem at hand.

Metrics May Affect What We Focus On

A common justification for our reliance upon measuring and counting in the workplace is the saying "what gets measured gets done," allegedly attributed to management theorist Peter Drucker. While he never, in fact, said this in the way that it has been interpreted,[28] this line of thinking argues that a manager needs to identify the desired results, plan to achieve them and establish yardsticks and measurements with which to measure the outcomes so that they can properly report upon the success of their actions (or not). Often, this simplistic and unreflective reliance upon metrics leads to what is (in government) often referred to as "feeding the beast." This refers to the ticking the box behaviour that adds little to no value but is required to remain in good standing career wise.

What Peter Drucker actually said was that what gets measured gets managed. In other words, we tend to manage based on the information that we have, whether or not the behaviours that are measurable are those that we would most like to encourage. Metrics often focus our efforts upon identified targets and performance indicators and in the process, predetermine what we are trying to accomplish, what we care about and what we are allowed to consider. This excludes all other valuations of organisational or social issues that might affect our work. This is not to suggest that plans and measurements are not important, just to caution that they are just part of the inquiry and should not be used to limit the exploration of what is going on.

Earlier, we discussed the dangers of reductionism when taken to an extreme. One of the downsides is that our reductionist tendencies may end up affecting what we prioritise and consider in our decision-making. One example is the major focus in the public sector on the levels of the national debt and deficit in determining appropriate levels of governmental spending. While clearly these are important considerations, understanding the condition and progress of a country is far more complex than just looking at two numbers. For example, it is clear that a country with zero debt and deficit is not in good shape if it has insufficient or crumbling infrastructure.

More importantly, however, if we consider this issue using the analogy of a company, the debt and deficit are merely two numbers in the financial statements of a country. No banker or executive (effective ones that is) would countenance running an organisation on just these two numbers. Managers would want to concern themselves with revenues, margins, depreciation, investments in new technologies, marketing, and customer relations as well as health of the workforce to name just a few. And yet, routinely, the discussion around fiscal sustainability for countries focuses all our attention on the size of the debt and/or deficit with nary a thought to the quality, quantity, accessible nature, or sustainability of the infrastructure of the country, the state of the environment, and the health of its citizens.

In fact, proponents of modern monetary theory suggest that the determination of what are excessive levels of national debt and deficit depends on factors such as whether the country is a currency issuer or user or how the income in the country is distributed. For example, in the period immediately following the Second World War, the United States debt was 120% of the gross domestic product (GDP), which today would scare silly most traditional prognosticators who warn of excessive resulting inflation levels. Indeed, according to the usual warnings of the dangers of overspending, the result should have been a disaster. Instead, this was "the same period during which the middle class was built, real median family income soared, and the next generation enjoyed a higher standard of living."[29]

Metrics Can Lead to the Denigration of Phronesis

In Chapter 3, the concept of *phronesis*, or practical judgement, was introduced. Where there are high stakes and we are under pressure to prove what we are saying, or to provide evidence to back up our assertions, practical knowledge can become discounted and often, disregarded. *Phronesis* or practical judgement becomes effectively invisible as it does not necessarily match with the metrics and cannot be measured, counted, or proved. Instead, numbers are considered necessary because we need objective evidence to help us to manage our anxiety sufficiently. While *phronesis* does not provide this type of assurance as it is neither certain nor truly objective, metrics also have limitations. And in a complex world, often the only guide that we have is the ability to identify the patterns of how we relate to one another—our practical knowledge. Despite this, objectivity and metrics, particularly in bureaucracies, have become de rigueur, and it has almost become undemocratic to rely on seasoned judgement as the basis for our actions.[30] Perhaps more to the point, one could argue that the move to almost universal quantification in social science and applied disciplines and the "push for rigor" came about in part as a result of the distrust of "unarticulated expert knowledge" and "suspicion of arbitrariness and discretion" that shape political culture.[31] In other words, to distrust of practical knowledge.

As metrics make employee experience invisible, the anxiety of those whose practical knowledge is discounted is increased. This adversely affects the interpersonal relationships of these team members which, in turn, can lead to increased self-silencing and the loss of their contribution to problem-solving. This may *further reduce* our trust in such judgement. As trust is reciprocal, when employees feel that they are not trusted, they are likely to lose their trust in their managers. Note the negative self-reinforcing cycle—relying on metrics to the detriment of practical knowledge—further reduces the likelihood that participants whose expertise is disregarded either will feel trusted or will trust others. In the absence of trust among colleagues, particularly in the high anxiety/high stakes world of politics, the siren song of numbers becomes almost irresistible with its promises of safety and certainty leading to our reduced capacity to explore productive doubt. Metrics increasingly become the only common ground we have.

This is directly contrary to the advice Peter Drucker gave to managers. While he believed that measuring results and performance was important for the effective functioning of an organisation, he viewed the fundamental and first priority for managers to be

> the relationship with people, the development of mutual confidence, the identification of people, the creation of a community. This is something only you can do . . . It cannot be measured or easily defined. But it is not only a key function. It is one only you can perform.[32]

Summing Up

We began this chapter with a review of the McNamara fallacy and a story about Robert McNamara's career and dedication to rational analysis of data as the fundamental way to manage effectively. Interestingly, in his retirement years, McNamara became involved in some of the extensive analysis of the Vietnam War. He was part of the 2003 documentary by Errol Morris titled *The Fog of War: Eleven Lessons from the Life of Robert S. McNamara*, which was in part based on his 1995 memoirs that he wrote together with Brian VanDeMark, *In Retrospect: The Tragedy and Lessons of Vietnam*. Some of the lessons that he identified are particularly apt for our work.

In brief, he recognised that rationality is not the immutable principle that he had always advocated. He admitted that humans are not machines and do not act like them. There are many social factors that numbers cannot convey. And thus, using reason does not necessarily mean being rational. Any type of plan is fallible because we cannot predict the future. Lastly, McNamara concluded that "in international affairs, as in other aspects of life, there may be problems for which there are no immediate solutions . . . . at times we may have to live with an imperfect, untidy world."[33]

Indeed, our work together can often be difficult, conflictual, and destabilising. We cannot predict or control and yet we are expected to do just that. We live in an imperfect and untidy world. Often, problems surface because of a breakdown in our expectations or a nasty surprise. Anxiety is inevitable in our complex world, and our fears of uncertainty often lead to the adoption of coping mechanisms and a rush to arrive at conclusions and certainty so that we can declare victory and move on.

In our rush to certainty, one of our coping mechanisms is often a default to metrics in our attempt to simplify our analysis of what is going on and to help us to manage our anxiety. Numbers are felt to be precise, accurate, and indisputable and thus make our decisions defensible and right. There are, however, limitations on what can be measured numerically, and numbers are often socially determined and thus not nearly as reliable or objective as their acolytes would represent. An overly simplistic use of metrics can also cause details and assumptions involved in their construction to become invisible or omitted and thus impair our ability to engage in an exploration of productive doubt. In the process, our reliance on metrics can also devalue or discount *phronesis* or practical wisdom in the workplace, which is sometimes our best line of defence in a complex world.

Often the biggest challenge in any problem-solving exercise is the determination of what the issue is that we need to address. One of the key lessons in crisis management is that the earlier and more effectively a problem is responded to often makes the difference between a metaphorical bump in the road or a full-blown crisis. Our rush to put the issue to bed, to declare victory and move on, can mean that we do not allow sufficient exploration of the problem. This may prevent us from understanding what is going on as well as what our options might be. In the result, we may well be sowing the seeds of future sleepless nights by prematurely declaring certainty and moving on!

The challenge for managers of an unreflective adherence to evidence-based as a value slogan is that it disregards the complex and nonlinear nature of the human experience and causes us to either narrow our ability to inquire into productive doubt or to close it down prematurely. And because our value slogans are so precious to us, we are very often unable to question their meaning or definition. In the process, as we lose the richness of our exploration of productive doubt, so too do we lose the information and the meaning that we would make of it.

The irony is inescapable. Our unsophisticated default to quantitative information and disregard of qualitative research prompted by our drive to avoid the perils and anxiety of uncertainty can often make a difficult situation worse and even increase the uncertainty that we collectively face. In a world that extols the values of innovation and creativity, we risk fettering our ability to engage in the exploration of productive doubt, thus reducing or preventing our ability to innovate and be creative.

This is not to say that metrics are not an important tool. Just that they, like all tools, have their limitations and are thus imperfect. Rather than a dogmatic approach, we need to take a more nuanced and informed view of their use that will allow us to reap their benefits leavened by an understanding of what they cannot and do not tell us.

Leading economist Mariana Mazzucato of the University College, London is well known for her studies on the economics of innovation and public value. She tells the story of a Jesuit order in the 15th century in which their money chest could only be accessed by using two keys: the key of the rector who was the guardian of the spiritual vision of the order and that of the bursar responsible for fiscal prudence.[34] Likewise, we need to hedge our intellectual bets more intelligently by considering both qualitative and quantitative forms of evidence in our work to make sense of what is going on.

Implications for Your Practice

1. How can you encourage inquiry into the meaning and collective understanding of the value slogan "evidence-based"?
2. In considering what evidence might be available or useful in your decision-making, how can you encourage your team to assess the contribution of both quantitative and qualitative evidence and the benefits and limitations of each.
3. When dealing with metrics and data, be careful about excessive reductionism, the use of proxies, and indices and averages. How are they constructed, and what assumptions are made in their development that may not be visible?
4. How can you be an intelligent consumer of evidence? Always be prepared to ask: Who says that? Why do they say that? What do they rely upon? What are they not saying perhaps because they do not see it? Might they have a vested interest in their interpretation of what is going on?
5. Consider how you can become aware of the social narratives that predominate in your workplace. How can you inquire into how they may be affecting the meaning that is made of a development?
6. Be cautious of how power and status can determine knowledge. There is often wisdom in those with positional power holding back with their opinions in order not to taint the discussion with premature certainty.
7. Always keep in mind the difference between "information about" and "understanding."
8. What is it in your workplace that everybody knows and thus no further exploration of perspectives is required or permitted or proof demanded? Be careful not to close down critical exploration of the accepted wisdom while at the same time holding the non-status quo to the highest evidentiary standards.

9. Be aware of how metrics can focus our attention on certain variables and obscure others.
10. How can you and your colleagues be prepared for the situation in which there is no good evidence that you can rely upon?
11. Remember that *phronesis* or practical judgement can be a key resource, allowing you to profit from the experience of those who may have seen this movie before.

Notes

1 Rick Nason, *It's Not Complicated: The Art and Science of Complexity in Business*, pp. 58–59 and 120–126.
2 *Defence: The Dilemma and the Design*, February 15, 1963, Time Magazine, https://content.time.com/time/subscriber/article/0,33009,829884,00.html.
3 Rick Nason, *It's Not Complicated: The Art and Science of Complexity in Business*, p. 121.
4 McNamara Fallacy, *Wikipedia*, https://en.wikipedia.org/wiki/McNamara_fallacy, accessed October 21, 2022.
5 Jon Krakauer, *Where Men Win Glory*, p. 246.
6 While Mark Twain is credited with this quote, it is not clear that he said it as there is no citation which can be found to prove it.
7 Doug Griffin, *The Emergence of Leadership: Linking Self-Organization and Ethics*, p. 183.
8 The accepted dogma is that scientific work in the natural sciences is based upon incontrovertible facts. However, as Chris Mowles observes on page 111 of his book, *Complexity: A Key Idea for Business and Society*, research shows that "scientific discovery is governed by chance, rivalry, personality and intense engagement with other scientists' ideas."
9 While evidence is clearly important in our work to make sense of what is going on, in complexity we may often find that we are not able to find evidence for what we want to know. As noted in this chapter, not everything can be measured, and nonlinear relationships mean that we cannot assume that if we know X then Y will occur. The American pragmatist John Dewey in *The Quest for Certainty: The Later Works, 1925–1953* preferred the term "warranted assertability" and "knowing" to that of "knowledge" or "belief" because he ascribed to the concept of *fallibilism*, (a term coined by American philosopher Charles Sanders Pierce) meaning that (1) propositions can be accepted even though they cannot be conclusively proven or justified, and (2) that neither knowledge nor belief is certain in an uncertain and always changing world.
10 John Dewey, *Experience and Nature*, at pp. 26–27.
11 Theodore Porter, *Trust in Numbers: The Pursuit of Objectivity in Science and Public Life*, pp. 97–101, 152, 194, 199–200.
12 Enoch J. Abbey, et al., *The Global Health Security Index Is Not Predictive of Coronavirus Pandemic Responses among Organization for Economic Cooperation and Development Countries*, National Library of Medicine.
13 Hlekiwe Kachali et al, *Are Preparedness Indices Reflective of Pandemic Preparedness? A COVID-19 Reality Check*.
14 Many have written on the problems of quantitative analysis and its application to the social sciences and our work to make sense of what is going on. Of note,

are two books by historians Jerry Muller (*The Tyranny of Metrics*) and Theodore Porter (*Trust in Numbers: The Pursuit of Objectivity in Science and Public Life*), which extensively survey the challenges and consequences of an unsophisticated reliance on metrics.

15 Chris Mowles, *Complexity: A Key Idea for Business and Society*, p. 33.
16 Ted Cadsby, *Closing the Mind Gap: Making Smarter Decisions in a Hypercomplex World*, pp. 73–87.
17 John Dewey, *Experience and Nature*, pp. 142–143.
18 See the 1937 report to the US Congress titled "Uses and Abuses of National Income Measurements," by Simon Kuznets, https://en.wikipedia.org/wiki/Gross_domestic_product#Limitations_and_criticisms.
19 John Dewey, *Experience and Nature*, p. 14.
20 Bourdieu, *Language & Symbolic Power*, p. 226.
21 For further on this point see Pierre Bourdieu, *Outline of a Theory of Practice*, pp. 164–165; Michel Foucault, *Power*, pp. 111–113; Bent Flyvbjerg, *Making Social Science Matter: Why Social Inquiry Fails and How It Can Succeed Again*, p. 226.
22 See Michel Foucault in *A Foucault Primer: Discourse, Power and the Subject*, Alec McHoul and Wendy Grace, p. 25.
23 Particularly (but not only) in the public sector, performance management has become an extremely costly, time consuming, and often difficult process that involves extensive documentation to specify what will be done in an annual period and then regular (formally often once or twice a year) documented conversations assessing performance over that time period. Several companies in the private sector have moved away from this type of system, finding it is too expensive for the value it conveys in return. These processes are individualistic between a manager and their employee. Collective goals may be incorporated but effectively, recognition and rewards are individually directed despite the reality that we perform as a collective. We are interdependent and can only achieve results through processes which depend upon the contributions of others. Even those that have demonstrated superhuman achievements, often are only able to do so because others stepped in and picked up some of their normal load. Or they are recognised for a high-profile achievement when it is the nature of their assigned role within the organization to take on these roles. At any one time, due to the non-linear nature of our environment, any one employee—regardless of level or location—might be the most important person in the department, performing the most vital function in terms of the health and security of the department and Canadians.

More problematically, this approach is focused on optimizing individual performance and can often trace its roots to Pavlovian and Skinnerian research in behavioural science, which assumes that the correct combination of rewards and punishments will lead to the desired behaviours. More recent research has suggested that the use of monetary and status rewards to motivate employees is simplistic and does not take into account the much more complex and nuanced factors that motivate individuals in their work. Author Michael Mechanic in his book *Jackpot: How the Super-Rich Really Live—and How Their Wealth Harms Us All*, (p. 33), for example, distinguishes between intrinsic and extrinsic rewards. Intrinsic has to do with self-acceptance, community mindedness, and meaningful relationships whilst extrinsic pursuit includes our desire to be attractive, popular, and have material things and financial successes. Extrinsic rewards which are the norm in our organizations do not correspond with how we are motivated. Instead, as American law professor and philosopher James Boyd White suggests in his book *Living Speech: Resisting the Empire of Force* (2006, pp. 41, 109, 208) based upon his research, our dignity individually and as a culture depends on being able to claim meaning for our lives and experience through inspiring work, connections with others, and a coherent way of imagining the world and one's role within it.

Even worse for performance management purposes, research suggests that extrinsically oriented people are more likely to behave selfishly (see Michael Mechanic, *Jackpot*, pp. 90–100) and that even the prospect of a reward can cause increased mistakes and decreased performance (see Henning Beck, *Scatterbrain: How the Mind's Mistakes Make Humans Creative, Innovative, and Successful*, p. 84 and Chapter 12). Testing and ranking processes which can reward individuals with increased access to resources and power and provide privileged access to the hierarchy (see Richard Wilkenson and Kate Pickett, *The Inner Level*, p. 32) have been found to increase both insecurities re self-worth and stress even for those thought to be the winners or high performers (see Harari, *Homo Deus*, pp. 195–200; Richard Wilkenson and Kate Pickett's, *The Inner Level*, pp. 25–26 and *The Spirit Level*, pp. 38–39). Perhaps even more problematically, the common form of pay for performance has been shown to encourage misbehaviour and gaming (see Raghuram Rajan's, *The Third Pillar*, at p. 197).

24 Theodore Porter, *Trust in Numbers: The Pursuit of Objectivity in Science and Public Life*, p. 214.
25 Ibid., p. 229.
26 Chris Mowles, *Complexity: A Key Idea for Business and Society*, p. 171.
27 Camilla Stivers, *Governance in Dark Times: Practical Philosophy for Public Service*, pp. 45–46.
28 See Paul Zak, *Measurement Myopia*, www.drucker.institute/thedx/measurement-myopia/, accessed October 22, 2022.
29 This is not to suggest that there are not negative consequences from high spending levels. The question that needs to be asked is whether the nation has the capacity to absorb this spending without increasing inflation. Issues such as corresponding taxation, where the spending is directed, distribution of income and so on become important. However, too often it is easier for policy makers to wave the flag of overspending and the myths about debt and deficit levels as political cover to deny investments that they do not want to make. For a more complete understanding the reader is directed to the book by Stephanie Kelton, former chief economist on the US Senate budget Committee and named by Politico as one of the fifty most influential people in the policy debate arena in America: *The Deficit Myth: Modern Monetary Theory and the Birth of the People's Economy, 2021*. Pages 8 to 12 summarise the myths that she examines and contains the information re debt/GDP after WWII at the top of page 10.
30 See Theodore Porter, *Trust in Numbers*, pp. 7–8.
31 Ibid., pp. 97–101, 152, 194–200.
32 See Paul Zak, *Measurement Myopia*, www.drucker.institute/thedx/measurement-myopia/, accessed October 22, 2022.
33 Rick Nason, *It's Not Complicated: The Art and Science of Complexity in Business*, pp. 124–126.
34 Mariana Mazzucato, www.wired.co.uk/article/mariana-mazzucato, accessed April 22, 2023.

Bibliography

Abbey, E.J., et al. (2020). *The Global Health Security Index Is Not Predictive of Coronavirus Pandemic Responses among Organization for Economic Cooperation and Development countries, National Library of Medicine. PLoS One, 15*(10), e0239398. www.ncbi.nlm.nih.gov/pmc/articles/PMC7540886/, accessed April 10, 2023.

Beck, H. (2019). *How the Mind's Mistakes Make Humans Creative, Innovative, and Successful.* Vancouver, Canada: Greystone Books.

Bourdieu, P. (1977/2015). *Outline of a Theory of Practice.* Cambridge, UK: Cambridge University Press.

Bourdieu, P. (1982/2003). *Language & Symbolic Power.* Cambridge, MA: Harvard University Press.

Cadsby, T. (2014). *Closing the Mind Gap: Making Smarter Decisions in a Hypercomplex World.* Toronto: BPS Books.

Defence: The Dilemma and the Design. (February 15, 1963). *Time Magazine.* https://content.time.com/time/subscriber/article/0,33009,829884,00.html, accessed February 23, 2023.

Dewey, J. (1929/1984). *The Quest for Certainty: The Later Works, 1925–1953.* Carbondale, IL: Southern Illinois University Press.

Dewey, J. (1929/2015). *Experience and Nature.* New York, NY: Dover Publications, Inc.

Flyvbjerg, B. (2001). *Making Social Science Matter: Why Social Inquiry Fails and How It Can Succeed Again.* Cambridge, UK: Cambridge University Press.

Foucault, M. (1994/2000). *Power.* New York, NY: The New Press.

Griffin, D. (2006). *The Emergence of Leadership: Linking Self-Organization and Ethics.* New York, NY: Routledge.

Harari, Y.N. (2015). *Homo Deus: A Brief History of Tomorrow.* Toronto: McClelland and Stewart.

Kachali, H., et al. (July 2022). Are Preparedness Indices Reflective of Pandemic Preparedness? A COVID-19 Reality Check. *International Journal of Disaster Risk Reduction, 77*, 103074. Published online May 27, 2022. doi:10.1016/j.ijdrr.2022.103074. www.ncbi.nlm.nih.gov/pmc/articles/PMC9135491/, accessed April 10, 2023.

Kelton, S. (2021). *The Deficit Myth: Modern Monetary Theory and the Birth of the People's Economy.* New York: Hachette Book Group.

Krakauer, J. (2009). *Where Men Win Glory* (p. 246). New York: Bloomsbury.

Kuznets, S. (1937). *Report to the US Congress Titled 'Uses and Abuses of National Income Measurements'.* https://en.wikipedia.org/wiki/Gross_domestic_product#Limitations_and_criticisms, accessed April 4, 2023.

Mazzucato, M. (2019). This economist has a plan to fix capitalism. Its time we all listened. *Wired.* https://www.wired.co.uk/article/mariana-mazzucato. accessed April 22, 2023.

McHoul, A., & Grace, W. (2007). *A Foucault Primer: Discourse, Power and the Subject.* New York, NY: New York University Press.

McNamara Fallacy. https://en.wikipedia.org/wiki/McNamara_fallacy, accessed October 21, 2022.

Mechanic, M. (2021). *Jackpot: How the Super-Rich Really Live—and How Their Wealth Harms Us All*. New York: Simon & Schuster.

Mowles, C. (2022). *Complexity: A Key Idea for Business and Society*. London, UK: Routledge.

Muller, J.Z. (2018). *The Tyranny of Metrics*. Princeton, NJ: Princeton University Press.

Nason, R. (2017). *It's Not Complicated: The Art and Science of Complexity in Business*. Toronto: Rotman—UTP Publishing.

Porter, T.M. (1995). *Trust in Numbers: The Pursuit of Objectivity in Science and Public Life*. Princeton, NJ: Princeton University Press.

Rajan, R. (2020). *The Third Pillar: How Markets and the State Leave the Community Behind*. London, UK: Penguin Books.

Stivers, C. (2008). *Governance in Dark Times: Practical Philosophy for Public Service*. Washington, DC: Georgetown University Press.

White, J. B. (2006). *Living Speech: Resisting the Empire of Force*. Princeton: Princeton University Press.

Wilkinson, R., & Pickett, K. (2009/2010). *The Spirit Level: Why Equality Is Better for Everyone*. London: Penguin Books.

Wilkinson, R., & Pickett, K. (2018). *The Inner Level: How More Equal Societies Reduce Stress, Restore Sanity and Improve Everyone's Well-Being*. New York: Penguin Books.

Zak, P. (2014). *Measurement Myopia*. www.drucker.institute/thedx/measurement-myopia/, accessed October 22, 2022.

Chapter 8

Meetings, Meetings, Bloody Meetings

Introduction

Film maker and social science researcher Deirdre Boden has written that

> It is through the telephone calls, meetings, planning sessions, sales talks, and corridor conversations that people inform, amuse, update, gossip, review, reassess, reason, instruct, revise, argue, debate, contest, and actually *constitute* the moments, myths and, through time, the very *structuring* of the organization.[1]

This suggestion, that we effectively talk our organisations into being makes sense if we take complexity seriously. It is our conversations that constitute how we work together, govern ourselves, and create knowledge and meaning in the midst of uncertainty and challenge. Through these interactions, the patterns of how we relate to each other emerge and organise our experience of being together, thus affecting both our formal and informal decision-making processes. Do we trust one another? Can we rely on our colleagues? Do we feel safe enough to have important discussions? Can we do business together? And shifts in these conversations constitute organisational change by altering these patterns.

The word "meetings" is another word for these conversations. Put simply, a meeting is a gathering of two or more individuals. They can be formal or informal, arranged or occur by chance and allow us to exchange information, solve problems, and make plans for future actions. While in this chapter we will concern ourselves with formal meeting processes, this is not to dismiss the importance of informal and unplanned conversations as their role cannot be underestimated. Regardless of whether our interactions address business or personal issues or are within or outside of working hours, all of them have an impact upon our relationships with each other. Serendipitous human interactions matter a great deal. For example, it is impossible to separate out the impact of a chance

DOI: 10.4324/9781003319528-12

encounter at the local park, as its effect upon the relationships of those involved will carry on throughout subsequent interactions. Or the chat may be the source of an idea that ends up changing our whole understanding and approach to an important issue. Or you may have a conversation that I refer to as a *buffering conversation* that takes place outside or on the sidelines of a formal meeting. Such a discussion can assist by explaining or softening an intervention in a meeting and thus help to repair or maintain relationships and expectations with colleagues as we continually negotiate our understanding of whether we can *trust* each other.[2] All this means that no conversation happens in a vacuum and every interaction leaves a trace.

At their best, meetings can be exercises in group *reflexivity* in which we collectively probe deeply into what is going on, how our and others' actions are affecting what is happening and how we should respond. They can be exciting and rewarding and create a stronger sense of belonging to the team. However, as the title of this chapter indicates, and a quick search on google will confirm, meetings generally have a bad rap. They are portrayed as time wasting, boring, and unproductive. This is perhaps not surprising as meetings are often ritualised in the sense that we go through the motions, say what is expected of us, and follow the implicit and unwritten scripts of our *habitus*.

In addition to sometimes being boring and non-productive, our fears of uncertainty can lead to us experiencing anxiety as part of our meetings. Learning and problem-solving, both of which are generally part of our meetings, can evoke powerful emotional responses which can range from the challenge and excitement of the exploration of new ideas to the fear of failure and humiliation. The latter can cause groups and individuals to seek ways to manage their anxiety, many of which are unproductive and serve only to prematurely close down the exploration of productive doubt.

Conflict is likewise a necessary part of our meetings as innovation and creativity do not happen if everyone is of the same opinion. When we face a new challenge or circumstances, we cannot expect that our old agreed-upon routines and solutions will work for us. This is challenging for us as conflict can be disruptive, and as we are interdependent, we need to stay in relation to get our work done. In reality, the traditional corporate advice often promotes the maintenance of harmonious relationships in the workplace,[3] and we are rewarded for being a team player and *playing nice* with others.

Conflict can range from the competitive and polarising (us versus them in which there is often a winner or loser) to the explorative and collaborative. Engaging in explorative conflict is key to our work to make meaning. It enables us to explore our assumptions and perceptions and to negotiate different interpretations about what is going on so that we can live with the simultaneous excitement, anxiety, and conflict of conversations that test the boundaries of what we know.[4]

Our anxieties and fear of conflict can cause us to adopt counterproductive coping mechanisms. In our rush to decision, we shut down exploration and discussion and accept the first satisfactory explanation, allowing us to achieve closure and move on to something more interesting and less threatening. We hand over the reins to consultants and experts who promise a track record of success and thus the sought-after certainty. And yet so often, in the words of Camilla Stivers, scholar and professor of public administration, the "analysis of human affairs by professional problem solvers takes the form of cramming reality into a preconstructed theory or worldview, which requires lopping off all the inconvenient aspects that don't fit,"[5] and we are worse off (both substantively and financially) than before.

We also eagerly seek certainty where there is none and rely on forecasts and make predictions in a world in which we cannot predict and determine outcomes. We might assert that we have found the right or best answer and become much too confident in the accuracy of our simplified interpretations based upon available data.[6] We may lapse into we/they[7] thinking. We have it right. They don't. Or take a dualistic approach in which there are only two contrasting, mutually exclusive choices, or realities which are viewed as bad/good or negative/positive, and in the process, we lose the middle ground and opportunity for nuance which is often needed in a complex environment. Or we are guilty of magical thinking, where we come to believe that if we feel strongly enough about something and wish hard enough for it, we can get the results we desire.[8]

Despite their many faults and challenges, meetings are how we discuss and resolve issues of mutual concern. They are not events that happen that interfere with the work, but particularly for knowledge workers, *they are the work*. The complexity of our existence makes it inconceivable that any one person can foresee all, understand all, or decide all, making it essential for us to pool our perspectives and capabilities. Our meetings can promote the generation of higher quality knowledge than any one individual can achieve. And even if the impossible happened and someone had the superpowers to do it all themselves, there is still the question of implementation, the fundamentally important conversion of lofty theories and ideas into action.

As American pragmatist John Dewey wrote, "All action is an invasion of the future, of the unknown. Conflict and uncertainty are ultimate traits."[9] As the many coping mechanisms that we adopt can be highly counterproductive, we need to place a priority on ways to manage the anxieties which are inevitably part of our meetings. This chapter explores that dynamic.

But first, a story about meetings in the early days of the Covid-19 pandemic in which we faced a world that, not to be too hyperbolic, felt like complexity on steroids—and with all the potential anxiety and conflict that such uncertainty can evoke.

All Hands on Deck

March 11, 2020, may have been the date of the declaration of the pandemic, but by then we were already in it up to our necks. As a department with responsibility for the delivery of benefits and services to Canadians, we knew that our world had changed drastically, and we needed to be at the top of our game. Not only that, but literally overnight as the lockdowns hit, we had to redesign many of our benefits programmes as well as develop and implement emergency response programming. Like the rest of the world, we also had to immediately move to a virtual way of working which up until then had been neither available nor accepted in the *habitus* of the department and for which we had neither the policies nor the technological capabilities or equipment.

Most of us moved home and worked from there using virtual meetings and processes. For the first few months, the usual schedule of departmental and committee meetings was put to one side while we wrestled with the many policy and programme challenges involved in supporting Canadians during this difficult time. We were deep into our emergency response processes. The departmental crisis response had been triggered which meant that the Departmental Crisis Management Team (DCMT) was constituted. Headed up by the chief operating officer of our delivery arm (COO), this group included the deputy ministers (department heads), all assistant deputy ministers (ADMs), and a few director generals (DGs) that were directly implicated in the response process. Each region had an equivalent organisation that reported up through the chief security officer of the department to the DCMT.

Every morning at 8:30 am Eastern Time, there was a 30-minute meeting called the "Standup meeting." It was generally held in the large boardroom used for senior management meetings, but now there were only a handful present. Generally, that included the COO and the lead deputy, a couple of ADMs, and a few others from the emergency preparedness team. The rest of us joined from home. The large virtual component was very new to us as in the past it was generally only regional executives that participated online from their offices. This format was repeated in the afternoon for the DCMT; however, this meeting was an hour and a half long, starting at 1:00 pm Eastern Time. The Standup was used as a quick review of where we were, what we knew, and the priorities of the day. The longer DCMT meeting was a further update, and the additional time used to discuss the thornier issues that needed an in-depth discussion. During the crazy rush of the first few months, we generally had these meetings on the weekends as well.

As significant a change as the virtual component was, however, it didn't stack up to the other differences in the way that the meetings were organised and conducted. Normally, our meetings had quite precise and detailed agendas. Reports were circulated in advance. Detailed PowerPoint decks were presented, and if time allowed, there would be discussion and questions. Now, there were no detailed agendas, at least to start with. Instead, the order of speakers was determined based upon what was a priority and/or what needed to be discussed early in the meeting as context for other issues.

Meetings generally began with an update from our chief security officer on the worldwide picture. Staff responsible for policy development would then speak to what was on their plate for the day: what had to be done, who was doing it, and what if any help was needed. Then it was the turn of the various ADMs such as benefits delivery and in-person services, IT, procurement, the chief financial officer, and human resources. Again, each updated the table on what was going on in their area of responsibility, what the concerns or issues were, and what was planned for the day. In the longer DCMT meeting, we had time to dedicate to more difficult issues. But this all evolved as a natural flow. Once the pattern was established, agendas were circulated but for the most part, they were the same every day. The DCMT afternoon meeting would have a little more detail, but they were still a far cry from the extensive and detailed agendas we were used to.

Presentations were also very different. We were accustomed to receiving highly polished PowerPoint presentations we called "decks" that were circulated in advance. At the meeting, those responsible for the issue would present them, often taking up a good proportion of the allotted time. Each of the decks would have been carefully prepared, considered, discussed, and manicured in previous meetings. The unwritten rule was that nothing was to be a surprise by the time it got to senior management. Discussion always started with compliments on the presentation. If there were concerns, it was expected that they would be taken up with the authors in advance of the meeting. Sometimes the deck was prepared to generate discussion of an issue and included a recommended course of action for approval. Other times, it was just an update for our information. We would have a good discussion (if there was time left after the presentation), and the report would be accepted, or decision made, and we would move on.

During these meetings, in addition to no or rudimentary agendas, there were no PowerPoint slides, at least in the first few months. In the hurly-burly of the pandemic with all that was going on, there just wasn't the time. Plus, everything was changing so quickly that we were continually working on a this just in basis! Reports to the meeting were verbal and to the point about what was going on, what we knew (or didn't), what was the most pressing issue of the day, and what we might need from others. Then on to the next one. We were kept on track by the meeting chair as we had to make good use of our time given the short timelines and often conflicting priorities.

The COO, who chaired these meetings, knew we were all stressed, as were our employees and families. Breaking with the usual more formal format, she would often start off with a quote, a personal story, or a joke to lighten the mood, including truly dreadful knock-knock jokes. One day she declared that it was funny hat day. Another meeting included making time to introduce our pets to the management table. If a team member was having a particularly difficult time, she would support them to take the time they needed to address the issue. None of this took much time but always served to lower the tension in the room. Despite the lack of the usual props, such as detailed agendas and PowerPoint presentations, these meetings were very effective, and we had sufficient time to discuss our priorities.

We often faced making decisions based on information that was either non-existent, incomplete, or unconfirmed. To some degree, this is always the case, but it was even more evident in the rapidly developing pandemic. Often, we found we had to make decisions knowing that the information the next day would likely contradict what we then had available to us. The COO would go round the table after an issue had been presented and pointedly ask if anyone had additional information, perspectives, or views that needed to be included, making it clear that she was depending upon us to surface our concerns.

If someone spoke up with a different perspective, it was listened to and responded to carefully. We spent more time engaging with the issues and less on airbrushing PowerPoint slides. We allowed productive doubt to be raised and explored collaboratively in the meetings. If anyone had a concern, it was discussed collegially rather than being glossed over. We all felt trusted, included, and critical to the effort. Our opinions mattered and were actively sought.

In our laser-like focus on all issues related to the pandemic, much of the regular work of the department was put to one side. As we progressed, we put in place new ways of delivering services, and we moved most of our employees to their homes, providing them with the resources they needed to do their work in this totally new way. We worked closely with the unions, sometimes harmoniously and sometimes not, but always with the joint intent of looking after the needs of Canadians and our employees. We developed policies and programmes as part of the federal emergency response that were brought into effect virtually overnight. It was unheard of to raise an issue as significant as the nature of the benefits payments and to be in front of Cabinet (the body of advisors made up from the House of Commons in Canada that sets the federal government's policies and priorities) two days later and implementing the programme within a couple of weeks. This type of policy work would normally take months or even years to come to fruition. But we did it because we had to. And we did it at the same time as we were innovating on many other fronts. And while we knew we couldn't always get it right (and indeed most of the time it was impossible to know what that might be), and that we didn't always have the information we needed, on balance the department acquitted itself well during these difficult and uncertain times.

The Blight of Ritualism

Just how different the meetings were during Covid is shown by an experience early in my tenure with a government department. Senior management were meeting to consider the following year's budget. Documents had been received only a few days in advance and showed significant pressures on one of the divisions due to a tax proposed by the chief financial officer (CFO) that would be imposed across the board. The head of the department introduced the issue and expressly asked everyone to be frank and raise their concerns. The affected division head spoke up, presenting their case, which was both reasonable and strong. There was little response in the meeting. Everyone conceded that while the tax was challenging, they would make it work, and the budget was approved as presented.

The individual who had spoken up, however, received a significant amount of push back as a result of their intervention, despite the fact that the head of the department had expressly invited those with concerns to speak up. What was going on here was that the meeting was a regular and ritualised aspect of governance and not a place of discussion and debate. The accepted order of things was that the chief financial officer had prepared the budget, and the head of the department had approved it after proper and wise consideration. There would be free and informed discussions and the proposal would naturally be approved as presented. The decision was already made. There was nothing further to say. The intervention was a direct and public challenge to the accepted rituals and, not unimportantly, to the authority and reputation of the head of the department as a careful and thorough decision-maker.

Rituals, a series of actions performed according to a prescribed order, are an important part of our *habitus*. They help us understand what to do, what to expect, and what is expected of us. However, rituals can also be counterproductive and reduce our effectiveness. German-born sociologist Lewis Coser identified how the "blight of ritualism" can be stultifying and serve to limit or close down exploration and debate, particularly in social arrangements that are habitual and patterned.[10] Often, our rituals are designed to increase control and productivity.[11] The "empty ritual of public bodies,"[12] ensures the gathering serves its intended purpose and minimises the risk of anything untoward happening. No one is taken by surprise. The hierarchy is unchallenged, and everyone sticks to the generally agreed-upon scripts dictated by the accepted and taken for granted requirements for participation according to the *habitus* of the group.

During the emergency response meetings, our rituals and usual scripts were disrupted. While clearly there were interventions that would still have been off limits, we, like the rest of the world, were in uncharted territory and thus needed to be more open than usual to new perspectives.

The Ritual of the Agenda

An important part of the ritual of meetings is the agenda, used to inform our participation, regulate the investment of time in particular issues, and allow participants to prepare. It also is an important control mechanism to keep the meeting and those attending on track. The challenge, however, is that "meaning-making argues with agendas and likes to break through time boxes."[13] We have all experienced the frustration of being told that what we are experiencing as an important discussion needs to be curtailed so that we can get back on track with the agenda. In our pursuit of good process, we prioritise the following of ritual and perceptions of efficiency over the exploration of productive doubt.

One of the ways in which our rituals had been shaken up during Covid, was in the lack of the usual detailed and carefully negotiated agendas. Instead, our discussions were built around an order of updates and debriefs that evolved during the first few meetings in this new format. It was clear what our task was at both the Standup and the DCMT gatherings. We all needed to know what was going on, what was the state of preparedness and/or implementation, what issues were being raised, and what we needed to do about them. And during the early days, that is what determined how the meeting was organised.

While we had limited available time, the COO always ensured that we could identify a new concern or disagree with a proposed action. Often, the order of speaking got juggled or a less important update abbreviated to make way for something that had been raised in the meeting. While the option had previously always been open to add something to the agenda, at least theoretically, it was certainly not the norm. Proposing alterations to the agenda often required significant status or courage as determining the programme was generally the purview of those with positional power.

Part of the reason we were more flexible and open during this period was that we were dealing with very urgent and emergent issues that involved us all. No one could argue that they were taken by surprise by a last-minute change to the agenda and hadn't had the chance to prepare for the discussion. If they were, it was generally because we were all surprised by recent developments. Thus, there was continued and express permission to raise issues that needed to be addressed as compared with the world pre-Covid in which formal agendas made such actions more difficult.

Think of it this way. In a complex world, there is no award for the tidiest agenda and meeting! Often a certain amount of messiness is inevitable in ambiguity[14] as we struggle with new concepts or perspectives, think out loud, or go down the proverbial rabbit holes of a different approach. Knowledge working is unruly, and you cannot know up front what is a productive or wasteful tangent.[15] And even what feels like an unsuccessful tangent can spark innovation and creativity. Contrary to common expectations, if we are truly engaged in listening, challenging, and working together to find a solution, we are unlikely to speak in perfect bullet points. However, if we trust in the good intent and competence of colleagues, this messiness can support our mutual exploration and discussion of difference.

There are alternatives to the usual agenda driven meetings. For example, in the Doctor of Management programme at the University of Hertfordshire, we held community meetings each day of our quarterly residential gatherings. In this format, we would sit in a circle and at the appointed time, the leader would note that we were starting. We would then sit together until someone had something to say to the group. The leader's role was largely for timekeeping purposes, although conceivably they would intervene if required. Sometimes we started with a bang, and other times there was a protracted period of silence before there was an intervention. However, during the meeting we were able to deal with very difficult and sensitive issues such as someone being afraid that they weren't going to be able to finish the programme. Expectations were clear that this time together was valuable, and faculty would often remark upon someone's failure to consult the group on an important issue. Our discussions provided critical support to all of us as researchers, helped us to negotiate our relationships with each other, and provided us with the opportunity to have the conversations that we needed to have.

There is another element to this which Sigmund Heinz Foulkes, the German-British psychiatrist and psychoanalyst credited with the development of group analysis, stressed. He claimed that creative organisational strategies were more likely to emerge in more "fluid, spontaneous forms of conversation . . . Such spontaneity is likely to be fostered through how the leader handles a situation, encouraging others to create and shape the situation rather than simply giving instructions."[16]

While this requires a dedication of time that feels significant, for groups that need to work together closely on a regular basis, the investment can be worthwhile. There are also slightly less time-consuming options. For example, tasks that don't need group interaction or that are more mechanical can be completed outside meeting spaces. You might also consider reserving a space on the agenda for open discussion in which the group can discuss whatever participants wish to talk about. While the first few times may feature awkward silences, in my experience the team will become comfortable with this approach, and it will often become the most productive part of the gathering.

Other options include a concerted focus on evaluating decisions and plans for their maintenance of optionality so that unanticipated consequences can be actively explored, and changes can be more easily made and off-ramps taken if it is determined that major changes are required. Scenario planning can be helpful in exploring how key uncertainties and assumptions might play out differently. Premortems, a methodology in which the group is asked to assume it is X years out and the project has been a disaster, can also encourage speculation on what might go wrong, effectively providing an opening for the surfacing of productive doubt by those with less power.

Obviously, some of these options may not be available due to the ongoing pressure of what needs to be accomplished. However, a question that is always important is "How do we know what we should be talking about?" Some items are no brainers and/or beyond our control. However, we must always be alert to the need to allow new concerns to be raised, even when they relate to items that we believe are routine. In a world of nonlinear relations, small things can help or hurt us disproportionately and a wise manager will ensure that there are both formal and informal ways to bring issues and concerns to the group's consideration.

The PowerPoint Trap

Another of the usual props for meetings which was missing from our early days in the emergency response was the ubiquitous PowerPoint deck. Pre-Covid, they were elaborate, carefully crafted and negotiated, airbrushed to perfection, and burnished with numbers, charts and graphs, and other data considered necessary in our evidence-based world. Their presentation often monopolised most of the allotted time. The rituals were followed, and discussion happened as expected because it was understood that any bothersome issues would have been worked out in advance. The important thing was that the meeting occurred, there was an opportunity to raise issues and to have a discussion, and the item was approved so that we could go on to the next step. The PowerPoint presentation was an important control mechanism to ensure that all occurred as planned.

During the early Covid days, however, we didn't have time for these decks. Instead, each speaker was responsible to distil the issue and identify the issues that others needed to be aware of or that they needed advice on.

One of the side benefits of the lack of these elaborate presentations was that space was opened up for practical knowledge or *phronesis*. In the absence of charts and data and pre-negotiated understandings, those with extensive lived experience of some of the issues we were debating were better able to share their perspective which enriched our discussions substantially.

As the months went by, however, PowerPoint decks crept back into the meetings. First, it was one slide, then a few. After the first six months, when decks had once more became the expected tool to frame discussions, the general (often unspoken) consensus was that the more polished and extensive the deck, the less satisfactory the discussion. Again, this is not to propose that these presentations cannot be helpful. However, managers need to avoid the trap of having a prop which is intended to *support and inform* the discussion, *dominate and constrain* our engagement with productive doubt instead.

What Does Success Look Like?

In our organisations, it is common to hear discussions about the importance of identifying the optimal or best solution. In the early days of Covid, however, sometimes victory looked suspiciously like surviving until the next day. Sometimes our progress seemed minor, such as getting computers delivered to workers at their homes. Other times, it was clear we had made huge strides as when we were able to conceive, propose, design, get approved, implement, and deliver a totally new support programme within a matter of weeks. There was zero talk about optimality during the Standup and DCMT meetings. This was not the world we were in, and we all knew it.

We have already discussed that what is the right thing to do is dependent upon the timing and the perspective of the person making the judgement. Another way of looking at this is what American political scientist Herbert A. Simon called *bounded rationality*, which we explored in Chapter 3. This concept, for which he was awarded the Nobel prize in 1978, is in opposition to the approach of traditional, classical economists who assume that decision-makers make rational decisions based upon achieving an optimal result. *Bounded rationality* suggests that what happens is that we make the decisions we are capable of in the circumstances based upon the information accessible to us and the time available, selecting a decision that is satisfactory and not necessarily optimal.

In our dynamic and ever-evolving world, what we consider a good result may well change. This plus the concept of *bounded rationality* suggests that we are not in a position of seeking an optimal solution. Neither the issues we solve, nor our objectives and goals are immutable end points. What we believe is perpetually subject to revision and any conclusions "can always be ruptured by unexpected contingencies."[17] Thus, we should always be prepared to hold both questions, proposed solutions, and even the desired end results lightly. Our goal, instead of elusive certainty, should be to determine how we can seek out a *good enough*[18] step to take together *for now*, acknowledging that in the future "we may be facing a completely different set of problems."[19] Thus in our meetings during the Covid emergency, we always knew that the uncertainty of the times was such that we could only do the best we could do at the time. Good enough became acceptable, and we actively monitored and adjusted our plans as necessary.

This does not mean that our work to plan, set objectives, and organise initiatives is useless. The statement that plans are of little importance, but planning is everything has been attributed to both Dwight Eisenhauer and Winston Churchill. Planning will never enable us to predict or determine what will happen in the future and thus what we need to do. We have already established that in complexity it is impossible to foresee the future. Instead, the process of planning is about developing understanding. The value is in the exploration that occurs and the opportunity to share and explore different perspectives. It is about building and strengthening relationships, which will, in turn, help us in our working together.[20] Strategic planning conversations, for example, may be one of the very few opportunities for us to engage in aspirational meaningful conversations about what we are doing, why it matters, and how we need to evolve.

How We Can Make Our Meetings More Productive

Having considered what success looks like, we also need to explore what is involved in making our meetings more worthwhile. While what happens in a meeting depends on all the participants, the influence of the individual serving as the chair is substantial. Their job is to facilitate the exchange of information and negotiation of differences and to manage both their own and other's anxieties which are necessarily a part of the exploration of differences.

Managing Conflict and Anxiety

Dr. Majken Askerland coined the term *friction competence*[21] to describe the ability to manage the tensions and frictions of our work and the inevitable power dynamics of the group so that we are able to make meaning together. While friction can be difficult and challenging for our relationships, without it, there can be no movement of thought. If participants can be supported in containing rather than submitting to or avoiding their anxiety, then the anxiety of the learning challenge may be tempered, and insight and creativity result. This does not deny the inevitability of conflict, but rather allows us to pursue explorative conflict in which we can negotiate our differences and find ways to move beyond our conflicting views and needs and "living in a grey goo of agreeable compromise" to a place where we can "integrate our perspectives and needs into something new . . . where we have the chance to make something better."[22]

At the beginning of Covid, we were five parts adrenaline and five to ten parts sheer terror as we, together with the rest of the world, were truly in uncharted territory. While we typically pride ourselves on being evidence-based, the data available to us was insufficient or being revised daily as the science progressed. We arguably had the best information that was available, but what we knew one day was often contradicted the next. Even so-called hard facts as to numbers of infections, hospitalisations, and deaths as a comparison between provinces and countries were totally dependent upon the openness of the jurisdiction and their readiness to release information and on how the data was assembled, which differed from one place to another sometimes significantly.

We were senior executives in a culture that prizes not only evidence but also a bias for action. Those who are considered management material find the right answers, take well informed decisions, and act decisively. In these early days of Covid, we were all too conscious of how high the stakes were for Canadians if we did not do our job well and knew that whatever we did would be judged by the often unkind lens of hindsight. Thus, while anxiety is always part of our work to solve problems, during this period, it was probably at unprecedented levels. All of this was on top of what each of us, in big and small ways, were going through in our personal lives.

The chief operating officer (COO) who was chair of the meetings worked hard to maintain our confidence. She modelled an atmosphere of calm and continually recognised how we were all doing our best in stepping up to these significant challenges. Despite the urgency of the situation, she bent over backwards to make sure that we all knew that our interventions and comments were important—and in fact necessary—to the organisational effort.

The COO's blend of personal touches, inspirational quotes, and humour helped us to manage the pressures and tension that we all faced. This supported us despite our anxiety so that we had the space to improvise and negotiate and find a way through the maze of impossibility that was Covid. Even her dreadful knock-knock jokes helped us relax, laugh, and recharge and strengthened our groupness when we needed it most as we negotiated our way through our areas of difference.

Perhaps most importantly, supporting us in managing conflict and anxiety allowed us to explore productive doubt. During the early days of Covid-19, the COO actively sought to unearth our concerns and questions, and she expressly placed the responsibility upon all of us to speak up if we saw issues that were not being addressed. Often those interventions would open an entirely new area of analysis or concern or perhaps challenge what we had taken for granted. However, in the urgency of the moment, we all valued—and the COO required—the surfacing of different perspectives. In the urgency of those difficult times, with her support and prompting, we were able to collectively carve out the needed space to discuss and reflect and function as a cohesive team.

Building Capacity and Trusting Relationships

A common style of management in many organisations is what is known as the command-and-control approach. Nothing happens without the say so of the boss. Interventions that do not accord with his or her view of the world are not welcome. Such autocratic leadership leads to the loss or reduction of knowledge because at any one time there are so many things going on and so many moving parts that the more eyes and minds on the issue the better.[23] Such a style can also cause disengagement and disempowerment of staff and perhaps, more importantly, is not conducive to the development of trusting relationships and the capacities of the team. If staff are never encouraged to challenge and be challenged or rewarded for speaking up in opposition to the orthodoxy of the group, they never learn how to do so safely, and the message will be that their perspective is not trusted. Often meetings are the only real opportunity to encounter a manager or leader in action. As the oft used expression "actions speak louder than words" says, how meetings are conducted will convey what the manager truly values and prioritises.

Instead, an apt metaphor to describe the role of a manager or chair of a meeting is as a facilitator or conductor, and their responsibility is to bring out the best in the group.[24] Thus, the active invitation by the COO in these meetings to raise doubts and concerns not only helped us to do a better job during a difficult period but developed the capacity of the team to explore productive doubt and demonstrated her values of inclusion and humility.

Facilitating Problem Definition

We deal with many issues every day. How are we doing? What do we need to know? What is going on? What is urgent? Important? Irrelevant? What do we want to happen? What results are we seeking? How do we make them happen, and how will we know when we have been successful? And in the words of Donald Rumsfeld, what are our unknown unknowns that might trip us up, and how might we even know what they might be (or sometimes that we have even been tripped up)?

Many of our conversations relate to the need to resolve a problem when there is a breakdown in our expectations. In the social sciences, there is almost never a distinct and defined problem,[25] so the first question is to determine what is going on and what has gone wrong. Sometimes this is the most significant part of the discussion. Labelling a problem is a consequential act[26] as the answers we get are often dependent upon the questions we ask. And in a changing world, both old answers and old questions are suspect.[27] How an issue is framed also determines the information that is and is not relevant, whose perspectives will be brought to bear upon its resolution, and how we will understand success. Often defining the problem is not easy as we need first to reduce the complexity of the situation so we can grasp what is going on (if that is even possible). In other words, there can be so much happening that it becomes difficult to identify what we should be concerned about and why.

Often those with positional power are the ones who determine what we notice and agree to work on as well as the nature of the discussion.[28] However, this can be problematic as we know that our very understanding and perceptions are determined by our history. What we will see others won't and vice versa. The risk of not including aspects that will subsequently become vital considerations—sometimes because we just don't see them— is very real. Thus, managers need to ensure that there are ways for all participants to bring their diverse perspectives to bear on the negotiation of the group's identification and understanding of the problem.

Once the problem has been defined, we are still not done as in our complex world, waypoints are continually shifting and what is easy or problematic one day may be quite the opposite the next. The problems we work on are always based upon our current understanding, which is always limited to the information available to us at the time, and thus they are just the *choice points that we are aware of*. Often what we know is not as important as what we don't know. As we are problem-solving, what is going on around us is continually evolving and our parameters changing. This requires us to be open to the possibility that our understanding of the issue needs to change as well. Our decision-making is, therefore, effectively incremental, or as the psychologist and philosopher John Shotter put it, understanding is always a process on the way.[29]

Often it is easier to be lulled into thinking that the problem is obvious and that the world will unfold according to our expectations and our decisions. We work so hard on our plans that we fall in love with them. The tools become our world, and the methodology is trusted to support the right discussions and result. What is often forgotten is that plans can act the same way as expectations in that they guide us to seek confirmation that the plan is correct. This positive feedback loop between behaviour and beliefs creates a self-fulfilling prophecy, which, in turn, confirms that we have done a great job at planning.[30] Our anxieties and fears of uncertainty are assuaged. In the absence of productive doubt, we are sentenced to unproductive certainty.

During Covid times, some of the problems we needed to address were clear. Others, such as the best way to protect our staff were not so obvious as the science about Covid-19 was not sufficiently developed. We needed to be open to discussion to try and figure out the next best steps that we could take. And once a decision was made, we still had work to do as the COO encouraged us to continually monitor and evaluate the situation so that we could adapt if circumstances required us to do so.

Summing Up and So What?

If, as Deirdre Bowden says, we talk our organisations into being, then clearly, we need to spend time thinking about the nature and quality of our conversations and our interactions with each other, particularly the formalised ones that take up a significant amount of our working time.

We started off with an exploration of the emergency management meetings early in the Covid-19 days in a federal government department where the usual processes and procedures were set aside due to the crisis. Instead, we had no (or abbreviated) agendas, no PowerPoint presentations, an openness to different perspectives, a shared sense of urgency, and a relational approach to how we worked together.

As our work together is often prompted by disruptions of our expectations and sometimes nasty surprises, we need to learn to manage our individual and collective anxieties rather than succumbing to the many counterproductive ways of dealing with them. An important aspect of the management role is thus the ability to manage our own and others' anxiety. Managers need to develop *friction competence*, the ability to manage the tensions and challenges of our sensemaking, so that we can collectively engage in the exploration of productive doubt. If we can learn to contain rather than give in to or avoid our anxieties so that we are able to "live with the simultaneous excitement and anxiety of conversations that test the boundary"[31] of what we know, innovation and creativity are possible.

We need to consider how we know/learn about what is going on and how we can explore the risks and opportunities involved without prematurely closing down our inquiry into productive doubt. To do that, we must feel that it is safe enough to ask questions and collectively explore, negotiate, and even challenge our assumptions and perspectives. We need to be open to the surfacing of productive doubt and be prepared to draw upon the practical knowledge of those in the organisation. While theories can be helpful in informing our actions, we need to deal with what is in our workplace and not what should be according to some authority or consultant.

We need to be aware of the tendency for meetings to be organised and controlled by rituals which govern what can and cannot be discussed and how the exploration of these issues can unfold. Part of the job of those leading meetings is to foster an interpersonal climate that makes it safe for participants to engage in an exploration of differences in what is, by definition, a conflictual process and where there are often paradoxical tensions inherent in the wicked problems we face.[32] An important element of meetings is the building of capacity and productive relationships to enable us to work together effectively. Mutual trust and respect are important, and part of our work is actively listening to and exploring the perspectives of colleagues.[33]

We discussed why problem definition and what success looks like are not straightforward in a world that is always changing and where what constitutes a right and good decision, as well as what will be effective, may change hourly. Our goal, instead of the elusive certainty, should be to determine how we can seek out a *good enough* step to take together *for now*, acknowledging that in the future "we may be facing a completely different set of problems." We need to think about how we can know/learn about what is going on or is happening with each other and in the world, and how we can explore risks and opportunities in a world in which the reality of what might be the best decision is evolving.

This is not easy work. We are engaged in a constant balancing act in a world that is constantly evolving and thus never in balance! We need to maintain a watch on what is going on to determine whether we need to revise or rethink our plans, opinions, and strategies. At the same time, we must avoid falling into what is often called analysis paralysis, or the inability to decide, in a vain attempt to obtain the perfect information and thus ensure that we have the right answer.

If the way that we work together today may well affect the way that we will work together tomorrow, then a group that is not accustomed or allowed to offer dissenting views or surface concerns, will be unlikely to do so in a moment of crisis or even when specifically requested. They will have learned that their perspective is not trusted and thus that it is a high-risk behaviour. Engaging in difficult or challenging conversations is something that one learns to do. If staff never have the occasion to develop these skills, they will be even less likely to be able to engage successfully even when and if the opportunity presents.

Thus, traditional decision-making and governance processes and their outputs have a role but are not sufficient in a complex world. Reliance upon them alone can create a *checklist culture* in that it is assumed that if we do all the prescribed steps, we will get the right result. Or at the very least, when the proverbial s**t hits the fan and everyone is somersaulting in duck and cover mode, we will be able to say that we did it by the book. Rather, how we work together and govern ourselves is a social, relational process that is ongoing and continuously evolving and determines how we will work together in the future.

This was well expressed by Kenneth Burke in his unending conversation metaphor in his book, *The Philosophy of Literary Form*.[34]

> Imagine that you enter a parlor. You come late. When you arrive, others have long preceded you, and they are engaged in a heated discussion, a discussion too heated for them to pause and tell you exactly what it is about. In fact, the discussion had already begun long before any of them got there, so that no one present is qualified to retrace for you all the steps that had gone before. You listen for a while, until you decide that you have caught the tenor of the argument; then you put in your oar. Someone answers; you answer him; another comes to your defense; another aligns himself against you, to either the embarrassment or gratification of your opponent, depending upon the quality of your ally's assistance. However, the discussion is interminable. The hour grows late, you must depart. And you do depart, with the discussion still vigorously in progress.

Implications for Your Practice

1. Beware the rush to certainty in meetings. As the job of sensemaking can be stressful, how can you as manager find ways to manage your own anxiety at the same time as you support colleagues in sitting in the fires of uncertainty? Be wary of those asserting that they have the answer or who otherwise seek to prematurely close down the exploration of productive doubt.

2. Conflict is also an inevitable aspect of sensemaking as without difference, there can be no innovation or creativity. Look for ways as manager to support the team to stay in relation with each other while they actively explore their different perspectives.

3. How can you develop your capacity for *friction competence* so that both you and your team are better able to manage the tensions and frictions of your work to make meaning?

4. How can you and your team be vigilant about the rush to certainty and dualistic or binary, we/they and magical thinking which are common coping mechanisms caused by our fears of uncertainty.

5. Keep in mind that a command-and-control environment is not only unwise in a complex environment where there is a premium on bringing different perspectives to the table but that it is not conducive to the development of trusting relationships and capacities of the team and the exploration of productive doubt. How can you work with your team so that they develop the capability to challenge and be challenged as the team negotiates a shared understanding of what is going

on? Accept that there may be times when your practical judgement tells you that you have to cut through the fog of discussion and make a decision. When you find you need to do this, try to do so in a way that is respectful of those participating in the debate.

6. Keep in mind that labelling something a problem is a consequential act. Try and restrain the rush to jump to conclusions about what is going on. Problem definition is a key time for the team to ensure good exploration and discussion so that as many perspectives as possible can be put on the table before labels become affixed and approaches constrained. Maintain an openness to adjusting the definition of the issue as events evolve.

7. Remember that the problems we work on are always based upon our current understanding, which is always limited to the information available to us at the time and thus, are just the *choice points that we are aware of*. How can you guard against falling in love with your plans or conclusions and instead hold them lightly and be open to revisiting when and if possible.

8. Try to include an appreciation for practical knowledge in your practice and ensure it is not suppressed or supplanted by the pseudo-scientific certainty of metrics.

9. Be conscious of how the ritual of our engaging with each other can serve to limit or close down the exploration of debate or lead to *check the boxes* types of behaviour, particularly in social arrangements that are habitual and patterned and therefore ritualised.

10. Consider the use of different techniques to build and supplement agendas and be flexible in your chairing of meetings so that the resulting conversations bring as many different perspectives to the table as possible. Ask yourself how you know what should be talked about and be open to incorporating the views of others. Consider alternatives such as community of inquiry or the use of an open agenda whenever possible. Protect time for discussion and exploration by moving work items that do not need synchronous interpersonal discussion and/or are more mechanical and automatic from meeting spaces.

11. How can you be judicious about the use of PowerPoint decks in your meetings. They should help frame and inform a discussion and not dominate or constrain it. Where possible, encourage individuals to bring discussions at an early stage, accepting that there may still be bugs to be worked out.

12. As perspectives and circumstances change, so may your objectives. Your goal should be to arrive at what is good enough for you and your team to take your next step together, knowing that tomorrow may bring a whole new set of problems. Keep in mind that how we interact today may well affect how we relate with one another and thus how we *will* work together in the future.

Notes

1   Deirdre Boden, *The Business of Talk: Organizations in Action*, p. 8.
2   Sara Filbee, *Trust and Its Consequences: A Regional Senior Manager's Experiences of Meaning Making in the Canadian Public Service*, pp. 100, 140.
3   See Ralph Stacey and Chris Mowles' book, *Strategic Management and Organizational Dynamics*, pp. 195–199.
4   Ibid., p. 357.
5   Camilla Stivers, *Governance in Dark Times: Practical Philosophy for Public Service*, p. 57.
6   Ted Cadsby, *Closing the Mind Gap: Making Smarter Decisions in a Hypercomplex World*, p. 88.
7   See Kenwyn Smith and David Berg, *Paradoxes of Life: Understanding Conflict, Paralysis, and Movement in Group Dynamics*, pp. 8, 54–57, 81 and 209.
8   John Dewey, *Human Nature and Conduct*, p. 18.
9   Ibid., p. 8.
10 Lewis Coser, *Social Conflict & the Theory of Social Change*, p. 199.
11 Elizabeth Ayer, *Meetings Are the Work*, March 3, 2023, The Edition, *The Medium*.
12 James C. Scott, *Domination and the Arts of Resistance*, p. 12.
13 Elizabeth Ayer, *Meetings Are the Work*, March 3, 2023, The Edition, *The Medium*.
14 Karl Weick, *Sensemaking in Organizations*, p. 186.
15 Elizabeth Ayer, *Meetings Are the Work*, March 3, 2023, The Edition, *The Medium*.
16 Ralph Stacey and Chris Mowles, *Strategic Management and Organizational Dynamics*, p. 358.
17 Chris Mowles, *Keeping Means and Ends in View—Linking Practical Judgement, Ethics and Emergence*, p. 553.
18 See discussion in Chapter 3 re the concept of *good enough*.
19 Chris Mowles, *Managing in Uncertainty: Complexity and the Paradoxes of Everyday Organizational Life*, p. 144.
20 What planners often miss is that planning is, in fact, a never-ending quest in all its different forms. The formal parts are an opportunity to question and debate before we go back to the humdrum everyday processes of implementing, testing, adjusting, and adapting. The methodology is arguably not important as it just sets the scene for the conversations and planning.
21 Personal conversations with Majken Askeland.
22 Elizabeth Ayer, *Meetings Are the Work*, March 3, 2023, The Edition, *The Medium*.
23 Karl Weick, *Sensemaking in Organizations*, p. 186.
24 Ralph Stacey and Chris Mowles, *Strategic Management and Organizational*, p. 358.
25 Mats Alvesson and Dan Kärreman, *Qualitative Research and Theory Development: Mystery as Method*, p. 112.
26 Karl Weick, *Sensemaking in Organizations*, p. 90.
27 Ibid., p. 186.
28 Ibid., p. 91.
29 John Shotter, *Conversational Realities: Constructing Life through Language*, p. 121.

30 Karl Weick and Kathleen Sutcliffe, *Managing the Unexpected: Assuring High Performance in an Age of Complexity*, pp. 43, 90, 153; also see Phaedra Daipha, *Masters of Uncertainty: Weather Forecasters and the Quest for Ground Truth*, pp. 214–215.
31 Ralph Stacey and Chris Mowles', *Strategic Management and Organizational Dynamics*, p. 357.
32 Roderick M. Kramer and Karen S. Cook, eds., *Trust and Distrust in Organizations—Dilemmas and Approaches*, p. 239.
33 Ted Cadsby, *Closing the Mind Gap: Making Smarter Decisions in a Hypercomplex World*, pp. 335–337.
34 Kenneth Burke's 'Unending Conversation' Metaphor, from *The Philosophy of Literary Form*, pp. 110–111.

Bibliography

Alvesson, M., & Kärreman, D. (2011). *Qualitative Research and Theory Development: Mystery as Method*. London, UK: SAGE Publishing.

Ayer, E. (March 3, 2023). Meetings Are the Work. *The Medium*, The Edition.

Boden, D. (1994). *The Business of Talk: Organizations in Action*. Cambridge, UK: Polity Press.

Burke, K. (1941). *The Philosophy of Literary Form*. Berkeley: University of California Press.

Cadsby, T. (2014). *Closing the Mind Gap: Making Smarter Decisions in a Hypercomplex World*. Toronto: BPS Books.

Coser, L.A. (1957). Social Conflict & the Theory of Social Change. *The British Journal of Sociology*, 8(3), 197–207. doi:10.2307/586859.

Daipha, P. (2015). *Masters of Uncertainty: Weather Forecasters and the Quest for Ground Truth*. Chicago: University of Chicago Press.

Dewey, J. (1922/2017). *Human Nature and Conduct: An Introduction to Social Psychology*. Globalgreyebooks.com.

Filbee, S. (2020). *Trust and Its Consequences: A Regional Senior Manager's Experiences of Meaning Making in the Canadian Public Service*. https://uhra.herts.ac.uk/handle/2299/26037.

Kramer, R.M., & Cook, K.S. (Eds.). (2004). *Trust and Distrust in Organizations: Dilemmas and Approaches*. New York, NY: Russell SAGE Foundation.

Mowles, C. (2012). Keeping Means and Ends in View—Linking Practical Judgement, Ethics and Emergence. *Journal of International Development*, 24, 544–555.

Mowles, C. (2015). *Managing in Uncertainty: Complexity and the Paradoxes of Everyday Organizational Life*. London, UK: Routledge.

Scott, J.C. (1990). *Domination and the Arts of Resistance*. New Haven, CT: Yale University Press.

Shotter, J. (1994). *Conversational Realities: Constructing Life through Language*. London: SAGE Publications Ltd.

Smith, K.K., & Berg, D.N. (1997). *Paradoxes of Life: Understanding Conflict, Paralysis, and Movement in Group Dynamics*. San Francisco, CA: Jossey-Bass.

Stacey, R.D., & Mowles, C. (2016). *Strategic Management and Organisational Dynamics: The Challenge of Complexity to Ways of Thinking about Organisations* (7th ed.). London, UK: Pearson Education.

Stivers, C. (2008). *Governance in Dark Times—Practical Philosophy for Public Service*. Washington, DC: Georgetown University Press.

Weick, K.E. (1995). *Sensemaking in Organizations*. Los Angeles, CA: SAGE Publishing.

Weick, K.E., & Sutcliffe, K.M. (2001). *Managing the Unexpected: Assuring High Performance in an Age of Complexity*. San Francisco, CA: Jossey-Bass.

Part 4

Reflections and a Challenge

Chapter 9

So, What Now?

Introduction

Our complex world is incredibly demanding. As public administration scholar Camilla Stivers observed, human affairs is where the wholly improbable happens regularly.[1] Or, colloquially, the truth is stranger than fiction. The patterning of our experience and how we relate to one another are always evolving. Our lives are perpetually under construction, and endings and beginnings merge into one another in a highly complex mix. We are surprised or confused as the unexpected occurs, keeping us in perpetual problem-solving mode. Nothing stays the same and tasks are never done. Any fix is only temporary as complex problems are rarely solved in a dynamic environment.[2] The inability to predict or determine results creates anxiety and challenges our need to control and to be right.

The difficult nature of our work as managers and leaders has attracted significant attention. In Chapter 1 we reviewed two common ways of understanding the work of management. Magico-mythical thinking looks to the heroic and charismatic individual leader who will bring their magic to the organisation and transform it. Or to the right answer or methodology, tools, and techniques that will guarantee success and solve our problems. Scientific management, based in part on the work of Sir Frederick Taylor, brings an individualistic understanding to the workplace and is premised upon the ability to analyse, predict, and control behaviour.

Neither of these traditional management prescriptions is likely to fit the bill. Any version which suggests that the manager can determine or control, can change the culture and ensure success or that relies upon magical or wishful thinking is unlikely to be helpful in a complex world in which it is impossible to predict or determine. Similarly, individualistic approaches to managing neglect the inescapable reality that we are fundamentally social and that we work and produce as a group. Likewise, depending on linear and non-complex processes, as well as many of the commonly accepted tools and techniques of management is also inadequate.

DOI: 10.4324/9781003319528-14

What this book proposes is a new perspective on managing in complexity, one that recognises the important role managers and leaders play but does not place inordinate emphasis upon any one individual. One that sees management as a negotiated and relational activity and that recognises our interdependence and that an individual only achieves through processes which are dependent upon the contribution of others.[3] One that incorporates social research and theory.

The genesis of this approach was PhD econometrician, Ralph Stacey's frustration that he (we) could not predict or foresee the future. After all, he was a smart guy and had access to the training and ability to develop all sorts of fancy economic models. This became his animating question in the field of management. What emerged from a process of study, discussion, and debate with colleagues at the University of Hertfordshire was a theory of what happens in a complex environment and has produced a rich and leading-edge body of research on the challenges of managing in complexity.

The theory, known as complex responsive processes of relating, draws upon the study of complex adaptative systems (CAS) in complexity science. CAS are computer programs which model complex systems with multiple agents (strings of code). What these agents can and cannot do in their interactions with one another are determined by rules developed by the computer programmer. When the programme is run, dynamic and ever-changing patterns of how the agents relate to one another emerge from their many interactions and organise what will happen between these agents in the future. What happens cannot be predicted even by the programmer. Similarly, in our workplaces, our dealings with one another, our conversations, our meetings, our writing, and our personal lives, all influence the themes of how we relate to each other. In turn, as we work together, we also affect these patterns in big and small ways, thus affecting our future dealings with one another.

Ralph Stacey and his colleagues drew heavily upon the work of pragmatic philosophers who are preoccupied with the human experience and propose that there can be no separating the subject and object of the experience. These scholars also explored the nature of problem-solving and how what is a right or good decision depends on who is making the judgement and when they are doing so.

If we base our view of what is going on upon the findings of complexity science, then we need to understand not only how individuals react (the study of psychology) but also processes of group dynamics. Stacey and his colleagues turned to the abundant literature on group analytic theory and the field known as process, or figurational, sociology that studies sociology from the perspective of group dynamics.

Considering complexity in our work of managing has many implications. The work of managers and leaders includes trying to understand what is going on in the workplace by exploring the themes that affect the patterning of our existence and organise how we relate to one another. This is not a simple task. There are no recipes nor hard and fast or proven rules to follow. No tools or techniques will ensure we are successful. Instead, management requires a combination of judgement, reasoning, emotion, and relating to one another. We need to be reflexive and take an ongoing view both on what is happening to us as individuals but also what is going on for us as a group.

This final chapter is an attempt to pull together thoughts on some of the key concepts related to this perspective on complexity. We close with some parting thoughts on the concept of leadership and thoughts on why complexity management is so important today.

Key Concepts for Complexity Managers

Management is a practice, much like the practice of law or medicine. Thus, while we can find helpful information in books, we must go beyond theories to application. This is not a spectator sport, but a practice to work on throughout our lives as we hone our skills and capabilities. As we do so, there are no rule books or guaranteed how-to directions to follow, but some of the implications of the research on complexity management explored in this book can guide us in our work. This chapter summarises ten of these concepts.

1. Keep the Paradox of the Individual and the Social in Mind

The paradox of the individual and the social means that the individual does not exist without the group and vice versa. We are social animals, and the individual and the collective are inseparable and interdependent. Our work together is both a social and collective endeavour as well as an individual one, and our approach to management and leadership must therefore reflect this reality. We need to keep both the group(s) and the individual(s) in mind. We cannot have one without the other. It is a both-and situation, where each is stronger if the other is valued and respected.

Many of our traditional management practices, however, are based upon an individualistic understanding of how we work together. Doug Griffin, in his book *The Emergence of Leadership*,[4] describes this perspective on leadership as one in which leaders are independent individuals and objective observers and formulators of visions. The American historian and political philosopher Hannah Arendt, wryly observed that the successful leader can "claim for himself what actually is the achievement of many" because after all, they are supposedly the ones who have made it all possible through their leadership![5]

We know, however, that no one is autonomous; we are all interdepend-ent. Our ethics and values, how we feel about each other, all emerge as patterns or themes that organise our experience of being together. Manag-ers may have more influence upon what will happen than other members of the team, but what is going on is still the result of what everyone is doing and thinking and saying and the themes that emerge from these actions. Thus, the effectiveness of an organization is profoundly conditioned by its history and social nature and not just by individual "high achievers."[6]

A successful manager needs to develop the capacity of *groupmindedness*, in which they recognise that leadership is a complex social process which is dynamic and ever-evolving as they and others interact and negotiate how they will go on together.[7] Managers are responsible to support members of the group, both individually and as a collective, in developing their own practice and understanding what is going on and what that will require of them. They need to consider what the group needs from them and, in turn, what they need from the group. Managers need to demonstrate *friction competence* and support the group in its exploration of different perspectives in a way that allows participants to stay in relation with each other despite the conflict, power dynamics and negative feelings that are often a part of the work.

Our actions as managers and colleagues are highly visible and thus have a disproportionate impact on how we relate to one another. Whether col-leagues feel we are trustworthy and, in turn, whether they feel they are trusted, will have profound implications for our ability to work together. It goes without saying that if I don't feel I can trust my boss, then I am unlikely to feel safe (or motivated) to bring a different perspective to the table, even though these different views might be exactly what the group needs to hear.

The leader is also responsible, as complexity theorist Chris Mowles counsels, to "step down gently from the pedestal upon which one has been placed so that participants in a group begin to realise their own agency and maturity." Their role as "rhetor, as politician, as storyteller in chief" is to help the group better understand who they are and what they stand for.[8] If we accept that no one person can see, know, and understand all, then the risks of the command-and-control approach to leadership are obvious. This way of managing impoverishes the ability to explore an issue by reducing access to different perspectives and information. It also does nothing to encourage and support employees in developing their experience, confi-dence in their capabilities, and trusting relationships to be able to more fully contribute to the work.

2. Develop the Capacity of Reflexivity

Managers need to notice themselves in relation to others, how they affect others, and, in turn, how they are affected by them. In other words, to exercise *reflexivity*. This requires that they work to take a view of the world which is not centred upon themselves but one in which they continually explore what is going on both for themselves and for others and include colleagues in that process of inquiry. This takes courage as it is often easier and feels safer to disregard or avoid the difficult conversations or to use one's positional power to try and escape accountability for the impact of one's actions. However, these interactions will still affect who we are together and addressed or not, will continue to inform the *habitus* or culture of the group for good or ill. Again, the way we work together today, what is supported, reinforced, and rewarded, punished, or ignored, may affect how we will relate to each other in the future.

It is generally considered poor form to act without thinking. We are admonished to think things through first. However, it is impossible to separate thinking and action in our ever-evolving and complex world, where we are perpetually encountering surprises. They are two sides of the same coin. We are always acting and reacting and (hopefully) thinking about what is going on and what we are doing. Instead of think, decide, and act, we need to engage in a never-ending loop of thinking about and questioning what is going on, being reflexive and letting this inform our actions.[9]

Living is, in fact, one giant research project. If you doubt this, watch a small child learn how to walk or manipulate a new toy. Trial and adjust, trial and adjust, always building on what the prior experiments in motion have taught them. This necessarily involves risk, trial and error, accepting that what has worked in the past might not work in the present, and learning to adapt. And once again, the best we can achieve is a reflexive engagement with productive doubt so that we, and others, can think about what we are doing, who we are becoming and how we feel about it.[10]

3. Operate Up in the Clouds and Down in the Weeds

In sociologist Norbert Elias's book, *The Society of Individuals*, he counsels that in order to understand what is going on for us in the social flow of life, we need to adopt the perspective of both the airman and the swimmer.[11] He argues that it is only from the perspective of the airman that one can gain some detachment and a relatively undistorted view of our history as well as an understanding of the environment, history, expectations, and context and how we are both forming and being formed by them. Everything, including historical trends, evolves and changes, and there is nothing inevitable about how we act and react to the processes in which we find ourselves. However, it is only by also adopting the perspective of the swimmer, directly in the weeds, who needs to act in the moment itself, that one can get beyond the general and theoretical and understand the many different pressures of a particular situation.

According to Elias, this means that we are always both involved and detached. By involved he meant highly emotional participation and by detached he referred to a less emotional, more aware, and reflective participation. What this says for us as managers is that we need to operate at both levels—up in the clouds and down in the weeds. Only then can we hope to bring about different outcomes as we explore what is going on and choose what to do about it. If we are better able to understand both our history and the patterning of our reality, and at the same time, pay attention to the pressures we are experiencing, there is no inevitability that things will continue in the same way.

As managers we are often expected to function at what is called the "big picture" level with an abstract knowing of theories, best practices, and other idealised concepts. We are told that professional managers don't necessarily need to understand what is going on in the depths of the organisation. For sure, it can be difficult to impossible to be fully conversant with the details of all that happens in large and complex organisations. However, management is a lot about acting (swimming) in the "blooming, buzzing confusion of everyday organisational life where our knowledge about what's going on is always going to be imperfect and where we can't predict the outcomes of our actions."[12] We need to be both detached and focus on universal principles and, at the same time, emotionally involved in and with the details of what is going on to function effectively.

4. Accept That We Cannot Be Either Truly Objective or Completely Rational and Unemotional

We are frequently admonished to be objective, to leave our personal troubles at the door and to keep our emotions out of our work. However, perfect objectivity and rationality are not possible. As we are part of the workplace, there is no stepping outside of the interactions in which we are engaged. We are part and parcel of what is going on. We are all affected by the patterning of how we relate to one another just as we in turn affect the themes organising our experience together. In the words of Thomas Nagel, there is no view from nowhere.[13] Likewise, we are unable to keep our emotions out of our work.[14] Neuroscientists have confirmed that emotion cannot be separated from cognition; the two are inseparably intertwined. In our conversations, therefore, while we may shift back and forth from involved detachment or detached involvement, there is no process external to what is going on in the discussion.[15] What is happening for us as we interact with others is driven by both emotion and rational contemplation. Both are an inescapable part of how we solve problems.

What we bring to our work together is a perspective that has been formed over the years based upon our experiences, our history, and our culture. We bring our emotions and our reasoning capability as well as what is going on for us in our personal lives. What we see is what we expect to see. What we do and do not notice and how we understand and interpret what is going on are influenced by our past. And this is also true for those with whom we work. The job of the manager is thus to enable others to bring their different views to the table so that we can try and make sure that as many values and perspectives as possible are in play. We need to resist the compulsion to rush to an early answer and prematurely terminate the exploration of what is going on. We are responsible, with colleagues, as indeed it is a shared responsibility, to consider the needs of the group and to make it safe to explore differences in a way that we can stay in relation with one another.

5. Take a Different Perspective on Time

The *living present* is a way of thinking about time. We act in the present based upon our history and experience and the themes that pattern how we relate to one another that have emerged as the result of past interactions. At the same time as the patterns of the past form us, through our actions we form both others and the themes of how we relate to one another. Our actions are informed by what we expect in the future, our hopes, wishes and, sometimes, our fears. As we act, we encounter responses and reactions which may cause us to affirm or question our expectations of the future. In the process, we may gain a new perspective which causes us to reinterpret how we understand our past. The experience of time is thus an ongoing dynamic process in which the past, present, and future are inextricably interwoven.

A related concept in complexity science is referred to as *path dependence* or sensitivity to initial conditions, in which prior choices may constrain and determine our future options. Both path dependence and a consideration of the *living present* are important to the complexity manager because how we relate to one another today affects the patterning of our existence and how we will see and react to one another in the future as well as the options that will be open to us.

One of the implications of seeing time from this perspective is that the way we work together may affect the way *we will work together* in terms of who we will become both individually and as a group. We thus need to think about who we are becoming in evaluating and determining our actions. This requires us to consider how our interactions with others will reward or reinforce, or in the alternative, sanction certain actions because as managers, we are in a position of high influence over what is considered successful behaviour in the workplace.

6. Take a Broader Perspective on What We Need to Know

Our processes of problem-solving depend on our understanding of what is going on so that we can decide what we need to or should do about the issue at hand. Thus, careful managers consider the evidence as they assess options, which can refer to either qualitative or quantitative research and data. Each can be helpful but also have limitations on what they can tell us. Indeed, in a complex environment, there may not be any available evidence for an initiative.

In many workplaces, being *evidence-based* is considered a necessity. However, there is a tendency to default to quantitative information in our drive for accuracy and certainty, which can drive us to restrict evidence to the use of metrics. This will give us the illusion that if we do X, then Y will be the result (and it will be sometimes but not necessarily so). We will also be able to monitor, measure, and report on our results and thus argue that we have demonstrated our effectiveness. If we take complexity seriously, however, the dangers and simplistic nature of this approach are clear. Instead, we need to be more open to a broader perspective on what we need to or can know.

Quantitative measures can never predict, nor can they convey an understanding of why what is going on is happening. As an important element of complexity is nonlinear relationships, we can never assume that if we do X then Y will happen. Collapsing our observations into one number whether in the form of indices or averages will often mask nuance and make helpful differences and information invisible. This approach is also dependent upon the assumptions used to create metrics, particularly in the case of indices. Sometimes there is no evidence or data for a proposition that we wish to understand. Even if others have developed the same programme or method and had great success with it, there is no way of understanding the social history and interactions that influenced the success, or otherwise of their implementation to determine if a similar approach will be successful in a different environment. Even if the numbers can tell us what, they cannot be used to understand the why or to describe the experience. And where deepening our knowledge involves the valuation of what is good and ethical, metrics are also unable to help us.

One of the problems with an evidence-based approach is that we are often inconsistent in its application and run up against an evidentiary double standard. For example, the *bright shiny toy syndrome* often means that someone in authority has become enamoured with some new and exciting transformational initiative, often couched as a best practice or from the toolbox of an external consultant. No evidence is required beyond the sales pitch once the boss has accepted the proposition. Likewise, if something is considered as a settled question in the relevant discipline or taken for granted in our *habitus*, once more, not only is no proof required, but often no questions or challenge to the dogma are welcome. Instead, any innovative or novel proposals often meet with a demand for the evidence that will prove that they are a good idea. Any benefit of the doubt will be resolved in favour of established knowledge.

When something goes wrong or we are surprised by a breakdown in our expectations, the first issue is to identify what the problem is that we need to solve. Sometimes this is obvious. For the most part in complexity, however, this is difficult as issues don't come with bows and labels on them. Further, as what is happening is determined by the patterning of our existence, it is unlikely to be just one thing that goes counter to our expectations, and there will often be more than one issue that we need to deal with at the same time. Often, the evidence that we rely upon shapes how we define a problem. At the same time, how the issue is framed will in turn determine what evidence is relevant, what is in scope, and who needs to be involved in its resolution. To paraphrase psychologist and philosopher John Shotter, if we are not careful about the ways in which research is used to form and shape our problems, we shall often be "investigating fictions of our own devising without recognising them as such."[16]

7. Value Phronesis in the Workplace

One form of knowing that goes beyond metrics is *phronesis*. This practical knowledge is the sound judgement and wisdom which develops over time through the accretion of experience. It is fundamentally important in complex environments, as it is based upon many years of experience with the patterns and rhythms of a field of expertise. It is like the feeling of having seen a movie before and having an idea of what might happen. While practical knowledge will still not allow prediction, it is often the best we have got to understanding when something is off kilter or is changing and what we might need to do about it.

Too often *phronesis* is disregarded and supplanted by the theoretical knowledge of those who are considered experts in the field. Much as with the passport officer in Chapter 3, however, *phronesis* is a fundamentally important asset for the organisation and needs to be supported, rewarded, and actively incorporated into our problem-solving processes. Those with the best grasp on what is going on are often lower in the hierarchy, described by author Michael Lewis[17] as L6 employees, (because he found that they were generally six levels down in the organisation). This form of knowing is the antithesis of context-free abstract knowing that is often the source of wisdom from so-called experts, consultants, and sadly enough, professional managers who do not have the hands-on experience of the work. Professor of organisational studies in the Warwick Business School in England, Davide Nicolini, suggests that it is not the real experts (those with long-term experience and practical knowledge) that use abstract knowledge but novices (including professional managers) who need to rely upon it in the absence of actual experience in the field.[18]

8. First Do No Harm[19]

Perhaps the wisest thing that a manager can do is to take care not to do harm in the workplace. This does not refer to criminal actions (although of course that goes without saying) but to unnecessarily increasing uncertainty and complexity. This can happen in any number of ways.

While managers often advocate for harmony and collaboration, many of the management processes and human resources practices lead to increased division and competition. A culture that pits one employee against another for promotional opportunities, compensation, or investment in their divisions can maximise uncertainty for all by adversely affecting the patterns of trust in the workplace and reducing the likelihood of collaboration on organisational challenges.[20] Likewise, a risk adverse culture often leads to the over-regulation of all employees to ensure that the small minority of individuals likely to defraud the organisation are controlled. This can have the unfortunate effect of sending the message that no one is trusted. This is not to advocate for a free-for-all, anarchic environment in which anything goes, but if the base assumption is that no one is trustworthy, then given that trust is reciprocal, neither is the leadership.

Another possibility of doing harm comes from managers who are rewarded for having a bias for action and immediately jumping into problem-solving and decision-making mode. This often results in the launch of new programmes and initiatives (often branded as transformational or whatever is the current management fad) and when nothing else can be thought of, reorganisations and renaming of companies and departments. Likewise, continued short-term thinking, unnecessary downsizing, and kick the can down the road[21] types of practices can all give the illusion of productive activity, but they generally generate more heat than light at best. At their worst, these actions can do significant damage to the organisation[22] and add additional issues which need to be dealt with, thus increasing the uncertainty we face.

The *big bang* approach to management is often attractive to managers because it is a way to demonstrate to stakeholders and bosses that they are adding value by taking bold action. However, any new initiative takes energy, time, and concentration on the part of both executives and employees to figure out what is going on, what might result, and, of course, to implement the proposed action. Any action also affects the patterning of what is going on and has an impact upon how we relate to one another. Superfluous actions risk adding additional complexity for perhaps no good reason. Continually announcing new initiatives as bright shiny toys or new management fads present themselves may also have the unanticipated result of teaching employees that this is just a kidney stone change: painful, but this too shall pass. You just need to wait management out.

Any interventions and initiatives have opportunity costs. When you pick one initiative, you are effectively rejecting others. It is often wise to do nothing or to take modest, small steps in an *anti-big bang approach*. The American economist and academic Charles Lindblom coined the term "the science of muddling through."[23] Considered one of the early developers and advocates of the theory of incrementalism in policy and decision-making, he advocated a theory of public policy-making which involved processes of interaction and mutual adaptation among many individuals with different values and interests and with different perspectives and information. This type of approach recognises that the best we can do at any one time is to figure out what is a good enough understanding to take the next step for now, knowing that we may well be dealing with completely different problems the next day.[24]

9. Welcome Productive Doubt

American playwright Wilson Mizner was known to have said, "I respect faith, but doubt is what gives you an education." In a complex world in which the unthought of often happens, the ability to question and to doubt is imperative for us as leaders and managers. Many times, I have heard senior managers say that they weren't afraid of what they knew, but of what they didn't know. While this makes sense, we also need to worry that we may not really know what we think we know. This places a premium upon providing safe space and opportunity for colleagues to surface their doubts and to collectively engage in an exploration of what pragmatist John Dewey referred to as productive doubt, to help us to reduce the unknowns and perhaps challenge the knowns.

Dealing with uncertainty can be anxiety creating and can lead to an almost irresistible compulsion to solve the problem, achieve certainty, declare victory, and move on. The use of positional power may inappropriately influence, curtail, or otherwise constrain necessary discussions and reduce our ability to explore productive doubt. It is all too easy to shut down the exploration of an issue. "We are pressed for time." "There is only so much time today." "Let's not rehash what has already been agreed upon."

And yet we know too well that what we are aware of or perceive is often determined by what we expect to see which, in turn, depends upon our history and our *habitus*. What one sees, others will miss and vice versa. In these uncertain times, an effective manager is often the one who is more able to "sit in the fires of uncertainty" and to encourage the group to sufficiently explore productive doubt and the many different values and perspectives at play. A manager's ability to manage their own anxiety as well as to support the group in doing so is a necessary part of their practice.

10. Hold Your Plans Lightly

Once we have decided what we are going to do, we need to hold these decisions and plans lightly. We need to accept that they are just our best judgement based on the information currently available to us and contingent upon the circumstances prevalent at the time of decision-making. Effectively, the inquiry should not be considered finished. Canadian writer, activist, and entrepreneur Liz Crocker suggests that we need to "live into the question," being prepared to continue monitoring what is happening and to adjust both the question and how we understand the situation as it evolves. Canadian Political Scientist Thomas Homer-Dixon recommends that often the best approach is to start simple, explore the possibilities, and figure out as you go, constantly recalibrating your plans and managing your doubts and fears.[25]

There are several ways to do this. Use of community of inquiry meetings or of open agenda approaches to noticing what is going on can be powerful ways of enabling team members to identify how our initiatives are progressing and when we might need to revisit or adjust. Evaluation of plans for maintenance of optionality and the use of methodologies such as scenario planning and premortems can also provide an opening for the surfacing of productive doubt by those with less power.

Parting Thoughts on Leadership in a Complex World

In this book, the terms leaders and managers have both been used. If we take complexity seriously, we know that what is going on is because of the themes or patterns that emerge from the multitudes of interactions that are going on all the time. These interactions are affected by our emotions, our evaluative criteria, our *habitus*, and power dynamics. While leaders have significant influence and are important to the organisation. They, like the rest of the organisation, are also formed by the patterning of how we relate to one another at the same time as they affect and are affected by the themes organising our existence.

Since at least the 1990s, we have been deluged by a flood of books, articles, and training programmes on leadership. Business coach Chris Westfall has estimated that we have collectively thrown an obscene amount of money (estimated at $366 billion) at the leadership development industry and yet have seen no improvement.[26] If anything, some would suggest that things have gotten worse. Given this adulation and focus on leadership, it is worth spending a few moments on the implications of this concept for the complexity of our work.

The concentration on leadership may be partly a result of our living in an individualistic age which celebrates charismatic individuals (and often rewards them handsomely) and looks to them to lead us through the trials and uncertainties of an increasingly complex world. Their high status, particularly in the private sector, has often been accompanied by significant, arguably excessive, rewarding of those in the executive suites.[27] The annual Executive Paywatch Report, a comprehensive database, tracks CEO-to-worker pay ratios for the past 20 years and shows that Standard & Poor's 500 CEOs averaged $18.3 million in compensation in 2021, which was 324 times the median worker's pay and an increase from the years 2019 and 2020.

The language of leadership has led to a cult-like flattering of the elite leader often propagated by those who by virtue of their positional power are able to determine how the stories are told. Anything and everything good about an organisation is associated with its leader and every social dilemma is seen as a failure of leadership.[28] Complexity theorist Chris Mowles suggests that we have collectively become addicted to the "one-armed bandit machine of leadership, permanently expecting miracles at the same time as anticipating the inevitable disappointment."[29]

What we have learned from research into the social impacts of income disparities in groups should sound a warning bell for the current adulation of leaders and leadership. Studies have shown that statistically those of higher socioeconomic status are increasingly self-oriented, self-interested, less empathetic, and prone to entitlement, narcissism,[30] and even unethical and antisocial behaviour. This can lead to a replacement of cooperation with status competition internally, resulting in a cutthroat environment, which, as we have already noted, decreases trust and the ability to collaborate and can thus increase the uncertainty and complexity of the workplace.[31] Other research suggests that subjects who are in positions of power for lengthy periods can act as "if they had suffered a traumatic brain injury—becoming more impulsive, less risk-aware, and, crucially, less adept at seeing things from other people's point of view."[32] One author rather alarmingly referred to leaders as the "psychopaths at the top."[33]

This research is not cited to say that leaders are inherently bad people, but merely to suggest that the way that we have organised ourselves has led to the development of unhealthy patterns in how we relate to one another. As previously suggested in these pages, people do what they believe will be successful based upon their history. They are formed by the patterns of relating in their *habitus* and continue behaviours that are rewarded and reinforced.

Research on income inequality also suggests implications for our ability to function in an uncertain environment. We have seen how our ability to explore productive doubt, to collaborate and to engage in an inquiry into our differences can be assets in complexity. It turns out that the more equal a society or group, the stronger their community life, the more that they will trust one another, and the more creative they will be as measured by the granting of patents. Studies have also found that small groups of employees in which members were paid equivalently, achieved more and had lower absenteeism.[34]

While this field of study is still evolving, the message is clear that the ability to collaborate is fundamentally important for how we work together. Animals whose social strategies are based upon cooperation, exhibit sympathy (an emotion closely related to empathy)[35] as that allows them to maintain relationships inside their social groups. In more unequal societies, empathy is often reduced, and people tend to view each other more ambivalently. Inequality is rationalised by seeing different groups as more or less deserving or moral. This is of concern as empathy is arguably the killer app for survival where cooperation is essential. Or as Sir Simon Baron-Cohen, British clinical psychologist and professor of developmental psychopathology at the University of Cambridge described it, empathy is a universal solvent. The good news is that the decrease in the ability of those with higher socioeconomic status to empathise with others in unequal societies is not inevitable. Studies have demonstrated that where the privileged are asked to think about egalitarian values, they tend to become more empathetic, less antisocial, more ethical, and less entitled.[36]

Why Complexity Management Matters

Today, we face arguably unprecedented levels of uncertainty and complexity due to several existential threats to humankind and the planet as we know it: the climate change emergency; high and increasing levels of income inequality;[37] the rising threat of authoritarianism and challenges to democracy; the continuing legacy of colonialism; questions of social justice and racism; and the impact of social media and big data upon how we live and work together. In times such as these, no matter what sector or field of endeavour we are engaged in, the uncertainties are greater than ever.

This book has explored how we work together and more particularly the role of managers and leaders in organisations, communities, and nations. We have seen how our fear of the inevitable uncertainty of our complex world often causes us to behave in counterproductive ways. With stakes as high as the future of our planet, it is even more essential than ever that we learn better ways to function in our work together. All of us, regardless of whether we are in the private sector, public sector, or civil society need to step up if we are going to make it through these turbulent times with a planet that we can recognise.

Taking complexity into account also means that we need to manage in a sustainable way, and not just for the exigencies of the moment. Our work together is a long game. But what would this more sustainable approach look like? Sustainable development has been described as one that "meets the needs of the present generation without compromising the ability of future generations to meet their own needs."[38] Another perspective is that known as the Seventh Generation Principle based on an ancient Haudenosaunee (Iroquois) philosophy that the decisions we make today should result in a sustainable world seven generations into the future. Sustainable management means that leadership is only temporary. We are not only responsible for what happens today but are also custodians and stewards of the future for generations to come.

Sustainable, by definition, means taking the long-term into account. Unfortunately, we have, all too often, taken a short-term view to drive our actions in all sectors and fields of endeavour. The very existence of the existential threats facing us is proof of that. As Mark Carney wrote in his book, *Value(s): Building a Better World for All*, we have continuously preferred the present over the future, and the short-term rather than any concept of inter-generational fairness. Our continued pursuit of efficiency in the short-term has led to organisations that are significantly less resilient to both internal and external shocks. Success has too often been individualistic and personal versus improving the happiness and welfare of others,[39] and research suggests that domination by self-fulfillers cannot sustain the strong identification with others that is required for public freedom and order.[40]

We have failed to invest in preventing climate change, strengthening democracy, addressing the levels of income inequality, and the lingering and powerful impacts of colonialism, social injustice, and racism. In too many countries, including the so-called developed world, we have systematically privileged the private sector, particularly large and powerful players, denigrated government and the public service, and impoverished civil society. As the extensive literature on income disparity shows, this has resulted in harm to all of us, but particularly those without power and clearly, future generations.

This research suggests that the more inequal a population, the lower the trust levels and the greater the damage to social cohesion, increase in status anxiety, and decrease in civic participation.[41] The reaction of those who feel left behind in the case of large societal wealth disparities and their effective exclusion from society has been shown to lead to their repudiation of social mores and expectations that no longer have any relevance for them—and worse, that are symbolic of the world that has rejected them. In the larger society, that is a recipe for populism and an increase in uncertainty and complexity. In our organisations this is likely to lead to an unmotivated and disengaged workforce. Consultants and managers of all stripes talk about the importance of engagement and communication, and yet in many companies, the loss of mutual interests and ties can lead to the loss of the social licence enjoyed by managers and can threaten both their authority and the development of a feeling of inclusion in the workforce and thus the sustainability of the organisation.

The more unequal a society, the more negative are the indicators of societal health.[42] This means that the health and welfare of those in the workplace are also under threat. For example, often discussed in human resources and management circles is what appears to be an epidemic of mental illness around the world. The Centre for Addiction and Mental Health (CAMH) points to the World Health Organization that suggests that it is the leading cause of disability worldwide with around 450 million people currently struggling with their mental health. In Canada, according to the statistics, mental illness affects more than 6.7 million people and one in two have or have had a mental illness by the time they reach the age of 40.[43] Just as worrisome, the WHO suggests that suicide is the fourth leading cause of death among 15–29 year olds, and those with severe mental health conditions are likely to die as much as two decades early due to preventable physical conditions.[44] Clearly, this is something that we all need to be concerned about.

Our Challenge

Before December of 2019, few had heard of the city of Wuhan, the capital of China's Hubei province, let alone thought that what happened there would affect them, their everyday reality, and their future. Today, Wuhan is a household name and recognised as the origin of the Coronavirus SARS-CoV-2 virus, which causes the disease known as COVID-19. The World Health Organization declared a public health emergency of international concern on January 30th, 2020 followed on March 11th by a declaration that the world now had a pandemic on its hands.

It is three years down the road that I am writing this final chapter. It is pretty clear that life has substantially changed for all of us worldwide as a result of the pandemic. Writer Peter C. Baker, a regular contributor to *The Guardian* wrote an article in March of 2020[45] on the field of study called "crisis studies" in which researchers and writers try to understand and perhaps project what might happen as the result of a particular crisis. He suggests that in a crisis, what is broken in society becomes apparent and "the fundamental reality of that community is laid bare. Who has more and who has less. Where the power lies. What people treasure and what they fear." While this can be extremely damaging and the nature of the responses may exacerbate such challenges, he suggests that when the "fabric of normality" is ripped open, we can "glimpse possibilities of other worlds" through the resulting hole that has opened up, worlds that may have previously been seen as impossible or unachievable up until that point.

It is impossible to say what the long-term impacts of Covid will be or indeed whether we as a species, both individually and as a species, will become more responsible inhabitants of the planet and rise to Peter Baker's challenge. In a world in which individuals, governments, and other institutions, as well as businesses and those in what is referred to as civil society, are all faced with the need to figure out what is going on, what is going to happen and what they need to or can do about it, the result will be a complex mix that none of us will be able to predict.

Obviously, there is a lot more to getting out of the mess we are in than managers and leaders taking a different approach to management. However, for us to not only survive but flourish, socially and economically, we need a new way of thinking about how this work is done. Such an approach needs to expressly consider both complexity and the needs of the future. And it needs to consider that we are truly all in this together. As the African proverb says, "If you want to travel fast, travel alone; If you want to travel far, travel together."

The threats to our very planet mean that it is time for us, individually and collectively, to decide who we want to become. The perspective on management explored in this book is an important step in the right direction.

Notes

1 Camilla Stivers, *Governance in Dark Times: Practical Philosophy for Public Service*, p. 101.
2 Ibid., p. 129.
3 Richard Wilkinson and Kate Pickett, *The Inner Level: How More Equal Societies Reduce Stress, Restore Sanity and Improve Everyone's Well-Being*, p. 255.
4 Doug Griffin, *The Emergence of Leadership—Linking Self-Organization and Ethics*, p. 205.
5 Hannah Arendt, *The Human Condition* (2nd ed.), p. 190.
6 Robert Putnam, *Bowling Alone*, p. 182.
7 Chris Mowles, *Complexity: A Key Idea for Business and Society*, p. 139.
8 Ibid., p. 140.
9 Ibid., at p. 16 on Hannah Arendt, *Thinking without a Bannister: Essays in Understanding 1953–1975*.
10 Ibid., p. 34.
11 Norbert Elias, *The Society of Individuals*, p. 12.
12 See Chris Mowles p. 104 of *Complexity: A Key Idea for Business and Society*. The reference to "blooming buzzing confusion" is a quote from William James describing his view of what an infant is exposed to in the early days of its life.
13 Thomas Nagel, *The View from Nowhere*.
14 Note that being critical of rationality or saying we cannot separate our cognition from our emotions, is not the same as advocating the abandonment of reason, i.e., the systematic consideration of our assumptions and investments.

15 See Norbert Elias' excellent discussion in his book, *Involvement and Detachment*.
16 John Shotter, *Conversational Realities: Constructing Life through Language*, pp. 104–105.
17 See Michael Lewis' book, *The Premonition: A Pandemic Story*.
18 Presentation to Complexity Management Centre Conference, June 2022.
19 This phrase is attributed to Hippocrates, often called the father of medicine, who wrote about 430 years before the rise of the Roman Empire. It does not, however, form part of the Hippocratic oath, although the latter does contain language that suggests that physicians should not cause physical or moral harm to their patients. The first known published version of this expression comes from mid-19th century medical texts and is attributed to the 17th century English physician, Thomas Sydenham.
20 Peter Marris, *The Politics of Uncertainty*, p. 5.
21 This expression refers to the types of practices that Robert Jackall in *Moral Mazes* described in which executives put off necessary investments and/or take actions which will have short-term benefits but in the long-term would be detrimental to the organization. This is generally in evidence where executives move frequently and thus have no problem leaving an unholy mess for those that follow them.
22 One example in the category of unnecessary or damaging actions was in one sector of a federal government department. There the sector head oversaw six downsizings during a period of two years, resulting in a deeply hurt and unmotivated workforce. While, in my view, this type of action should be considered evidence of incompetence and poor leadership in the extreme, the reward for this sector head was to be promoted to the deputy minister ranks.
23 Charles Lindblom, *The Science of "Muddling Through,"* 1959.
24 Chris Mowles, *Managing in Uncertainty: Complexity and the Paradoxes of Everyday Organizational Life*, p. 144.
25 Thomas Homer-Dixon, *Commanding Hope*, pp. 210–215 in a chapter titled "A Message from Middle Earth" writes about the strategy that the fellowship formed to achieve the mission of destroying the "One Ring" to keep it out of the hands of The Dark Lord Sauron in *The Lord of the Rings*.
26 Chris Westfall, *Leadership Development Is a $366 Billion Industry: Here's Why Most Programs Don't Work*, www.forbes.com/sites/chriswestfall/2019/06/20/leadership-development-why-most-programs-dont-work/?sh=7722706c61de.
27 Those defending significant pay disparities often suggest that elevated compensation levels are warranted because of hard work, skills, and competencies of those at the top. Significant research, however, suggests that where one ends up in life and the hierarchy, and one's abilities, interests, and talents, are mostly determined not by inherent capabilities and hard work, but by where the individual started and the opportunities and privileges that were available to them. Even more depressing, there is also research to suggest that the higher up the corporate ladder one is, the lower is the evidence of their contribution. Nassim Nicholas Taleb, *Fooled by Randomness: The Hidden Role of Chance in Life and in the Markets*, p. 254.
28 Chris Mowles, *Complexity: A Key Idea for Business and Society*, p. 172. Mark Learmonth, Professor Emeritus at Durham University, UK, is another researcher who has taken a critical approach to the consideration of "leadership" in academic and business literature. See Mark Learmonth and Kevin Morrell's book, *Critical Perspectives on Leadership: The Language of Corporate Power*.

29 Ibid., p. 127.
30 Michael Mechanic, *Jackpot: How the Super-Rich Really Live—and How Their Wealth Harms Us All*, p. 165.
31 Richard Wilkinson and Kate Pickett, *The Inner Level: How More Equal Societies Reduce Stress, Restore Sanity and Improve Everyone's Well-Being*, pp. 76–89.
32 Jerry Useem, *Power Causes Brain Damage*, July/August 2017, Scientific American.
33 Richard Wilkinson and Kate Pickett, *The Inner Level: How More Equal Societies Reduce Stress, Restore Sanity and Improve Everyone's Well-Being*, p. 82.
34 Ibid., pp. 158–161, 254–255, also see Richard Wilkinson and Kate Pickett, *The Spirit Level: Why Equality Is Better for Everyone*, p. 225.
35 Empathy is the ability to experience the feelings of another person which goes beyond sympathy, which is caring and understanding for the feelings of others.
36 Richard Wilkinson and Kate Pickett, *The Inner Level: How More Equal Societies Reduce Stress, Restore Sanity and Improve Everyone's Well-Being*, pp. 91–95.
37 The increases in income inequality in our society belie the fact that 90% of the time that humans have been anatomically modern, equality has been the norm. Ibid., p. 27.
38 Mark Carney, *Value(s): Building a Better World for All*, pp. 493–496.
39 Ibid., p. 127.
40 Charles Taylor, *Sources of the Self: The Making of the Modern Identity*, p. 508.
41 Richard Wilkinson and Kate Pickett, *The Inner Level: How More Equal Societies Reduce Stress, Restore Sanity and Improve Everyone's Well-Being*, pp. 65–89.
42 For an excellent exploration of this phenomenon and the research behind it, see Richard Wilkinson and Kate Pickett's books, *The Spirit Level* and *The Inner Level*.
43 The Crisis Is Real, *CAMH*, www.camh.ca/en/driving-change/the-crisis-is-real, accessed December 10, 2022.
44 World Health Organization, www.who.int/health-topics/mental-health#tab=tab_1, accessed December 11, 2022.
45 Peter C. Baker, *We Can't Go Back to Normal: How Will Coronavirus Change the World?*, The Guardian (Tuesday, March 31, 2020, 0:600 BST).

Bibliography

Arendt, H. (1958/1998). *The Human Condition* (2nd ed.). Chicago: The University of Chicago Press.
Arendt, H. (2018). *Thinking without a Bannister: Essays in Understanding 1953–1975*. New York, NY: Knopf Publishing.
Baker, P.C. (Tuesday, March 31, 2020, 0:600 BST). We Can't Go Back to Normal: How Will Coronavirus Change the World? *The Guardian*.
CAMH. *The Crisis Is Real*. www.camh.ca/en/driving-change/the-crisis-is-real, accessed December 10, 2022.
Carney, M. (2021). *Value(s): Building a Better World for All*. Toronto: Penguin House Random Canada Limited.
Elias, N. (1983/1987). *Involvement and Detachment*. Oxford, UK: Basil Blackwell Ltd.
Elias, N. (1987/1991). *The Society of Individuals*. Oxford, UK: Basil Blackwell Ltd.
Griffin, D. (2006). *The Emergence of Leadership: Linking Self-Organization and Ethics*. New York, NY: Routledge.

Homer-Dixon, T. (2020). *Commanding Hope: The Power We Have to Renew a World in Peril*. Toronto: Penguin Random House Canada Limited.

Jackall, R. (1988). *Moral Mazes: The World of Corporate Managers*. New York: Oxford University Press, Inc.

Learmonth, M., & Morrell, K. (2019). *Critical Perspectives on Leadership: The Language of Corporate Power*. New York: Routledge.

Lewis, M. (2021). *The Premonition: A Pandemic Story*. New York: W.W. Norton.

Lindblom, C.E. (Spring 1959). The Science of 'Muddling Through'. *Public Administration Review, 19*(2), 79–88.

Marris, P. (1996/2009). *The Politics of Uncertainty: Attachment in Private and Public Life*. New York: Routledge, Taylor & Francis Group.

Mechanic, M. (2021). *Jackpot: How the Super-Rich Really Live—and How Their Wealth Harms Us All*. New York: Simon & Schuster.

Mowles, C. (2015). *Managing in Uncertainty: Complexity and the Paradoxes of Everyday Organizational Life*. London, UK: Routledge.

Mowles, C. (2022). *Complexity: A Key Idea for Business and Society*. London, UK: Routledge.

Nagel, T. (1989). *The View from Nowhere*. Oxford, US: Oxford University Press.

Putnam, R.D. (2000). *Bowling Alone: The Collapse and Revival of American Community*. New York, NY: Simon & Schuster.

Shotter, J. (1994). *Conversational Realities: Constructing Life through Language*. London: SAGE Publications Ltd.

Stivers, C. (2008). *Governance in Dark Times—Practical Philosophy for Public Service*. Washington, DC: Georgetown University Press.

Taleb, N. N. (2004). *Fooled by Randomness: The Hidden Role of Chance in Life and in the Markets*. New York: Random House Trade Paperbacks.

Taylor, C. (1989). *Sources of the Self: The Making of the Modern Identity*. Cambridge, MA: Harvard University Press.

Useem, J. (July/August 2017). Power Causes Brain Damage. *Scientific American, 320*(1), 24–26.

Westfall, C. (June 20, 2019). *Leadership Development Is a $366 Billion Industry: Here's Why Most Programs Don't Work*. www.forbes.com/sites/chriswestfall/2019/06/20/leadership-development-why-most-programs-dont-work/?sh=7722706c61de, accessed April 10, 2023.

Wilkinson, R., & Pickett, K. (2009/2010). *The Spirit Level: Why Equality Is Better for Everyone*. London: Penguin Books.

Wilkinson, R., & Pickett, K. (2018). *The Inner Level: How More Equal Societies Reduce Stress, Restore Sanity and Improve Everyone's Well-Being*. New York: Penguin Books.

World Health Organization. www.who.int/health-topics/mental-health#tab=tab_1, accessed December 11, 2022.

Bibliography

Abbey, E.J., et al. (2020). The Global Health Security Index Is Not Predictive of Coronavirus Pandemic Responses among Organization for Economic Cooperation and Development Countries, *National Library of Medicine*. *PLoS One*, *15*(10), e0239398. www.ncbi.nlm.nih.gov/pmc/articles/PMC7540886/, accessed April 10, 2023.

Alvesson, M., & Kärreman, D. (2011). *Qualitative Research and Theory Development: Mystery as Method*. London, UK: SAGE Publishing.

Alvesson, M., & Spicer, A. (2012). A Stupidity-Based Theory of Organizations. *Journal of Management Studies*, *49*, 1194–1220. https://doi-org.ezproxy.herts.ac.uk/10.1111/j.1467-6486.2012.01072.x.

Alvesson, M., & Spicer, A. (2017). *The Stupidity Paradox: The Power and Pitfalls of Functional Stupidity at Work*. London: IPS-Profile Books.

Arendt, H. (1958/1998). *The Human Condition* (2nd ed.). Chicago: The University of Chicago Press.

Arendt, H. (2018). *Thinking without a Bannister: Essays in Understanding 1953–1975*. New York, NY: Knopf Publishing.

Ayer, E. (March 3, 2023). Meetings Are the Work. *The Medium*, The Edition.

Baker, P.C. (Tuesday, March 31, 2020, 0:600 BST). We Can't Go Back to Normal: How Will Coronavirus Change the World? *The Guardian*.

Baldwin, J.D. (1988). Habit, Emotion and Self-Conscious Action. *Sociological Perspectives*, *31*(1), 35–58. https://doi.org/10.2307/1388950.

Barber, K. (2004). *The Canadian Oxford Dictionary* (2nd ed.). Oxford, UK: Oxford University Press.

BBVA. (May 22, 2015). *When Lorenz Discovered the Butterfly Effect*. www.bbvaopenmind.com/en/science/leading-figures/when-lorenz-discovered-the-butterfly-effect/, accessed February 5, 2022.

Beck, H. (2019). *How the Mind's Mistakes Make Humans Creative, Innovative, and Successful*. Vancouver, Canada: Greystone Books.

Boden, D. (1994). *The Business of Talk: Organizations in Action*. Cambridge, UK: Polity Press.

Bourdieu, P. (1977/2015). *Outline of a Theory of Practice*. Cambridge, UK: Cambridge University Press.

Bourdieu, P. (1982/2003). *Language & Symbolic Power*. Cambridge, MA: Harvard University Press.

Brezzi, M. (2022). *All You Need Is Trust: Informing the Role of Government in the COVID-19 Context*. www.oecd.org/gov/all-you-need-is-trust-statistics-newsletter-12-2020.pdf, accessed August 24, 2022.

Brinkmann, S. (2017). *John Dewey: Science for a Changing World*. London, UK: Routledge.

Brown, A.D., Colville, I., & Pye, A. (2015). Making Sense of Sensemaking in Organization Studies. *Organization Studies, 36*(2), 265–277. https://doi-org.ezproxy.herts.ac.uk/10.1177/0170840614559259.

Burke, K. (1941). *The Philosophy of Literary Form*. Berkeley: University of California Press.

Burke, K. (1966). *Language as Symbolic Action—Essays on Life, Literature and Method*. Berkeley, CA: University of California Press.

Burkitt, I. (1999). *Bodies of Thought: Embodiment, Identity & Modernity*. London, UK: SAGE Publishing.

Burkitt, I. (2012). Emotional Reflexivity: Feeling, Emotion and Imagination in Reflexive Dialogues. *Sociology, 46*(3), 458–472. https://doi-org.ezproxy.herts.ac.uk/10.1177/0038038511422587.

Burkitt, I. (2014). *Emotions and Social Relations*. Los Angeles, CA: SAGE Publishing.

Cadsby, T. (2014). *Closing the Mind Gap: Making Smarter Decisions in a Hypercomplex World*. Toronto: BPS Books.

CAMH. *The Crisis Is Real*. www.camh.ca/en/driving-change/the-crisis-is-real, accessed December 10, 2022.

Carney, M. (2021). *Value(s): Building a Better World for All*. Toronto: Penguin House Random Canada Limited.

Coser, L.A. (1957). Social Conflict & the Theory of Social Change. *The British Journal of Sociology, 8*(3), 197–207. doi:10.2307/586859.

Daipha, P. (2015). *Masters of Uncertainty: Weather Forecasters and the Quest for Ground Truth*. Chicago: University of Chicago Press.

Damasio, A.R. (1994). *Descartes' Error: Emotion, Reason and the Human Brain*. London: Picador.

Davis, W. (2009). *The Wayfinders: Why Ancient Wisdom Matters in the Modern World*. Toronto: House of Anansi Press, Inc.

Defence: The Dilemma and the Design. (February 15, 1963). *Time Magazine*. https://content.time.com/time/subscriber/article/0,33009,829884,00.html, accessed February 23, 2023.

Dewey, J. (1891). Moral Theory and Practice. *International Journal of Ethics, 1*(2), 186–203. www.jstor.org.ezproxy.herts.ac.uk/stable/2375407.

Dewey, J. (1922/2017). *Human Nature and Conduct: An Introduction to Social Psychology*. Globalgreyebooks.com.

Dewey, J. (1929/1984). *The Quest for Certainty: The Later Works, 1925–1953*. Carbondale, IL: Southern Illinois University Press.

Dewey, J. (1929/2015). *Experience and Nature*. New York, NY: Dover Publications, Inc.

Elias, N. (1908/1978). *What Is Sociology?* New York, NY: Columbia University Press.

Elias, N. (1983/1987). *Involvement and Detachment*. Oxford, UK: Basil Blackwell Ltd.

Elias, N. (1987/1991). *The Society of Individuals*. Oxford, UK: Basil Blackwell Ltd.

Elias, N. (1989/1996). *The Germans*. New York, NY: Columbia University Press.

Elias, N. (1994). *The Civilizing Process*. Oxford: Blackwell.

Elias, N., & Scotson, J.L. (1965/1994). *The Established and the Outsiders: A Sociological Enquiry into Community Problems* (2nd ed.). London, UK: SAGE Publishing.

Feldman Barrett, L. (August 25, 2021). *This is how your brain makes your mind*. MIT Technology Review. https://www.technologyreview.com/2021/08/25/1031432/what-is-mind-brain-body-connection/ accessed October 16, 2023.

Fenton-O'Creevy, M., Soane, E., Nicholson, N., & Willman, P. (November 2011). Thinking, Feeling and Deciding: The Influence of Emotions on the Decision Making and Performance of Traders. *Journal of Organizational Behavior, 32*(8), 1044–1061.

Filbee, S. (2020). *Trust and Its Consequences: A Regional Senior Manager's Experiences of Meaning Making in the Canadian Public Service*. https://uhra.herts.ac.uk/handle/2299/26037.

Filbee-Dexter, K., Pittman, J., Haig, H.A., Alexander, S.M., Symons, C.C., & Burke, M.J. (2017). Ecological Surprise: Concept, Synthesis, and Social Dimensions. *Ecosphere, 8*(12). doi:10.1002/ecs2.2005.

Flyvbjerg, B. (2001). *Making Social Science Matter: Why Social Inquiry Fails and How It Can Succeed Again*. Cambridge, UK: Cambridge University Press.

Foucault, M. (1994/2000). *Power*. New York, NY: The New Press.

Foulkes, S.H. (1964). *Therapeutic Group Analysis*. London: George Allen & Unwin.

Fukuyama, F. (1996). *Trust: The Social Virtues and the Creation of Prosperity*. New York, NY: Free Press Paperbacks.

Gadamer, H.G. (1960/2013). *Truth and Method*. New York, NY: Bloomsbury Academic.

Griffin, D. (2006). *The Emergence of Leadership: Linking Self-Organization and Ethics*. New York, NY: Routledge.

Harari, Y.N. (2014/2016). *Sapiens: A Brief History of Humankind*. Toronto: McClelland and Stewart.

Harari, Y.N. (2015). *Homo Deus: A Brief History of Tomorrow*. Toronto: McClelland and Stewart.

Hardin, R. (2006). *Trust*. Cambridge, UK: Polity Press.

Hare, B., & Woods, V. (August 2020). Survival of the Friendliest. *Scientific American, 323*(2).

Homer-Dixon, T. (2020). *Commanding Hope: The Power We Have to Renew a World in Peril*. Toronto: Penguin Random House Canada Limited.

Hurley, R. (2012). *The Decision to Trust: How Leaders Create High-Trust Organizations*. San Francisco, CA: Jossey-Bass.

Jackall, R. (1988). *Moral Mazes: The World of Corporate Managers*. New York: Oxford University Press, Inc.

Janis, I. (1972). *Victims of Groupthink: A Psychological Study of Foreign-Policy Decisions and Fiascos*. Boston, MA: Houghton Mifflin.

Janis, I. (1982). *Groupthink: Psychological Studies of Policy Decisions and Fiascos.* Boston, MA: Houghton Mifflin.

Jaques, E. (1951). *The Changing Culture of a Factory.* Tavistock Institute of Human Relations. London: Tavistock Publications. ISBN 978–0415264426. OCLC 300631.

Jones, G.T., & George, J.M. (1998). The Experience and Evolution of Trust: Implications for Cooperation and Teamwork. *The Academy of Management Review, 23*(3), 531–546. doi:10.5465/amr.1998.926625.

Kachali, H., et al. (July 2022). Are Preparedness Indices Reflective of Pandemic Preparedness? A COVID-19 Reality Check. *International Journal of Disaster Risk Reduction, 77*, 103074. Published online May 27, 2022. doi:10.1016/j.ijdrr.2022.103074. www.ncbi.nlm.nih.gov/pmc/articles/PMC9135491/, accessed April 10, 2023.

Kelton, S. (2021). *The Deficit Myth: Modern Monetary Theory and the Birth of the People's Economy.* New York: Hachette Book Group.

Kimmerer, R.W. (2013). *Braiding Sweetgrass: Indigenous Wisdom, Scientific Knowledge, and the Teachings of Plants.* Minneapolis, MN: Milkweed editions.

Krakauer, J. (2009). *Where Men Win Glory.* New York: Bloomsbury.

Kramer, R.M., & Cook, K.S. (Eds.). (2004). *Trust and Distrust in Organizations: Dilemmas and Approaches.* New York, NY: Russell SAGE Foundation.

Kuznets, S. (1937). *Report to the US Congress Titled 'Uses and Abuses of National Income Measurements'.* https://en.wikipedia.org/wiki/Gross_domestic_product#Limitations_and_criticisms, accessed April 4, 2023.

Learmonth, M. & Morrell, K. (2019). *Critical Perspectives on Leadership: The Language of Corporate Power.* New York: Routledge.

Lewis, M. (2021). *The Premonition: A Pandemic Story.* New York: W.W. Norton.

Lindblom, C.E. (Spring 1959). The Science of 'Muddling Through'. *Public Administration Review, 19*(2), 79–88.

Malpas, J., Arnswald, U., & Kertscher, J. (Eds.). (2002). *Gadamer's Century: Essays in Honor of Hans-Georg Gadamer.* Cambridge, MA: MIT Press.

Marris, P. (1996/2009). *The Politics of Uncertainty: Attachment in Private and Public Life.* New York: Routledge, Taylor & Francis Group

Mazzucato, M. (2019). This economist has a plan to fix capitalism. Its time we all listened. *Wired.* https://www.wired.co.uk/article/mariana-mazzucato, accessed April 22, 2023.

McHoul, A., & Grace, W. (2007). *A Foucault Primer: Discourse, Power and the Subject.* New York, NY: New York University Press.

McNamara Fallacy. https://en.wikipedia.org/wiki/McNamara_fallacy, accessed October 21 2022.

Mead, G.H. (1923). Scientific Method and the Moral Sciences. *International Journal of Ethics, 33*, 229–247. www-jstor-org.ezproxy.herts.ac.uk/stable/2377331.

Mead, G.H. (1938). *The Philosophy of the Act.* Chicago, IL: University of Chicago Press.

Mechanic, M. (2021). *Jackpot: How the Super-Rich Really Live—and How Their Wealth Harms Us All.* New York: Simon & Schuster.

Menczer, F., & Hills, T. (December 2020). The Attention Economy: Understanding How Algorithms and Manipulators Exploit Our Cognitive Vulnerabilities Empowers Us to Fight Back. *Scientific American, 323*(6), 54–61.

Mengis, J., Nicolini, D., & Swan, J. (2018). Integrating Knowledge in the Face of Epistemic Uncertainty: Dialogically Drawing Distinctions. *Management Learning, 49*(5), 595–612. https://doi-org.ezproxy.herts.ac.uk/10.1177/1350507618797216.

Mercier, H., & Sperber, D. (2017). *The Enigma of Reason*. Cambridge, MA: Harvard University Press.

Milotek, H. (April 24, 2018). The Almosts and What-Ifs of 'Sliding Doors', *Haley Milotek*. www.theringer.com/movies/2018/4/24/17261506/sliding-doors-20th-anniversary, accessed February 5, 2022.

Misztal, B.A. (1996). *Trust in Modern Societies: The Search for the Bases of Social Order*. Maldan, MA: Blackwell Publishers.

Mowles, C. (2012). Keeping Means and Ends in View—Linking Practical Judgement, Ethics and Emergence. *Journal of International Development, 24*, 544–555.

Mowles, C. (2015a). *Managing in Uncertainty: Complexity and the Paradoxes of Everyday Organizational Life*. London, UK: Routledge.

Mowles, C. (2015b). *Rethinking Management: Radical Insights from the Complexity Sciences*. Surrey, UK: Gower Publishing Limited.

Mowles, C. (2022). *Complexity: A Key Idea for Business and Society*. London, UK: Routledge.

Mukherjee, et al. For Teams, What Matters More: Raw Talent or a History of Success Together? *Kellogg Insight*. Kellogg School of Management at Northwestern University. https://insight.kellogg.northwestern.edu/article/talent-versus-teamwork-for-successful-teams, accessed June 17, 2022.

Muller, J. Z. (2018). *The Tyranny of Metrics*. Princeton, NJ: Princeton University Press.

Nagel, T. (1989). *The View from Nowhere*. Oxford, US: Oxford University Press.

Nason, R. (2017). *It's Not Complicated: The Art and Science of Complexity in Business*. Toronto: Rotman—UTP Publishing.

North, D.C. (1990). *Institutions, Institutional Change, and Economic Performance*. New York: Cambridge University Press.

Porter, T.M. (1995). *Trust in Numbers: The Pursuit of Objectivity in Science and Public Life*. Princeton, NJ: Princeton University Press.

Putnam, R.D. (2000). *Bowling Alone: The Collapse and Revival of American Community*. New York, NY: Simon & Schuster.

Putnam, R.D. (with Leonardi, R., & Nanetti, R.Y.). (1993). *Making Democracy Work: Civic Traditions in Modern Italy*. Princeton, NJ: Princeton University Press.

Rajan, R. (2020). *The Third Pillar: How Markets and the State Leave the Community Behind*. London, UK: Penguin Books.

Richer, F. *Where Our Thoughts Come from: How Microemotions Affect Spontaneous Thought*. https://theconversation.com/where-our-thoughts-come-from-how-microemotions-affect-spontaneous-thought-177241, accessed April 10, 2023.

Scott, J.C. (1985). *Weapons of the Weak: Everyday Forms of Peasant Resistance*. New Haven, CT: Yale University Press.

Scott, J.C. (1990). *Domination and the Arts of Resistance*. New Haven, CT: Yale University Press.

Scott, J.C. (1998). *Seeing Like a State: How Certain Schemes to Improve the Human Condition Have Failed*. Durham, NC: Yale Agrarian Studies Series.

Shaw, P. (2002). *Changing Conversations in Organizations: A Complexity Approach to Change*. New York, NY: Routledge.

Shotter, J. (1994). *Conversational Realities: Constructing Life through Language*. London: SAGE Publications Ltd.

Simon, H.A. (1964). On the Concept of Organizational Goal. *Administrative Science Quarterly, 9*(1), 1. doi:10.2307/2391519.

Simon, H.A. (1991). Bounded Rationality and Organizational Learning. *Organization Science, 2*(1), 125–134. www-jstor-org.ezproxy.herts.ac.uk/stable/2634943.

Smith, K.K., & Berg, D.N. (1997). *Paradoxes of Life: Understanding Conflict, Paralysis, and Movement in Group Dynamics*. San Francisco, CA: Jossey-Bass.

Smith, L., Wetherell, M., & Campbell, G. (2018). *Emotion, Affective Practices, and the Past in the Present*. New York, NY: Routledge.

Stacey, R.D. (2003/2010). *Complexity and Group Processes: A Radically Social Understanding of Individuals*. New York: Routledge.

Stacey, R.D., & Mowles, C. (2016). *Strategic Management and Organisational Dynamics: The Challenge of Complexity to Ways of Thinking about Organisations* (7th ed.). London, UK: Pearson Education.

Stamps, J., & Lipnack, J. (February 2009). A Measure of Complexity: Organizations as Complex Adaptive Networks. *NetAge Working Papers*. www.netage.com/pub/whpapers/whpapers/WP_Complexity.pdf, accessed January 6, 2023.

Stivers, C. (2008). *Governance in Dark Times—Practical Philosophy for Public Service*. Washington, DC: Georgetown University Press.

Stockdale, K. (2021). *Hope under Oppression*. New York: Oxford University Press.

Suchman, A.L. (2011). Organizations as Machines, Organizations as Conversations: Two Core Metaphors and Their Consequences. *Medical Care, 49*(12, Suppl. 1), S43–S48. doi:10.1097/MLR.0b013e3181d55a05.

The Sunday Times. (October 31, 1987). Interview for 'Woman's Own' ('No Such Thing as Society'). *Margaret Thatcher Foundation: Speeches, Interviews and Other Statements*. https://briandeer.com/social/thatcher-society.htm, accessed April 25, 2023.

Sztompka, P. (2006). *Trust: A Sociological Theory*. New York, NY: Cambridge University Press.

Taleb, N. N. (2004). *Fooled by Randomness: The Hidden Role of Chance in Life and in the Markets*. New York: Random House Trade Paperbacks.

Taylor, C. (1989). *Sources of the Self: The Making of the Modern Identity*. Cambridge, MA: Harvard University Press.

Taylor, F. (1911). *The Principles of Scientific Management*. New York, NY: Harper & Brothers.

Toulmin, S. (2001). *Return to Reason*. Cambridge, MA: Harvard University Press.

Townley, B. (2008). *Reason's Neglect: Rationality and Organizing*. New York, NY: Oxford University Press.

Useem, J. (July/August 2017). Power Causes Brain Damage. *Scientific American, 320*(1), 24–26.

Victor, D., & Stevens, M. (April 10, 2017). United Airlines Passenger Is Dragged from an Overbooked Flight. *The New York Times*.

Wardrup, M.M. (1992). *Complexity: The Emerging Science at the Edge of Order and Chaos*. New York, NY: Simon & Schuster Inc.

Weber, M. (1905/2002). *The Protestant Ethic and the Spirit of Capitalism*. London, UK: Routledge Classics.

Weber, M. (1922/1978). *Economy and Society: An Outline of Interpretive Sociology*. Los Angeles, CA: University of California Press.

Weick, K.E. (1995). *Sensemaking in Organizations*. Los Angeles, CA: SAGE Publishing.

Weick, K.E., & Sutcliffe, K.M. (2001). *Managing the Unexpected: Assuring High Performance in an Age of Complexity*. San Francisco, CA: Jossey-Bass.

Westfall, C. (June 20, 2019) *Leadership Development Is a $366 Billion Industry: Here's Why Most Programs Don't Work*. www.forbes.com/sites/chriswestfall/2019/06/20/leadership-development-why-most-programs-dont-work/?sh=7722706c61de, accessed April 10, 2023.

Wetherell, M. (2014). *Affect and Emotion: A New Social Science of Understanding*. Los Angeles, CA: SAGE Publishing.

White, J. B. (2006). *Living Speech: Resisting the Empire of Force*. Princeton: Princeton University Press.

Wilkinson, R., & Pickett, K. (2009/2010). *The Spirit Level: Why Equality Is Better for Everyone*. London: Penguin Books.

Wilkinson, R., & Pickett, K. (2018). *The Inner Level: How More Equal Societies Reduce Stress, Restore Sanity and Improve Everyone's Well-Being*. New York: Penguin Books.

Wired Magazine. www.wired.co.uk/article/mariana-mazzucato, accessed April 22, 2023.

World Health Organization. www.who.int/health-topics/mental-health#tab=tab_1, accessed December 11, 2022.

Zak, P. (2014). *Measurement Myopia*. www.drucker.institute/thedx/measurement-myopia/, accessed October 22, 2022.

Zaraska, M. (October 2020). All Together Now. *Scientific American*, *323*(4), 64–69.

Index

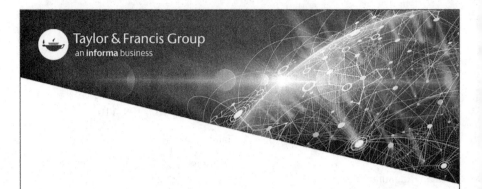

Printed in the United States
by Baker & Taylor Publisher Services